European Unity in Context
The Interwar Period

European Unity in Context
The Interwar Period

Edited by Peter M.R. Stirk

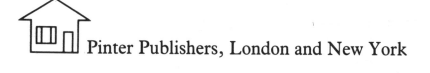 Pinter Publishers, London and New York

© Peter M.R. Stirk, 1989

First published in Great Britain in 1989 by
Pinter Publishers Limited
25 Floral Street, London WC2E 9DS

ISBN 0-86187-987-2

British Library Cataloguing in Publication Data

A CIP catalogue record for this book is available from the British Library

Library of Congress Cataloging-in-Publication Data

European unity in context: the interwar period / edited by Peter M.R. Stirk.
   p.   cm.
  Includes index.
  ISBN 0-86187-987-2
  1. Europe—Politics and government—1918–1945. 2. Europe—
Economic conditions—1918–1945. 3. Europe—Social conditions—20th
century. 4. Europe—Civilization—20th century. 5. European
cooperation.   I. Stirk, Peter M.R., 1954–
D727.E925   1989
940.5—dc19   88-39082
                                    CIP

Typeset by Florencetype Ltd, Kewstoke, Avon
Printed and bound in Great Britain by
Biddles Ltd, Guildford and King's Lynn

Contents

1 Introduction: Crisis and Continuity in Interwar Europe

Peter M.R. Stirk

The chapters in this book are a selection from the papers presented at the conference 'European Unity in Context: Problems and Perspectives of the Interwar Period', which was held at the University of Hull in 1987. From the perspective of the postwar world and the relative success of the European Community it is easy to forget the deeper roots of European unity and the enormity of the obstacles which had to be overcome in order to bring it about. One possible consequence of this neglect of the past is the under-estimation of the enormity of the obstacles which still confront Europe. This volume may help to recall these dimensions of our recent past. The range of topics and states covered and the divergence of judgement is appropriate to reflection on the context of European unity, for Europe was and is a multi-faceted phenomenon at best. At worst it succumbs to Bismarck's dismissive note, 'Anyone who talks of Europe is wrong—a geographical notion'.[1] In the contemporary world, what Europe means is superficially self-evident. It means Brussels and Strasbourg, the Commission and the Parliament. Although the degree of unity achieved by the European Community is often, and rightly questioned, as is the right of this Community to the title 'European', there are institutions which are European and not simply German, British, French and so on. National governments put forward candidates for European office only to find that 'their' men can display an irritating and apparently unanticipated independence. In other words, they act as Europeans rather than as representatives of their nations. This is far from always being the case but it happens often enough to make the idea of Europe tangible. In the interwar period the lack of any European institutional identity meant that Europe itself seemed to change shape along with the proposals, problems and dreams which temporarily brought it into focus. Europe had to compete with other claimants to people's loyalty and identity—most obviously the nation-state but also alternative forms of

1

transnational unity, class, race and local or regional community. Despite the claims of their respective advocates none of these claimants enjoyed invariable and unqualified loyalty. Moreover ideological loyalty, difficult enough to establish in the first place, often had to compete with material interests which pointed in a different direction. The conflict or combination of ideology and interests at one level in turn influenced the conflict or combination of ideology and interests at another level. How people thought of their nation and its interest determined how they thought of Europe and the European interest, or whether they thought of Europe at all. Similarly the claims of class and race could displace those of the nation or state. At the end of the period, however, the nation-state remained the predominant focus of loyalty, national interest the predominant guide to action. Looking back upon the cause of Europe in the interwar years there is a temptation, a misguided one, to regard these years in the same way that the men of the Renaissance regarded the medieval era: as a period of unmitigated darkness and destruction.

The war which broke out in 1939 brought to an end a troubled period of European history. It was not greeted with the enthusiasm which accompanied August 1914 but was accepted with greater or lesser readiness as a long-awaited fate. The immediate judgement on the interwar period was blunt and harsh and has not been greatly mitigated since. From the perspective of 1940 the prominent federalist and pro-European R.W.G. Mackay concluded that: 'In 1919 peace was restored by a Treaty which has provided some of the causes of the present war, and ushered in a period in the history of the world in which the nations, passing rapidly from one crisis to another, have lived in a perpetual condition of insecurity and anarchy.'[2] Another contemporary, E.H. Carr, entitled his seminal survey of international relations between the wars which was first published in 1939 *The Twenty Years Crisis*. The title of a more recent commentary, published in 1976, by S. Marks indicates the reason for the harshness of the judgement upon the interwar period: *The Illusion of Peace*. Paradoxically, it was the very expectations of international peace, of the victory of democracy and self-determination, and of a land fit for heroes that led to the retrospective condemnation of governments and ideologies with such vigour. The end of the First World War had appeared to usher in a new era in which the old vices of international power politics were to be swept away in favour of a new international system. The League of Nations was to establish international order by a process of collective decision-making and collective enforcement. The Covenant of the League of Nations did not actually envisage the end of war, but it did distinguish between just and unjust wars. It provided, indeed, for the pursuit of war in order to punish or constrain those who were judged by the League and its articles to have launched unjust wars. In the eyes of

President Wilson, violators of international law and peace could not be tolerated with equanimity. Neutrality was not an option in such cases. All states were obliged to join in opposition to the pariah. States who violated international law were to be regarded as criminals deserving of punishment in much the same way as individuals who transgressed the laws of their countries were designated as criminals. This was, at least, one understanding of the purpose of the League and the nature of the new international order. Alongside it, and often indistinguishable from it, was the expectation of peace, of the arbitration of international disputes, and, more importantly, of the disappearance of disputes. That the causes of wars might actually evaporate is one of the most striking aspects of the 'illusion of peace' in the interwar period.[3] It was assumed by some that the international order could be so arranged, and indeed was being so arranged, that no state would have an interest in going to war. For the sceptical E.H. Carr this represented an irresponsible extension of nineteenth-century utopianism in a period in which the historical presuppositions of that utopianism had vanished. This expectation of peace was, he claimed, based upon the doctrine of the harmony of interests which in turn was closely associated with the principle of self-determination. A world in which each nation could determine its fate through its own state would be one in which no state, or part thereof, had an interest in war.

That no such harmony existed was apparent before the ink was dry on the Covenant. The wish that it did was, however, stubborn. Statesmen and publicists sought, with varying degrees of sincerity, to make reality conform to the wish by reforming the League or extending the commitments associated with it. Indeed, the League was scarcely born when proposals for strengthening it, namely the Draft Treaty of Mutual Assistance of 1923 and the Geneva Protocol of 1924, were made, albeit without success. By 1928 the cause of the League was being vigorously propagated beyond the confines of the League itself. On 24 September 1927 a Polish proposal prohibiting wars of aggression and enjoining the pacific settlement of international disputes had been adopted by the General Assembly of the League. Not long after, in February 1928, the Pan-American Conference passed a similar resolution. By this time enthusiasm for the idea of outlawing war, or at least wars of aggression, was mounting rapidly. An initial, and limited, suggestion of the French Premier, Briand, which was actually intended to induce greater commitment by the United States to the security of France, culminated over a year later, in August 1928, in a more expansive treaty condemning wars of aggression. This treaty, the Kellogg Pact, was soon signed by nearly all states of any significance and even prompted an analogous Soviet initiative, the Litvinov Protocol, which was intended to bring the principles of the Pact into effect along Russia's eastern borders prior to the general ratification.

Global peace and the League of Nations were two of the illusions of the interwar period. A third was the idea of Europe. The idea of Europe has a long pedigree which is often difficult to distinguish from the quest for peace and a league or federation of nations. Indeed, the three tended to mean much the same thing so long as European politics could plausibly be regarded as world politics. The idea of Europe had been gaining ground even before 1914 but the sheer carnage of 1914–18, compounded by the feeling that the war was a civil war between kindred, European, nations gave it added impetus. Of course the war had been more than a European one after the involvement of the United States in hostilities. Similarly peace and the league of nations ceased to be purely European. An influential book by two Italians, Giovanni Agnelli and Attilio Cabiati, raised the question in its very title: *European Federation or League of Nations?* (1918). The League won out because there was more to the League than the pursuit of an illusion. In one sense it reflected a real and significant trend. In the words of the American historian, W. McDougall: 'The eclipse of Europe itself was manifested in Wilson's dream of a world system. Europe would merge into the world to be governed, not by principles derived from its own experience, but by universal intuitive principles—the Open Door, national self-determination, and collective security.'[4] The principles may have been over-ambitious or innappropriate but the eclipse of Europe was real enough. It was recognised by pragmatic statesmen and visionaries alike. Both the ageing Clemenceau and the young prophet of a united Europe, R.N. Coudenhove-Kalergi, agreed that the havoc and carnage of the First World War had, temporarily at least, impoverished Europe by comparison with the emerging colossus on the other side of the Atlantic. At the end of the war Frenchmen and Germans looked to the United States for material aid and protection. Germans hoped that they would be protected from French vengeance in the immediate future, and had less right to be disappointed than they pretended, given American defence of their territorial integrity. Frenchmen looked for protection in the more distant future against a newly resurgent Germany. Both needed, and continued to need for some time, financial support from the economic giant. Nor did the American presence disappear. Recent research has shown that the United States played an active role in Europe throughout the 1920s and into the early 1930s. American economic prosperity was dependent upon the establishment of an Open Door, or free trade, policy on a global scale. On this both President Wilson and his successors were agreed. Differences arose only over the question of whether or not this policy required American commitment to the League of Nations.[5]

Yet US involvement was ambiguous. The new superpower did decline to join the League and isolationist distaste for embroilment in the archaic and internecine affairs of Europe did restrict the activity of its leaders. This fact was of decisive importance for the character of the interwar period. For in a sense this was a period during which the judgement of history enunciated in the First World War, namely the emergence of America as the world power, was temporarily suspended. Europe appeared to have regained or maintained its pivotal role in the world. Vast tracts of the globe seemed like appendages of European states. These states themselves spoke, and occasionally acted, as if the prewar equilibrium could be restored and even improved. Equilibrium was not restored and the end of the period was marked by a war in which an even stronger America allied with the Soviet Union asserted their status as the new superpowers. According to De la Porte, the First World War witnessed another, related, judgement.[6] The European states were no longer capable of restoring any form of stable equilibrium between themselves. Stability could be achieved only by external intervention. To that extent the interwar period was precisely that. It was a period in which the old European system stood condemned and was merely waiting for the unpronounced date of execution.

It is in fact difficult to find indicators of long-term stability in the wake of the First World War. A new and potentially unstable map was drawn up for Eastern and Central Europe. The Habsburg Empire had disappeared entirely, leaving a truncated core, Austria, whose economic viability was in doubt from the outset and whose political identity was also uncertain. Some sections of the German-speaking population did not intially want an independent Austria at all and called for *Anschluss* with the German state to the north. The Allies took perverse recognition of this desire when, by the Treaty of St Germain (September 1919), they imposed upon the new state the obligation to preserve its own independence and integrity. Of the various characteristics and motives ascribed to states under the old system self-preservation had always been predominant. Yet here was a state whose interest in self-preservation was assumed to be so weak that it had to be bound by international treaty to pursue this 'interest'. Elsewhere in Eastern and Central Europe the desire for independence was not in doubt. Nor was the threat irredentist claims posed to peace. As early as 1921 Czechoslovakia, Yugoslavia and Romania formed one of the more stable alliances of the period, the so-called Little Entente, in defence against Hungarian claims against them. Respect for minorities had been written into the peace treaties in an effort to manage the inevitable conflicts in a region whose linguistic and national complexity rendered almost any conceivable boundaries open to question, but to no avail.

Territorial changes in Western Europe had been comparatively slight, slighter than some wished. The major powers, France and Germany, remained united. German territorial losses, both in the west and the east, did not disguise its economic, and potentially its military, superiority over the victor, France. The threat posed by German economic power to a postwar France had been noted even during the war by the organisation representing French coal and steel interests, the Comité des Forges. In 1917 this association had argued that French industry would need access to both German coal and German capital if postwar German hegemony were to be prevented. It had already called for territorial annexation beyond the Saar and Alsace-Lorraine. French territorial claims, and the even more far-reaching schemes for the fragmentation of Germany and the separation of the Rhineland, had to be restricted in the face of opposition from France's allies. Annexation and fragmentation were, even then, not the only French option. Parallel to this policy ran another, namely the attempt to obtain Anglo-American commitment to the defence of French security. Something of both of these policies was incorporated in the peace treaties, though less than the French desired. Ultimately the difference of interest between France and her wartime allies proved fatal to French ambitions. The final attempt to exert the punitive provisions of the Versailles Treaty by occupying the Ruhr in 1923 collapsed in the face of German opposition, British suspicion of French hegemony, and the American need for a prosperous Germany as part of the world economy.[7]

If Germany could not be constrained it might, however, be possible to dissolve the threat by pursuing the path of conciliation. While German foreign policy was under the control of Stresemann and like-minded politicians and officials this option appeared plausible. The Locarno Treaty of 1925, by which Germany accepted its western borders as established by the peace treaties, raised hopes of the revival of a concert of Europe—hopes that were to resurface throughout the remainder of the 1920s and even into the 1930s. Yet doubts and fears were to persist on both sides. The spirit of cooperation was limited on the French side by the desire for security, which effectively meant either limitations on German sovereignty or a system of alliances which would ensure that in the event of conflict more than France's inadequate resources could be mobilised against Germany. On the German side the spirit of cooperation was limited by the desire to be rid of the affront of reparations and by the refusal to accept the eastern borders on the same basis as in the west. These problems were significant, but during the 1920s it was at least possible to see them as part of a slow but essentially peaceful revision which remained within the framework of the Versailles Treaty. Revision and fulfilment did not seem to be inevitably incompatible. The shock of the depression effectively removed fulfilment from the agenda. Revision was the order of the day. Versailles was no longer relevant save as a propaganda weapon. The only questions were how far and by what means was the revision to take place.

The management of revision was complicated by nationalism and the competition of conflicting international ideologies. There was of course nothing new in nationalism itself. There does, however, seem to have been a change in the climate around the turn of the decade. The authoritarians of the *Tatkreis* dated it from the Hague conference which was called to sanction the Young Plan of 1929 for the rearrangement of the payment of reparations by Germany. The British Chancellor of the Exchequer had narrow-mindedly, and successfully, sought to enlarge the British share of the receipts and threatened to abandon the French if they refused to acquiesce. Ferdinand Fried, a member of the *Tatkreis*, could scarcely conceal his delight:

> In August Snowden had been misunderstood by the whole conference. In August: that was before the crack which ran through this conference, before Europe's sudden turn towards domestic politics and therefore towards one's own nation, towards the new and sober objectivity in politics. Before then one believed so casually in a Pan-Europe, in a borderless community of all nations, all democrats and all socialists. One thought of horizontal stratification, not of vertical stratification.[8]

The German swing to revision at any price under Chancellor Brüning went hand in hand with the collapse of the international economic order and the general retreat behind the walls of tariff barriers. The change was not instantaneous. The words of the *Tatkreis* were as much prophetic as they were descriptive. But by the time the World Economic Conference of 1933 met the world market had gone. Even Britain had opted for protection within its imperial bloc at the Ottawa Conference of 1932.

The simple sentiment of nationalism was not always reliable if only for the reason that the actual nationality of groups was disputable. Thus some French politicians sought, unsuccessfully as it turned out, to promote separatist identity in the Rhineland and in Bavaria, to the advantage of French security interests. They had mistakenly calculated that Rhenish or Bavarian identity would prevail over German indentity or, as they saw it, loyalty to the Prussian state.[9] The Spanish Falangist José Antonio Primo de Rivera feared that separatist nationalism might become a reality in his own country and issued equivocal judgements about the spirit of nationalism. He disavowed emotion on the grounds that it favoured local patriotisms, that is, regional autonomy and separatism. Spanish unity, as opposed to Catalan unity, lay in the pursuit of an imperial destiny which was, in some opaque way, to be neither motivated by 'a vague feeling' nor to be 'something aridly intellectual'.[10]

Conflicting international ideologies were no novelty either, though again there was a change in intensity, dating this time from the Bolshevik revolution in Russia. International fascism was soon added to international communism. Both phenomena cut across the national community. Their conflict took the form of a civil war within the nation and subsequently of a civil war which did not recognise the boundaries of territorial states. Hence, the interwar period has been seen, not least by some of its contemporaries, as one that witnessed a manichaean struggle between the ideologies of fascism and communism over the apparently sickly body of liberal democracy. Democratic forms of government have never lacked critics nor prophets of the crisis of democracy. In the interwar period, however, criticism was given added bite by the existence of alternative systems with explicitly claimed to have transcended the old forms of liberal democracy. Both the Soviet Union and fascist Italy presented themselves, albeit to varying degrees, as harbingers of a new future. Many who did not desire to imitate these foreign forms nevertheless sympathised with the criticisms made of the old democracies. The latter encouraged, it was said, naked egoism and the elevation of party interest above the national interest; they lived not by virtue of their own effort but from that of their colonial subjects; they neglected their poor and forgot the men who had sacrificed life, limb or career in the war, and so on. The list of criticisms was endless. What was probably more important than any of the individual points was the general presumption and feeling that the old democracy had had its day. This sentiment received a considerable boost as the financial crash of 1929 compounded the problems of falling raw material and food prices. The depression, with the attendant waste of human and material resources, was regarded as a scandal and, by many, as a final demonstration of the failings of democracy.

Once the demise of liberal democracy was accepted the rhetoric of fascism or communism provided a ready alternative. With what degree of sincerity it was used can only be determined case by case. There were cases where the conflict between the major ideologies seemed fairly clear cut, pre-eminently in the Spanish Civil War where national socialist air power and Italian fascist soldiers fought the International Brigade and the agents of Comintern. Even there, however, the clarity of the manichaean conflict dissolves on closer inspection. The indigenous champion of the fascist cause, General Franco, regarded the Spanish falangists with some suspicion and even they disapproved of the efforts of one of their number, Gimenez Caballero, to interpret Spanish falangism as part of a wider Mediterranean fascism.[11] Sincere or not, the rhetoric of international ideological conflict was widespread. It endowed the conflicts in Europe with the character of a civil war. The language of domestic conflict, of the horizontal divisions whose end Fried claimed to discern in 1930, seemed to expand across the frontiers.

In the ideologically unstable interwar period these two countervailing trends, intensified nationalism and the inflation of the language of domestic conflict, could fuse into some strange configurations. According to E.H. Carr,

This then is the basic reason for the overwhelming importance of international politics in the post-War epoch. The conflict between privileged and unprivileged, between the champions of an existing order and the revolutionaries, which was fought out in the nineteenth century within the national communities of Western Europe, has been transferred by the twentieth century to the international community. The nation is now, more than ever before, the supreme unit round which centre human demands for equality and human ambitions for predominance.[12]

For Carr, then, the nationalist trend had subsumed the internationalist, horizontal conflict at the same time as the latter was inflated beyond its original realm. The radical realignment of traditional cleavages coolly analysed by Carr often acquired vivid and fantastic shape. At the beginning of the period, amidst the advance of the Red Army on Warsaw and internal conflict in Germany, the strange phenomenon of National Bolshevism was born. In the words of McDougall, 'Haunted by the spectre of a German-Russian coalition, French and British officials perceived in National Bolshevism a conspiracy of revenge against the Entente. Newspapers in France printed lurid scenarios of Cossack hordes led by the Prussian General Staff crushing Poland, then bursting across the Rhine.[13] The incongruity of such images should not blind us to their significance. Many believed that the incongruous was not only possible but necessary.

Confronted with this plethora of images some chose to discount the increasingly confusing ideological battle and to orient themselves strictly on the basis of *Realpolitik*. There was much to recommend itself in such a strategy. That some ideologues had a tenuous grasp of reality was as evident as the sincerity of others was suspect. But it was not always a reliable guide to the behaviour of people and states. Interests could prove to be as slippery as ideologies, or perhaps we should say that the interests of some had become so ambitious that they escaped calculation by the traditional methods. This goes some way to describing the now infamous policy of appeasement, that last expression of the illusion of peace before the advent of war. Premier Blum, leader of the French Popular Front, told the German Minister of Economics and supposed focus of the moderate faction amongst the German government, Schacht, that 'we cannot achieve anything if we treat ideological barriers as insurmountable'.[14] The underlying assumption was that revisionist claims, especially those of Germany, could be accommodated by judicious and limited concessions without tearing apart the basic international order. The victims of these adjustments could easily be regarded as the problem. Indeed, it has been suggested that the British dissatisfaction with the League of Nations in the 1930s arose from the inability of that institution to secure the compliance of these states to the dispensations worked out by the great powers. This sort of logic need not be seen as the expression of that cynical disregard of smaller powers which was openly trumpeted by fascists. It was rather a logic which tolerated injustices in the hope of averting greater ones. Whether or not it was a justifiable logic depends very much on whether or not the larger democratic states had much option to do otherwise, and that is disputed.

The imminent collapse of the international order was aggravated by the very agreements which were to have guaranteed it in another way. The obligations which states had accepted exceeded their ability to fulfil them. The problem was well expressed by the November 1935 report of the British Defence Requirements Sub-Committee:

> we feel bound to bring to notice the very serious effect of the system, in its present stage, on our own defence requirements as illustrated by the Manchurian and Abyssinian episodes . . . In 1932–33, and again in 1935, owing to our obligations under the Covenant and the position we occupy as the one great sea-power remaining in the League, we had no alternative but to play our part—inevitably a leading part—in disputes in which our national interest was at most quite secondary . . . On each occasion we have come within sight of war and aroused the bitterness of old friends and allies . . .[15]

The combination of limited resources and extensive commitments or ambitions threatened to turn every diplomatic dispute into a crisis. War in Europe did not actually erupt for twenty years and during that time the order established by the peace treaties had been substantially abandoned. In retrospect, then, it seems more appropriate to talk in terms of the 'crumbling' or 'unravelling' of that order. Yet each stage of the dissolution brought one state or another 'within sight of war'.

Diplomatic crises were but one form of crisis which confronted people and states in the interwar period. According to Arnold Toynbee the threat of war, like much earlier threats of divine retribution, could be met with fortitude or resistance. The events of 1931, which he called the *annus terribilis*, were of a different order: 'The catastrophe . . . which Western minds were contemplating in 1931 was not the destructive impact of any external force but a spontaneous disintegration from within; and this prospect was much more formidable than the other.'[16] As has been suggested, the sense of crisis of which Toynbee wrote had many roots, several of which long predated the *annus terribilis*. The instability of the European system of states, the hesitancy of the one great superpower, the inflammation of nationalism, the conflict of international ideologies, and the radical attempts to redraw the ideological map, all contributed to a diffuse sense of crisis. There was a sense of being on the verge of a new era to which the old categories would not apply. With the depression fear and anxiety jostled alongside the anticipation of a new order. It was not merely the severity of the crisis, and especially of unemployment, that was the problem, though this was bad enough. It was rather the idea that the crisis was, so to speak, permanent. An international conference held in 1931, whose main aim was to initiate a statistical and factual study of unemployment fluctuations, justified the urgency of its considerations on the grounds that '[t]he fear of recurrence becomes then a question even more important that the extent of unemployment at any one time . . .'[17] As anxiety added urgency to anticipation many sought to strike out into uncharted waters. The future, it was said, lay in neither capitalism nor socialism but in a Third Way.

The sense of crisis, of standing amidst the ruins of one order and gazing out at the outlines of a new world, led to a re-examination of the basic units of domestic and international life. The boundaries of political power, economies and political identity seemed either fragile or inconsistent. There were two main responses to this situation. One was to reaffirm the nation-state, to strip it of the links binding it to an anarchic world economy and an impotent and discredited system of international obligations. The corollary of this isolation was the consolidation of internal indentity and unity. The other strategy was to sacrifice the idea of the nation-state in favour of a larger form of political and economic organisation. The League of Nations was one, imperfect, alternative which actually did more to reaffirm the model of the nation-state than to supplant it. The fascist New Order and communism were others whose ability to transcend the boundaries of the states which harboured them was stronger than their ability to transcend the interests of those states.

Despite these prevailing and ultimately fateful divisions important strands of European unity were forged during the 1920s and managed to survive the *annus terribilis*, though they grew weaker or vaguer during the 1930s. The survival of the idea of Europe was partly due to its elasticity. It could be and was appropriated by individuals of diverse ideological inclinations. By the same token it could superficially unite fundamentally incompatible spirits until some event, point of emphasis or tactics revealed the underlying discord. As the small groups of advocates of European unity reached out to the men who controlled the levers of power or surveyed the international scene in the hope of discerning some pattern of alliances which might provide the core of a unified Europe, the very idea of Europe took on a different shape. Something of this confusion, or, to be more charitable, evolution, is evident in the career of Coudenhove-Kalergi. His book, *Pan-Europa*, published in 1923, inaugurated a life-long career of advocacy of European union. Although there is considerable dispute concerning the influence of his ideas upon decision-makers, both within the interwar period and afterwards, there is no doubt that he achieved a high profile. Adolf Hitler, for instance, paused to pour scorn upon the ideas of the Count. His movement attracted the official support of Chancellor Seipel of Austria and of Briand of France as well as Eduard Beneš of Czechoslovakia. The first Pan-European Congress was held in Vienna in October 1926. Others followed and by May 1936 Coundenhove-Kalergi had even organized a Pan-European Agrarian Congress. During the mid-1930s he repeatedly met Mussolini and other Italian fascists in a vain attempt to promote a Rome–Paris axis. It is perhaps proof of his enthusiasm for the idea of Europe, if not of the quality of his judgement, that he was pleasantly surprised to find, in 1938, that the editor of an Italian fascist journal entitled *Anti-Europa* was nothing of the sort. The editor, Asvero Gravelli, assured Coudenhove-Kalergi of his sympathy and support for his ideas. The title he said was a misnomer! Coudenhove-Kalergi's credulity should not, however, be too harshly condemned. Some fascists and even some national socialists took the international pretensions of their respective doctrines quite seriously.

It was also in 1938 that Coudenhove-Kalergi relaxed his previous exclusion of Britain from the envisaged Pan-Europe and placed his hopes in a Paris–London axis. His original attitude to the role of Britain was one of the points of dispute with other movements, especially the *Verband für europäischen Verständigung*. The latter was not actually formed until the autumn of 1926 but had existed in different forms from 1924. Its leader, Wilhelm Heile, considered the exclusion of Britain to be both wrong-headed and counter-productive. He was certainly right about the latter for the officials of the German Foreign Office reacted coolly to Coundenhove-Kalergi's frequent approaches in part at least because of the German need for British support in their efforts to revise the Versailles settlement. The role of Britain was not the only point of dispute. Personality clashes and sectarianism were promoted by the difficulty of trying to establish international structures for the respective movements. A more fundamental disagreement was whether to focus upon influencing key statesmen and officials, as Heile wanted, or to build up a popular mass movement, as Coudenhove-Kalergi wanted. This dispute was actually somewhat irrelevant since Coundenhove-Kalergi, consistent with his own aristocratic philosophy, did spend much of his time seeking out influential figures and signally failed to create a mass movement.[18]

Although the movements for European union were usually far removed from the levers of power they were far from out of tune with their time. Coudenhove-Kalergi's Europe was characterised in part by cultural and geopolitical considerations which proliferated in the interwar years. Anthropological or cultural reflections tended to take a pessimistic turn. According to some versions Western or European man was in irreversible decline. The future belonged to the slavic type, the Eastern, yellow or Chinese type. Islam was resurrected as yet another alien and threatening force. Advocates of European unity tended to reassure their readers that the cause was not yet lost. A united Europe could still salvage the threatened cultural and anthropological heritage. There was of course nothing new in this. Well before the First World War the image of 'Pan' movements had been widely propagated. The first Pan-Slavic Congress had been held in 1848. Pan-Germanism was undoubtedly the most effective of these movements. Others, of lesser import, included Pan-Americanism, Pan-Islam, Pan-Mongolians, Pan-Latinism and Pan-Turanianism. Some were little more than figments of overheated imaginations. Most were used either as negative or positive images to inculcate narrowly nationalistic ambitions. Yet they helped to make it acceptable to conjure up global images of distinctive and conflicting blocs of peoples. Whether such imagery could provide any real basis for European unity is doubtful. Stresemann was surely right to say that whoever sought to build a United States of Europe on the basis of some theory of human 'types' was misguided and neglected the real issues which could lead to progress in the economic and political solidarity of peoples.[19]

Geopolitical arguments affected to stand nearer to the realities of economic and political power. Often working upon a global scale, geopoliticians dispensed with the boundaries of existing states. In the cruder versions calculations of surface area, population, population density and so on were used to invoke the need for expansion and/or unification. The political weakness or division of the supposed blocs, their economic underdevelopment, were no impediment to the strength of the image. From the European perspective there was indeed a kernel of truth in these speculations, if not in the methods and arguments used to support them. European powers which had thought of themselves as the fulcrum of the world were increasingly confronted by new non-European states with wide-ranging ambitions. The emergence of the United States on to the world stage in the Spanish–American war of 1898 and of Japan in the war with China of 1894–5 shook European complacency. After the First World War the manifest superiority of the economy of the United States became a commonplace argument for European union. Indeed, a British Foreign Office memo of May 1930 drawn up in considering the Briand plan observed,

> it may well be that what he [Briand] has in mind is not only, and perhaps not even primarily, further military and political security for France (though no doubt he does desire this) but also such regrouping and consolidation of European finance and industry as to assure France and the rest of Europe against the ever-growing strength of non-European and especially American competition. This is primarily what has always been meant by the 'United States of Europe' or 'Pan-Europe' and without this it is hard to see that the word 'Pan-Europe' can mean anything at all.[20]

Whereas the geopoliticians tended to dismiss existing boundaries and states in the interests of the underlying realities of population, resources, space and so on, federalists confronted the problem of the state and especially the nation-state head on. As T. Schieder has pointed out, the idea of the nation-state as the natural and final form of political organisation had never gained unqualified acceptance even in the nineteenth century.[21] Critics of the nation-state discerned two flaws, both of which were amplified by the events of 1914–18. In the first place, war itself appeared to be the inevitable outcome of an anarchic system of states in which each member of the system recognised no obligation beyond its own will and interests. The Peace Treaties compounded the problem by multiplying the number of states and hence the potential points of conflict. The exigencies of the First World War had also enabled those states which had weathered the storm to extend the power of the state within its own boundaries. Military and economic mobilisation along with war propaganda had weakened the individual, the family, and regional cultures in the face of the awesome power of the impersonal centralised state. Federalist theories, then, could have a dual focus. Looking outwards they offered federation as an alternative to the internecine wars of Europe. Looking inwards they offered federalism as a means of protecting the individual and his particularist communities against the domestic leviathan. Those who stood in the tradition of Proudhon could readily argue that the two strategies went hand in hand. Since it was centralised states that were presumed to make wars decentralist federalism would be conducive to peace. But exactly the converse movement could be derived from the desire to avoid war. Only a federal power, ultimately on a global scale, which possessed its own means of coercion could enforce peace between members of the federation. Centralisation, not decentralisation, was the answer. Hence the British federalist Curtis was to argue that the *de facto* strength of the British Empire lay in the fact that in questions of war and peace there was a single decision-maker, Great Britain.[22]

Such fundamental differences of goals within the federalist camp were further complicated by the need to relate federalism to the evident problems of the day. In Central and Eastern Europe the distinction between centralist and decentralist strategies, between federalist criticism of the nation state and advocacy of the nation-state, became blurred. When M.H. Boehm wrote his article on federalism for the *Encyclopaedia of the Social Sciences* he claimed that 'The added factor of a large and compact German speaking territory in Czechoslovakia might well suggest to that country a reform along federal lines; this however the Czechs oppose'.[23] It is difficult not to see in this the assertion of German hegemony at the expense of the Czechoslovak state. Whether or not the suspicion is justified in this case it is true that federalism as a slogan was turned into a propaganda weapon on behalf of powerful states in much the same way as the idea of Europe was. Thereby of course some varieties of federalist theory were more or less permanently discredited.

On the other hand, the federalist traditions were broad enough and diverse enough to provide arguments for men who would brook no compromise with the ambitions of individual states or nations. Federalist doctrines were important to the idea of Europe because they provided these men with sets of principles and constitutional proposals within which the idea of Europe could be articulated.

Proposals for customs unions fulfilled the same function but with the added advantage that they were taken more seriously by political and bureaucratic élites. Customs frontiers, vastly increased by the post-war settlement, had long been seen as an obstacle to prosperity. By comparison with the vast internal market of the United States they seemed downright suicidal. In the mid-1920s small groups of economists and businessmen formed to advocate customs unions. In 1924 an International Committee for a European Customs Union emerged. Its first Congress, which was not held until June 1930 in Paris, was attended by French ministers and officials. The *Mitteleuropäische Wirtschaftstag* had held its first Congress in September 1925. One of its leaders argued for a purely economic cooperation, shorn of the burden, as he saw it, of political union. This sort of attempt to circumvent the problem of the existence of sovereign states was common amongst businessmen and would-be planners. Yet politicians, too, seriously considered various forms of customs union; probably more seriously than they considered the schemes for federation. Indeed, it is difficult to decide which is the more striking: the sheer number of proposals for customs unions or the fact that with the rare and highly limited exception they failed. Many of these unions were not European in scope. One of the most touted sub-European regions was the Danube. This was prominent on the agenda because substantial economic unity had previously existed, by courtesy of the existence of the Habsburg Empire, and because of the prolonged economic distress of the region in the interwar years. In the crisis years of 1929–33 the schemes extended from full-scale federation and customs union to more limited ones for a system of internal preferential tariffs between the states concerned. All were dependent to some extent on wider international agreement to provide markets for the region's agricultural products and financial credit. Individual schemes were feared either by the Germans, who rightly saw French proposals as attempts to shore up their system of alliances and to block German economic penetration and political influence, or by the French, who rightly worried about German designs to construct an extended *Mitteleuropa*. The outcome was paralysis and perpetuation of the problems. The cause of customs union teetered on the verge of success with the Ouchy Convention of 1932 which envisaged a reduction of tariffs by 10 per cent per annum over five years. Although signed by Belgium, The Netherlands and Luxembourg it was never ratified, partly because of British opposition and partly because of the failure of other states to join.

It is worth asking whether these sub-European customs unions, or the more politically motivated idea of Scandinavian union, would have furthered the cause of wider European union. During the interwar period many federalists and free traders assumed that they would not only encourage European union but would serve as stepping-stones to global federation or free trade. In retrospect the assumption seems dubious. After all the British federal tradition and associated system of economic preferences pointed towards unification of the Empire at the expense of European union, as is clearly indicated by the British response to the Briand plan. On the other hand, the idea of European union fed on the association of European union with these wider goals of global government and free trade in much the same way as it fed on the desire for universal peace.

The same sort of elasticity can be found in another phenomenon which was taken at the time as a symbol, and mechanism, for unity, namely the development of cartels. The most famous of these was the *Entente Internationale de l'Acier* which was finally signed in November of 1926 after over two years of protracted negotiation. The agreement regulated the production of steel by German, French, Belgian and Luxembourg firms on the basis of agreed quotas. Producers paid into a central treasury on the basis of their level of production with supplementary payments serving as a penalty for exceeding the agreed quotas and rebates as a reward for underproduction. Although the agreement was a private and non-governmental one, both the French and the German governments had been involved in the complex and multi-faceted negotiations which issued in the steel agreement and a general trade treaty between France and Germany. The underlying cause of the agreement was the excessive capacity of the European steel industry but wider implications were soon drawn. An American observer commented, 'the conclusion of the European steel agreement has been hailed by some of its sponsors as the greatest recent economic development and a first step toward the formation of an "Economic United States of Europe".'[24] The most European minded of these sponsors was Emile Mayrisch, head of the Luxembourg steel group ARBED. Amidst the negotiations for the steel agreement he had helped to set up the German–French Study Committee. Intended initially to promote Franco-German understanding, the Committee soon acquired an anti-American streak. Mayrisch himself intended to expand its aims to include the promotion of European union. It should not be forgotten, however, that the parties to the agreement had fought long and hard over the size of their respective quotas. Some accepted it only when their preferred strategy of protective tariffs failed. Moreover, despite the anti-American rhetoric which the agreement inspired the producers were not averse to concluding agreements with American firms, and actually succeeded in incorporating the Americans in 1938. The idea of the cartel, like those of peace, free trade and federation, tended to expand to global dimensions. Nevertheless, it remains true that the general trend towards the formation of cartels and especially those affecting French and German industries did encourage the idea of European union. In some quarters businessmen and technocrats were thought to be capable of achieving what politicians could not. The cultivation of petty prejudice and self-seeking widely associated with party politics was to be circumvented or even replaced by the rational management of technology and markets.

The Memorandum which Briand submitted on 17 May 1930 set out from exactly the opposite assumption. It bluntly proclaimed the 'General sub-ordination of the Economic Problem to the Political'.[25] That Briand was planning to launch some sort of European initiative was known as early as the September 1928 Geneva Protocols for the Liquidation of War. His intentions became clearer in June 1929 when he met Stresemann in Madrid and broached the idea of some form of federal bond. The idea gained a wider audience in July through a series of speeches amidst mounting press speculation. Briand formally launched his initiative on the 5 September 1929 at the Tenth Ordinary Session of the League Assembly. Speaking again of 'some kind of federal bond', Briand placed the economic dimension first: 'Obviously, this association will be primarily economic, for that is the most urgent aspect of the question . . . Still I am convinced that, politically and socially also, this federal bond might, without affecting the sovereignty of any of the nations belonging to such an association, do useful work . . .'[26] It was soon agreed that the French should draft a memorandum expanding upon such ideas and that other governments should respond prior to further discussion. The priority of economic considerations did not reappear in the actual Memorandum of 17 May 1930. There was a return to the customary French concern for security, or rather the underlying concern which had motivated the initiative emerged into the open. What did reappear was the curious notion of a federation which did not affect the sovereignty of the participant nations. Of the various replies only the Dutch reply drew attention to this, clearly stating that the unlimited sovereignty of states was incompatible with the federal idea. The crucial replies of the three other major European powers, Britain, Germany and Italy, were largely critical. In the ensuing discussions in Geneva in September it was no surprise therefore to find that their representatives, Henderson, Curtius and Grandi, were happy to divert the initiative by setting up a Commission of Inquiry for European Union within the framework of the League of Nations. The intent, successful as it turned out, was to diffuse the European focus of the plan, by drawing out the global dimensions of the various issues with which the plan dealt. The world beyond Geneva was hardly auspicious anyway. Between September 1929 and September 1930 the world economic crisis had erupted, amidst the September 1930 discussions the *Reichstag* election, which was to increase greatly the vote for the NSDAP, took place, and the *annus terribilis* of 1931 was only months away.

The crisis of 1931 may have buried the Briand plan and any reasonable prospect of European unity which entailed the reconciliation of France and Germany but it did not bury the idea of Europe. The idea survived in many of its manifold forms. It survived in the perverse form of the national socialist New Order in which the worst vices of geopolitical calculation and pseudo-anthropological identity were revealed. It also survived amongst small groups of federalists who saw federation as an alternative to an obsolete system of states and federalism as an ideology which would unite people against the New Order without pitting them against each other in the aftermath of the war. It was, however, the war and the over-reaching ambition of the New Order which were to give the federalists their chance. In retrospect it appears that despite the instability of the European system between the wars, despite the diplomatic and economic crises, despite fears of the imminent dis-integration of society summed up by Toynbee, the crises of the interwar period were not severe enough. The existing states had too much to recommend them. Concentration of power and authority, control of armies and sources of revenue, and regulation of the economy were all embodied in the state. To surrender any of this on behalf of Europe or even of a lesser form of union was more than could be reasonably expected. Only in the wake of defeat and occupation were the existing states sufficiently shaken to allow the emergence of new, European, institutions. Even then the process had to be pushed along by the new superpowers who put their own stamp upon the idea of Europe.

The foregoing issues are explained in depth by the contributors to this volume. Ralph White shows how the impact of the First World War drove Coudenhove-Kalergi to Wilsonianism and, as his faith in that illusion faded, to the idea of Europe. Coudenhove-Kalergi's continental perspective was strengthened by a somewhat legalistic belief in the efficacy of pacts and treaties, but he was, above all, a visionary. Despite intermittent insights into the mechanisms of power politics the idealist never came to grips with *how* Europe was to unite. The Marxists examined by R.N. Berki provide a strong contrast to the idealism of the cosmopolitan aristocrat, Coudenhove-Kalergi. They thought in terms of the harsh realities of interests and conflict. This perspective still left open a variety of approaches to Europe. In the 1920s the assertion of the impossibility of unity in the light of inter-imperialist rivalry predominated. In the 1930s European unity appeared as an anti-Soviet strategy of reactionary capitalism. Yet there was also the ideal of a socialist Europe, of a revolutionary and united Europe, facing up to the challenge of the United States. A revolutionary Europe, however, soon ceased to be a realistic alternative and gave way to Stalin's 'socialism in one country'. A socialist Europe appeared more and more as yet another illusion of the interwar period.

That interest might point to European unity was recognised by politicians and businessmen. In Britain, as Robert Boyce argues, it was the businessmen rather than the politicians and officials of the Foreign Office who were convinced of the imminence of European unity. Again the American challenge loomed large in their calculations. That Europe would unite did not mean that Britain would unite with Europe. The Empire still beckoned as a viable and, for some, preferable alternative. Nevertheless, business opinion came to believe in 1929 that Europe must, and would be, united economically. Economic considerations are also prominent in Peter Krüger's article. It is, indeed, to the specific problems and plans which exercised the power-holders that he insists we should look if we want to know what Europe was like and might have been like. Both articles reveal that the debate about European unity was much more widespread than might be suspected from a consideration of the pro-European movements alone. Yet despite the pro-European inclinations of the Weimar politicians and despite the expectations of the British businessmen the nation-state remained the basic unit of political power and legitimacy. As the decade turned the prospects of European union grew darker and, from the perspective of 1935, could seem totally forlorn. *Europa* was in decay in the eyes of the novelist and anthropologist, Robert Briffault. The world of *Europa*, which is presented by George Lehman, resembles in some ways the world from which Coudenhove-Kalergi sprang. It is aristocratic, cosmopolitan and European. In Briffault's work it is also a world of the past. Contemporary Europe was fractured by violent nationalisms.

Nationalism and national identity held out against class, culture and even interest as the integrating factors of the interwar period, albeit not without a struggle. David Kirby explains how complicated this could be in the smaller states of Europe which were burdened by legacies and ambitions which outstripped their meagre resources. He also reminds us that the nation is not as 'natural' as its self-appointed representatives like to pretend. Equally important the nation was not necessarily the same thing for its prophets and its less exalted members. There is a difference between the image which the former seek to impose and the image which the latter perceive. The nationalism of the German national socialists, described by P.M.R. Stirk, was an extreme form of such imposed identities. It purported to be the most natural form of power and identity, to be superior to the individual, the state and international law. Yet alongside this natural form ran the claims of the movement to create a martial community. The tension between these two approaches grew as the national socialist ideologues turned their attention to international relations and the idea of a New Order in Europe. In the end the ideology of the New Order prefigured its practice and vice versa: domination by a self-appointed élite became the model for Europe as it was the model for Germany.

German national socialists were not the only enthusiasts of a New Order. Whereas they put the *Volk* or Core-State at the centre, radicals in Western Europe espoused planning as both a technical and moral way forward. This New Order, which is presented by M.L. Smith, was to provide a 'third way' as an alternative to the polarisation between communism and fascism which seemed to be on the agenda in the 1930s. Another, more specific, alternative to the mounting conflict was offered in Scandinavia. Here, neutrality bolstered by Nordic unity was, as Anthony Upton explains, to guard against the political ambitions of a resurgent Germany and Russia. Despite some public sympathy for the ideal of Nordic unity, which even extended to governmental circles, the more othodox interests of state prevailed and the ideal collapsed, temporarily at least, amidst the Second World War. If the exigencies of war induced a retreat into the boundaries of one's own state in Scandinavia they posed a different threat to the advocates of a third way in Western Europe. Like the German authoritarians some of the latter chose the path of collaboration with the national socialist New Order and consequently tarnished the alternative for which they had argued earlier. Others chose a different path and survived to reoffer their ideas at the end of the war. So too did the federalists. The roots of federalist and personalist ideas and the complex network of individuals and arguments which sustained them are traced in the contributions by John Loughlin and John Pinder. John Loughlin shows how Proudhonian federalism was taken up by a small group of young men and developed as a humanitarian response to the overwhelming authority of the state and the manifold crisis which they believed they faced in the 1930s. In England and Italy a different type of federalism prevailed. This more politically and institutionally oriented federalism, which went back to Hamilton, was to be at its strongest in Italy at the end of the war and has continued to influence many prominent advocates of European union. John Pinder unravels the threads which lead from the anglo-saxon federalists to the Italian opposition to Mussolini, showing how deeply indebted the latter were to the former. In these articles on federalism, as in many of the other contributions, the elements of continuity between the prewar and postwar worlds are clear. The same arguments and sometimes practically the same plans for or against European union persisted. Yet so too did some of the same problems. It also behoves us to recollect the costs of the progress that has been made and to ask, as Peter Krüger insists we should, what the cost of further progress will be. By the same token we must ask what the costs of the failure to make further progress will be.

Notes

1. Quoted in James Joll, 'Europe: an historian's view', *History of European Ideas*, Vol. 1 (1980), p. 7.
2. R.W.G. McKay, *Federal Europe*, (London, Michael Joseph, 1940), p. 28.
3. The phrase 'illusion of peace' occurs throughout Sally Marks, *The Illusion of Peace: International Relations in Europe 1918–1933* (London, Macmillan, 1975).
4. Walter A. McDougall, *France's Rhineland Diplomacy, 1918–1924* (Princeton, Princeton University Press, 1978, p. 3.
5. For a summary and interpretation of this view, see Gilbert Ziebura, *Weltwirtschaft und Weltpolitik 1922/24–1931* (Frankfurt-on-Main, Suhrkamp, 1984).
6. A.W. De Porte, *Europe between the Superpowers* (New Haven, Yale University Press, 1979), esp. pp. viii–ix.
7. McDougall, *France's Rhineland Diplomacy*, op. cit. pp. 250–379.
8. Ferdinand Fried, 'Hintergründe der Haager Konferenzen', *Die Tat*, Vol. 21 (1930), p. 899.
9. McDougall, *France's Rhineland Diplomacy*, op. cit., esp. pp. 113–26.
10. Hugh Thomas (ed.), *José Antonio Primo de Rivera. Selected Writings* (London, Cape, 1972), pp. 102–3.
11. Douglas W. Ford, 'The Forgotten Falangist: Ernesto Gimenez Caballero', *Journal of Contemporary History*, Vol. 10 (1975), pp. 3–18.
12. E.H. Carr, *The Twenty Years Crisis, 1919–1939* (London, Macmillan, 1939), p. 291.
13. McDougall, *France's Rhineland Diplomacy*, op. cit., p. 137.
14. Quoted in Anthony Adamthwaite, 'France and the coming of war', in Wolfgang J. Mommsen and Lothar Kettenacker (eds), *The Fascist Challenge and the Policy of Appeasement* (London, Allen and Unwin, 1982), p. 248.
15. Quoted by R.A.C. Parker, 'The failure of collective security in British appeasement', in Mommsen and Kettenacker (eds), *Fascist Challenge*, op. cit., p. 24. See Parker's article for the British attitude to the League of Nations given above.
16. Arnold J. Toynbee, *Survey of International Affairs 1931* (Oxford, R.I.I.A. 1932), p. 5.
17. M.L. Fledderus (ed.), *International Unemployment* (The Hague, I.R.I., 1932), p. 18.
18. For Coudenhove-Kalergi's ideas, see Carl H. Pegg, *Evolution of the European Idea 1913–1932* (Chapel Hill and London, University of North Carolina Press, 1983) and the chapter by Ralph White in this volume.
19. Quoted by Walter Lipgens, 'Europäische Einigungsidee 1923–1930 und Briands Europaplan im Urteil der Deutschen Akten', *Historisches Zeitschrift*, Vol. 203 (1966), p. 66.
20. *Documents on British Foreign Policy, 1919–1939*. Second Series, Vol. 1, p. 328.
21. T. Schieder, 'Idee und Gestalt des übernationalen Staates', *Historisches Zeitschrift*, Vol. 184 (1957), pp. 336–66.
22. Lionel Curtis, *World War. Its Cause and Cure* (London, Oxford University Press, 1945), pp. 54–6.

23. M.H. Boehm, 'Federalism', in Edwin A. Seligman (ed.), *Encyclopaedia of the Social Sciences*, Vol. 7 (London, Macmillan, 1932).
24. Louis Domeratzky, *The International Cartel Movement* (United States Department of Commerce Trade Information Bulletin, No. 556, 1928), p. 38.
25. The Memorandum can be found in *International Conciliation*, Special Bulletin, 1930.
26. Quoted in Pegg, *Evolution of the European Idea*, op. cit., p. 119.

2 The Europeanism of Coudenhove-Kalergi

Ralph White

Count Richard Coudenhove-Kalergi was the founder of the Pan-European Union, the first and best known of the Europeanist groups to emerge after 1918. Although the movement survives to this day, its greatest achievement lay in its trail-blazing evangelism from its birth in 1923 to 1939. Coudenhove-Kalergi's Europeanism was essentially a phenomenon of the interwar years.

It was also both original and idiosyncratic. Churchill, in his foreword to Coudenhove-Kalergi's later memoir, characteristically entitled *An Idea Conquers the World*, noted: 'The resuscitation of the pan-European idea is largely identified with Count Coudenhove-Kalergi. The form of his theme may be crude, erroneous and impractical, but the impulse and the inspiration are true.'[1] This distinction tells us much of the distinctiveness of Coudenhove-Kalergi's Europeanism. Perhaps it was inevitable that an extraordinary man, having devoted his life to propagating an idealistic solution to centuries-old problems of Europe's peace and prosperity, should have provoked the charges of impracticability and unrealism. Yet, as we shall see, Coudenhove-Kalergi was both visionary and *grand simplificateur*: in his Europeanism we find a refusal to be boxed in by contemporary notions of reality, or to be intimidated by the gulf between what is and what ought to be. It is not surprising that more prosaic and limited schemes of European union also surfaced in the interwar years, some by way of reaction, and that the Pan-European Union proposals were not the only ones from within the liberal-democratic or bourgeois camp.

Coudenhove-Kalergi turned to the idea of a federal union of Europe in the aftermath of the First World War. That he did so was the result of the effect upon a person of his generation, ancestry and upbringing of the traumas of the war and the postwar crisis in Europe. In this assessment we shall consider first his remarkable background, together with his experiences during and after the war, which precipitated his conversion to Pan-Europeanism, and then his European credo as set forth in his treatise *Pan-Europe,* written in 1923.

Born in 1894, Coudenhove-Kalergi was a member of the European intelligentsia that has been called 'the generation of 1914'[2]: those whose formative years were spent in the two decades preceding the outbreak of the war and to whom the experience of those years, capped by that of the war itself, gave a sense of special identity. This expressed itself in a restlessness with the basic structures and values of bourgeois Europe after 1918, and in the support of significant numbers of the European intelligentsia for such radical alternatives as communism, fascism and—in Coudenhove-Kalergi's case—Pan-Europeanism. His form of radical departure never gained anything like the mass support or success of the others, or even the Leage of Nations; yet it remains an important aspect of its origins that Pan-Europeanism emerged as one of the number of brave new worlds embraced by men of Coudenhove-Kalergi's generation in the characteristic mood of despair and hope about Europe's future that prevailed after 1918.

If Coudenhove-Kalergi shared his era with his contemporaries, he shared little else. The distinctiveness of his Pan-European response to the common experiences of his generation reflected the singularity of his background. It is only through being aware of these personal circumstances that we can understand the source of the precocious cosmopolitanism, the talent for 'thinking in continents', that provides the key to Coudenhove-Kalergi's Pan-European thought and action. It was no idle comment when he described himself as one 'born and educated for internationalism'.[3]

Coudenhove-Kalergi was a child of the aristocracy of the Austro-Hungarian Empire and inherited the traditions of that class and that multinational polity. These traditions were important but not unique—unlike the story of his own family and background. Thomas Mann's description of him as a 'Euroasiatic type of noble cosmopolite' pinpoints his remarkable origins. The Coudenhoves could trace their lineage to the oldest nobility of medieval Brabant; by the end of the eighteenth century they moved to Austria where the son of the first count married a Baltic baroness, and one of *their* sons married the Kalergi heiress. The Kalergis added breadth to the proven depth of the Coudenhove line, and a fortune. Cretan in origin, the family had acquired connections of one sort and another with the Norwegian, Russian, British, German, Polish and French aristocracies. The history of the Coudenhove-Kalergis was itself an achievement in international relations: intermarriage and migration elevated their European identity far above national ties. This process was fortified when the Coudenhove-Kalergis took to the diplomatic profession, in the service of the Austro-Hungarian Empire in the late nineteenth century. This was a prelude to the transcending of not only national but European confines. Their penchant for cosmopolitanism assumed global proportions when Heinrich Coudenhove-Kalergi, head of the Austrian Legation in Tokyo, married the Japanese Buddhist Mitsuho Aoyama, in 1892. Count Richard was their second child.

In 1906 the family returned to Europe, to its seat, the castle and estate of Ronsperg in Bohemia: the infant Richard and his elder brother were accompanied by their Japanese nurses. In his memoirs, Coudenhove-Kalergi describes an idyllic childhood, sheltered and serene, at Ronsperg in the years before 1914. His father, whom he revered, retired from diplomacy and devoted himself to his estates. A scholarly country nobleman with a beautiful Japanese wife, he created at Ronsperg a pattern of civilised family life remarkable for its fusion of Oriental and European souls and culture.

Great broadmindedness and tolerance enabled this community to live at peace, Coudenhove-Kalergi recalls; his family was devoutly catholic in both senses of the word. Outside the castle walls, the Czech and German borders limiting the estate, and the hostility of the Czechs and Sudetens, emphasised the force of nationalism: 'In striking contrast to the national hatred that surrounded it,' he remembers, 'Our castle was an oasis of international spirit.'[4] Further, Coudenhove-Kalergi claims that because of the many contacts his family had with the East, 'we were conscious of the fact that Europe represented, above all national dissensions, a single branch of humanity. Europe seemed to be anything but a union from the mere European point of view. Only on a world wide background did this unity manifest itself.' Indeed, the reality of the differences between the continents of East and West—which his family experienced for themselves in their daily life—led them to sense that the different national groups in Europe 'all belonged to the one great paternal class of Europeans, children of a single race, a single continent, a single civilisation and a single destiny'.[5]

On the evidence of his memoirs, therefore, Coudenhove-Kalergi gained three insights from his upbringing at Ronsperg which were crucial for his later Europeanism: a global perspective; a sense of the substance of continental rather than purely national kinships; and a feeling for the unity and identity of the peoples of continental Europe, for all their national divisions and conflict. These were intimations mediated through family and childhood experience, not articulated yet as academic analysis or political programme: but enormously significant all the same. Paradoxically, Coudenhove-Kalergi's formal education was purely European. His father, for all his personal and cultural ecumenicity, did not wish his children to become intellectual hybrids; the Japanese nurses were sent home, and Richard was educated as an Austrian, a Christian, and a European. It was this combination of a conventional formal training with an extraordinary informal upbringing, this fusion of continentalism and globalism, that shaped

Coudenhove-Kalergi and made possible his Pan-Europeanism. It enabled him, later, to see, in a remarkable way, Europe and its problems, from both within and without.

For the moment his formal education continued along highly traditional lines. In 1908, at the age of 14, he began to study at the Theresianum Academy in Vienna. This was the Empire's Eton, and it sought to perpetuate the ideals of the Austrian monarchy among pupils drawn mainly from the children of titled families. When he graduated, in 1913, he thought his vocation was to be a professor of philosophy. In fact he was able to pursue his philosophical and historical studies at the University of Vienna during the First World War, for a lung affliction gained him exemption from military service. By 1917 he had gained a doctorate in philosophy and was writing his first book, on the aesthetic basis of ethics. But in 1917 also occurred the seminal events—the revolutions in Russian and America's entry into the war—that transformed his interest in the war and in politics to such an extent that by November 1918, at the age of 24, Coudenhove-Kalergi was ready to forsake his projected academic career for a lifetime of politics. It was this process of immersion in the public world from 1917 onward that exposed the potency of the unconventional internationalism in his outlook and led him to define his Europeanism.

Before the war, Coudenhove-Kalergi's interests in public affairs had been limited. At school, he remembers, he was conscious of the cosmopolitan culture of Vienna, and of the internationalism of the aristocracy, the Jewish intelligentsia and the social democratic working classes. But the appeal of extreme nationalism and anti-semitism to the middle classes was also clear, not least to the pro-Germans, the Christian Socialists, and to Adolf Hitler, his Viennese contemporary. He participated in Viennese society without great relish, with the notable exception of meeting and subsequently marrying the actress Ida Roland; otherwise he preferred to spend his free time at Ronsperg.

The First World War he regarded as a crime and a folly. He wrote to Ida Roland in August 1914 that

> I do not consider the terrible murders and cruelties now raging in all parts of the world the most tragic elements in the World War. What is more terrifying than anything, perhaps for centuries to come, is the awakening of the aggressive tendency of nationalism which is nothing but the apparently vanishing religious fanaticism, reappearing under a new form.[6]

This nationalism was not the liberal variety of the earlier nineteenth century, but racial, anti-semitic Germanism: 'I am afraid there are no more cosmopolitans left in Europe,' he lamented. The guilt for this lay with scholars like Gobineau and Chamberlain rather than with war-minded statesmen. He added in filial admiration, 'My father must have foreseen all this when, in conscious opposition to Chamberlain, he fought anti-semitism. I wish to continue his work on a vaster scale.'[7] This did not mean, however, that he believed that only the Germans were aggressors. If he inherited his father's distaste for anti-semitism, he also accepted the traditional Austrian apprehension of Russia. Behind the struggle between Austro-Hungary and Serbia he saw the clash of Pan-Germanism and Pan-Slavism: he believed that both Germany and Russia needed the Danube basin as a springboard to European hegemony. This fear of an underlying Russian threat to Europe was to colour the development of his Pan-Europeanism, as will be seen.

Although Coudenhove-Kalergi remained a convinced and consistent opponent of the war, it was not until 1917 that events stirred him to political involvement. The collapse of Tsardom and the entry of the United States enabled him to see the war in clear-cut moral and ideological terms with which he could identify: the Allied cause was at last a genuinely democratic one. He found himself a passionate supporter of Woodrow Wilson, the American President, whose fourteen-point programme for peace commanded, he thought, widespread popular support in Europe and America. This commitment to Wilsonian democracy and internationalism as the key to the future was sharpened by the rise of Lenin and the Bolsheviks. Although Coudenhove-Kalergi acknowledged the importance of social and economic justice, and conceded the radical criticisms of capitalist society on this score, individual liberty remained his highest ideal. Further, he retained his conviction that liberal democratic regimes were capable of what he called 'social evolution', i.e. of redressing social and economic grievances. Thus his existing apprehension about Russian expansionism was supplemented by doubts about Bolshevism: doubts that were greatly intensified as the regime consolidated its position.

As the war drew to its close in 1918, therefore, this view of Soviet Russia as an increasingly alien threat strengthened Coudenhove-Kalergi's belief in the great and immediate need for a Wilsonian settlement. His view of the radical urgency of a Wilsonian solution was a Central European one: it reflected not only the proximity of Soviet Russia and the appeal of communism but, even more, the dramatic collapse of existing and often centuries-old political structures as a result of the war. The Tsarist, Hohenzollern and Habsburg monarchies had all been swept away. Coudenhove-Kalergi experienced for himself the final disintegration of the Austro-Hungarian empire in the space of a few weeks in the summer of 1918, as aggressive nationalisms conspired to destroy what had been a viable economic, geographical and political unit. The resulting political instability, economic chaos and social misery which Coudenhove-Kalergi saw for himself, not least in Vienna, he took to be a symptom of the European situation in general.

An old regime—that of semi-feudal, authoritarian, imperial Central and Eastern Europe—had gone. Wilson's democratic and internationalist pre-scriptions for peace offered hope of a new European and world order, in the midst of tragedy and despair. Coudenhove-Kalergi proclaimed that this was 'the world for which I had been born and educated'. His political education, he said, was now accomplished: he had broken with 'the prejudices of my class, with all national imperialisms, and with the narrow outlook of capitalism'. It was to the enormous task of reconstructing a Wilsonian new world that, Coudenhove-Kalergi believed, his origins and upbringing called him, and to which he would now devote his life. It was in this commitment to Wilsonian principles that Coudenhove-Kalergi declared himself to be at one with his generation. He assumed that most young men and women in Europe shared his faith in Wilson in 1918:

> We all felt that the crumbling world of imperialism and semi-feudalism was linked to the old generation, responsible for the terrible war and that it was now up to our own generation to build a new and brighter world on sounder and more moral principles . . . That it was up to us to build a new and better Europe on the ruins of the old.[8]

This is not, of course, Pan-Europeanism. It was the *failure* to achieve a Wilsonian peace in 1919, and the calamitous (as Coudenhove-Kalergi saw them) consequences for Europe and the world, of the peace treaties, that led him in the early 1920s to abandon the vision of a new world order as an immediate and practicable enterprise. Instead he turned to the ideal of a united states of Europe. His Pan-Europeanism was a response to the perceived inadequacy and failure of the peace settlement; it was the reaction of a frustrated Wilsonian.

Coudenhove-Kalergi reacted practically as the decline in Wilson's influence exposed his own impotence. He set about making a name for himself by contributing articles to journals, mainly in Germany and Austria, and by publishing his first book, on *'Ethics and Hyper-Ethics'*. He soon found material to sink his teeth into as a writer on public affairs: the results of the Paris peace conference. His analysis of the peace settlement was pessimistic and prophetic; it provided the immediate stimulus for his conversion to the idea of a federal Europe.

He agreed that a new Europe had indeed emerged from Paris, but it was not the Europe of his dreams. Instead he found Europe 'more torn, more dismembered, more divided by hate than ever before'. This was no new order but a new and dangerous disorder, a chaos, which he contrasted to the relative international stability of Europe before 1914, and which he saw as an expression of undisciplined and (in the case of the victors) vindictive nationalism. He was appalled at the creation of 'a dozen Alsace-Lorraines'—

the artificially created successor states of Central Europe which nourished national hatreds and provided seedbeds of future war. He was shocked at the treatment of Germany, especially economically, and the incentive thereby created for future conflict betwen France and Germany. To Coudenhove-Kalergi, the twenty-six states of Europe constituted an anarchy which the League of Nations was powerless to restrain. Wars, he noted, continued, between Russia and Poland, between Greece and Turkey. This encouraged those discontented with the peace settlement, the revisionists, above all Germany, and defenders of the treaties, above all France. He had nightmare visions of a war between a revisionist alignment of Germany, Russia and Italy, on the one hand, and France, Poland and their allies, on the other, a war that would destroy finally Europe and its Western civilisation.

Again, one can see that this pessimism about the prospects for peace in Europe was especially fuelled by the situation in Central Europe. And this was not just political, not just a matter of the probability, perhaps the inevitability, of war, but also economic and social, a question of the chaos and misery Coudenhove-Kalergi found in postwar Vienna. It was in the divided lands of the old Austro-Hungarian empire that he found the problems, in their acutest form, that beset postwar Europe: rampant and conflicting nationalisms, the oppression of minorities, the creation of tariff barriers. In turn these threw up the great problems that confronted Europe in the years after the peace settlement: the danger of European war; the danger of terrible economic collapse; and the danger of Bolshevism, due not least to the incapacity of the democratic regimes to handle these questions. A new and radical solution to the international anarchy and economic dismemberment of postwar Europe had to be found: for Coudenhove-Kalergi it lay in the notion of a federal union of the continent.

Between 1920 and 1922 his thinking on Europeanism became clearer. He was deeply convinced that, although the structure and performance of the League of Nations undermined belief in the immediate possibility of a Wilsonian world order, history was passing, perhaps had passed, out of the age of the local national state. He remained unshakeably sure that the era of nationalism was over, despite the potency of its contemporary forms. Coudenhove-Kalergi's origins, upbringing and values committed him to the primacy of international identity and kinship. So he came to the view that history, which to him meant world history, was in an intermediate stage, that of continental or super-continental federations. Although Coudenhove-Kalergi was to refine the details of this 'thinking in continents' considerably, the basic assumption was articulated from the early 1920s onward, and was central to his Pan-Europeanism. For Europe stood between the continental giants, a continent herself, but unorganised; instead, she was divided into nearly thirty sovereign states, each following the political and economic laws of the jungle.

Thus Coudenhove-Kalergi came to believe, by 1922, that a federation of all continental states of Europe was the only solution to Europe's international-political and economic problems, was the prerequisite for her defence and survival in a world of continental federations, and was compatible with a scheme of world order based on the League of Nations. Negatively, he was sure that if Europe failed to reorganise on a federal basis, a second European war would follow. So he studied other, earlier, experiments in federalism, as well as proposals for European union. Despite individual projects for uniting Europe produced over the centuries, he found no present organisation for the study or promotion of the idea. And he saw clearly enough that European public opinion tended to be dominated by either national sentiments, or, if international, by the universalist values of the League of Nations. A major programme of propaganda and education had to be launched, to create a popular sense of regional European identity and solidarity, as a necessary preliminary to the establishment of a federal Europe; and this in turn required the creation of a Pan-European organisation and movement. It was to these tasks that Coudenhove-Kalergi, by the end of 1922, was devoting the main part of his energies.

Early in 1922 Coudenhove-Kalergi wrote a draft of his Pan-European programme for two leading European papers: The *Neue Freie Presse* of Vienna and the *Vossische Zeitung* in Berlin. In the spring of 1923 he produced the definitive statement of his Europeanism in his book *Pan-Europe*, which was published in October of that year. It became the first of a regular series of Pan-European publications from the movement's own publishing house, which was set up in Vienna, and which was the cornerstone of the movement's publicity and propaganda.

Although the definition and application of Pan-Europeanism as set out in *Pan-Europe* varied subsequently according to circumstance, the book contains the essentials of Coudenhove-Kalergi's creed. It was programmatic and propagandist, a guide to basic principles intended to create sympathy and support for the idea of a federal European union. It was not a scholarly historical or philosophical monograph and should not be read as such, but as the intended manifesto for a movement. It fused the diagnosis of Europe's current discontents which had preoccupied Coudenhove since 1917 with the global vision inherited from his origins and upbringing, with remarkable results.

The profound flaws in Europe's internal organisation were now set in the context of Europe's external position; these contemporary ills had even more fateful consequences, and were in need of even more radical treatment, when seen in the light of the decline of Europe's world position, and of the rise of great non-European continental-federal powers. This setting of Europe's problems in an intercontinental, global framework, reflected Coudenhove-Kalergi's capacity to see Europe from within and without and is the essence of his Pan-Europeanism.

The foreword immediately set the scene with the argument that 'whilst the rest of the world is making daily progress, Europe is going steadily downhill'. The cause of this decline was not natural or 'biological' but political, a matter of Europe's senile political system, not the senility of its peoples—who remained qualitatively 'the most productive human reservoir in the world'. But Europeans were looking backwards, and Coudenhove-Kalergi called for the reorganisation of Europe out of its present anarchy. It is clear that the 'organisation' Coudenhove-Kalergi had in mind here was that of the relationship between states of Europe, a problem ignored as utopian compared to the relationship between classes, a question which, he acknowledged, dominated public debate. This led the writer to formulate the 'European question' thus: 'can Europe, so long as its political and economic disunion lasts, maintain its peace and independence, with respect to the growing World Powers; or is it bound, in order to preserve its existence, to organise itself into a Federal Union?'[9]

Thus the linkage of Europe's internal weaknesses and external vulnerability was immediately established, which enabled the case for a federal union to be presented as one of peace, security and even survival *vis-à-vis* the external world, as well as a resolution of Europe's domestic problems. Further, on a practical level, this consolidation of Europe into a politico-economic federation would only be possible if the idea was transformed from utopia to reality by mass support. In turn, this led to a generational appeal: 'I call upon the youth of Europe to accomplish this task'.

Coudenhove-Kalergi devotes half his treatise to an assessment of Europe's changing relations with the outside world, and half to Europe's internal state. In both cases a federal Europe is embraced as a necessary, perhaps inevitable solution in an argument that bounds from a pessimistic view of Europe's decline in the world and a vivid and tragic sense of the internal state of the continent, to a compelling and hopeful vision of Pan-Europe as it should and could be. His analysis is urgent, stronger on the desirability of federalist change than on its practicality, on ends rather than means, on outline rather than detail. Some issues are grasped unexpectedly, others are ignored or skirted; prescient insights comingle with naïve or questionable assertions.

The first half of the work tells us far more about Europe's global position and especially Pan-Europe's relations with Britain, Russia, America and the League of Nations than it does about European union itself. The transformation of Europe's position in the world was fundamental to Coudenhove-Kalergi's thinking, and his explanation of this reveals a characteristic interplay of orthodox and unusual elements. He cites first, and more familiarly, the decline, since the nineteenth century, of the 'world hegemony' of the leading European powers. When he identifies these as not only Britain but Russia (as a 'European World Empire'), Asia (primarily through the rise of Japan) and America north *and south*, we sense the author's distinctive view. For, he argues, these world powers were not traditional European-style great powers writ large, but *new kinds* of world power grouping, which he refers to variously as 'continental-federations' or 'people's empires', functioning as 'planetary fields of force': the key examples being the British Empire, the Russian Empire, Pan-America and the Chinese Republic—which Japan reinforced to form an Asian or 'Mongolian' bloc.

This political regrouping of the extra-European world was reinforced by a scientific factor: the speeding-up of travel and communications had the effect of shrinking states and bringing them closer. The nation-state as it had historically evolved had become too small to stay independent: 'it must be supplemented or completed by the establishment of federations'.[10] Here the author moved characteristically from an observed historical or current tendency to a federalist imperative.

Thus Europe had moved from the centre of the world stage to its periphery. Individual European states and peoples were asserting their sovereignty and independence, going 'atomic' whilst the rest of the world integrated. So Europe had not only lost its hegemony, but would lose its independence and remaining prosperity if disunity continued. He later argued that, economically and militarily, a united Europe would be one of the strongest world powers, and culturally would remain the world leader.

There were two further stings in this tail. Until and unless this 'European question' was resolved, there could be no world peace. As long as Europe remained an unfederated jumble of peoples and states, she remained a power keg of conflict. And, second, the European question would only be settled either by voluntary uniting of the European peoples, or by imposition, by force, possibly by Russian conquest. The choice between a federal future and the alternatives could not have been put more starkly.

It was necessary for Coudenhove-Kalergi to define the extent, the frontiers of his Pan-Europe if he was to complete his analysis of the external dimension. He argued that 'the concept Europe arose from a blending of geographical, political and cultural elements', each of which had been defined, and distinguished from the others, differently, in the past: this explained the varying history of Europe's frontiers. The key to the frontiers of Pan-Europe was political-cultural; this exposed the importance of Coudenhove-Kalergi's commitment to Western liberal democracy, for Pan-Europe embraced all the *democratic* states of continental Europe. Russia excluded herself because of her non-democratic political system, and Britain excluded herself because of her extra-European world role. Coudenhove-

Kalergi greatly exaggerated the 'liberation of Eastern Europe' whereby West European liberalism and nationhood had been extended throughout the Continent, to provide a homogeneous political base for Pan-Europe.

Britain and British policy were central to Coudenhove-Kalergi's Pan-European scheme of things. He was acutely conscious that Britain was part of Europe, and that her attitude to any proposal of Pan-Europe might be decisive. Because of Britain's imperial and Atlantic ties Coudenhove-Kalergi opted for 'Little Europe', without England but—this was strongly emphasized—not against her. England must agree with the principle of Pan-Europe and be able to join, if she decided to accord it a priority greater than her other links. The writer emphasized that Pan-Europe must aim, with England, to be a mainstay of world peace and a step towards world organisation. England, he knew, traditionally opposed the union of Europe under a single leader or nation; so by removing the possibility of a hegemony over Europe, Pan-Europe would enable England to sustain her neutrality. Pan-Europe would thus be able to offer England continental peace, prosperity and safety from a Russian threat.

'The menace' of Russia was then considered. No single European state would be a match for an organised and industrialised Russia; the only way of overcoming the danger of a Russian invasion was by European consolidation. A race was commencing between Russia and Europe as to which should first recover from its breakdown: if Russia recovered economically and Europe remained politically split, she would come to dominate Europe, 'Red or White'. The answer (as with England) lay in a security pact, this time guaranteeing the protection of the European land frontiers; this was to be backed up by a compulsory treaty of arbitration among all states of Europe. The first would ensure peace between Russia and Europe, while the second would prevent Russian interference. The author's faith in pacts and treaties is touching—yet he was shrewd enough to stress the possibility of links developing between the Soviet Union and Germany.

Finally, Coudenhove-Kalergi asserted Russia and Pan-Europe's interdependence in the economic sphere, which should tend to peaceful political relations. For European and world disarmament depended on Russia and Europe forging a lasting peace: and if Europe reorganised, Russia would realise the futility of a war and would be ready to disarm: the path to universal disarmament would then be clear. We can see here, as elsewhere, how the pessimism with which Coudenhove-Kalergi discussed the circumstances—in this case the Russian menace—which justified and necessitated Pan-Europe stood in stark contrast to the optimism of his assessment of the benefits it would confer.

Next the author turned to the question of Europe and America. Again he pressed the case that 'To its (federal) unity America owes its unexampled rise: to its disunion Europe owes its unexampled decline'.[12] Specifically, in world markets Europe would be unable to compete with America. The only solution was threefold: the economic federation of continental Europe's democracies; the cooperation of a Pan-European customs union with Russia; and disarmament throughout the continent. And this solution was itself only possible on the basis of a political union of the European states, which would replace war by a compulsory court of arbitration and a joint guarantee of frontiers. Again, the underpinning of Coudenhove-Kalergi's geopolitical 'thinking in continents' with legalistic belief in pacts, unions, treaties, courts and guarantees is notable.

If the United States was essentially an example of the economic case for federalism, Pan-America was *the* political inspiration for Pan-Europe. Coudenhove-Kalergi prayed for a European statesman to lead the way by convening a Pan-European conference along the line of recent Pan-American ones, and for a Pan-European bureau, again on the Pan-American model. He believed that had such a bureau been in existence in 1914 it could well have stopped the First World War breaking out: another expression of his faith in the impact federal organs would have.

Finally, on the external front, Coudenhove-Kalergi considered Europe and the League of Nations. Although sympathetic to the League's purpose in theory, he objected to the 'inorganic', 'mechanical' structure of the League's membership, based as it was on the abstract principle of *any* single state's right to apply, irrespective of size or any other consideration. He also found it unsatisfactory as a European institution: it was no substitute for Pan-Europe. Neither Germany nor Russia were members. Even if they were, the situation would remain that the League enabled non-European member states to meddle in European affairs. Europe must oppose this League tutelage; Europe was for Europeans; a European Monroe doctrine should be proclaimed.

Instead, the League should be reformed so that it dealt only with intercontinental problems: Europe's own problems should be left to Pan-Europe. So Coudenhove-Kalergi advocated the autonomy of Pan-Europe within the League, as part of its restructuring on regional lines. He was to have difficulty fending off the charge that his Pan-Europeanism was fundamentally hostile to the League, and that his proposals for regional restructuring were little more than a smoke-screen.

Many of the themes developed in the second part of Coudenhove-Kalergi's treatise on the internal state of Europe have been encountered already. In particular he focused on the question of war and peace, the present political and economic situation of the continent, the key role of Franco-German relations, and the problem of nationalism.

The author claimed more urgently than ever that 'At this moment Europe is rushing headlong towards another war',[13] the evidence he cites being the current diplomatic and military preparations for war of the states of Eastern and Central Europe. Again Coudenhove-Kalergi demanded a series of legally binding measures: the necessity for these arose from the nature of any future war, which would far surpass the First World War in terror and destruction. He certainly shared the anti-war feelings of many of his era, and this was reinforced by the conviction that only one state would gain from European war—Russia. He managed to combine the question—begging assertion that the European states would be infinitely better off today had they held their peace conference in the spring of 1914, not 1919—with the insight that it was 'absurd optimism' to think that experience of the last war would stop European states going to war again.

So, more genuine guarantees of peace were necessary to render war between European states as inconceivable as war within the United States or the British Empire. Only a 'pan-European Federation, by the introduction and joint guarantee of a compulsory court of arbitration, can definitely secure the internal peace of Europe.' Once European peace was achieved, the road to world peace lay open: treaties of arbitration between Pan-Europe and the other world powers would be necessary to guarantee intercontinental peace.

Economically, meanwhile, the continent had gone backwards: the success of the nationalist demagogues at the peace conference meant that a liberated Europe contained the germ of economic decay. These economic problems, it was argued, would have to be discussed and settled at Pan-European conferences. Thus, Europe had to rebuild its devastated regions, restore the morality of work, and prepare the way to a continental customs union. Coudenhove-Kalergi was sure that European peoples would 'gladly' relinquish some of their sovereign powers in order to save themselves from famine, bankruptcy and war. And if common sense should fail to create Pan-Europe, necessity would do so, pronounced the author, again fusing the desirable and the inevitable.

Coudenhove-Kalergi's realism was, however, straightway evident in his insistence that the present-day frontiers of Europe, as defined in the peace treaties, would be very hard to change. Therefore Pan-Europe must start from the present territorial arrangements and attack the present system of customs unions, so that the economic regions of Europe would be fused in one economic entity, which alone would keep pace with the United States. This principle of building up to a continental federation by integrating smaller regional units also applied on the political front: Coudenhove-Kalergi cited the Little Entente, and the Scandinavian countries, as examples of such regional groupings already in existence.

Coudenhove-Kalergi then confronted what he called the greatest obstacle to Pan-Europe: the thousand-year rivalry of France and Germany. Now their fates were enjoined—they would sink or swim together, taking Europe with them. France's problem was security, which could be achieved by policies of either the annihilation of Germany, or conciliation. It clearly mattered enormously to Coudenhove-Kalergi's Pan-Europeanism that France should pursue a conciliatory policy, not least the aim that Germany should become 'the bulwark against the Russian peril'.

Coudenhove-Kalergi depicted Germany as also facing a choice between revenge or understanding. The former carried the awful prospect of another war against France, with Germany allied to Russia. Hence the necessity, from a Pan-European standpoint, of Germany pursuing a policy of understanding, with implications akin to those of France opting for a similar course. In both countries the only options were therefore either what Coudenhove-Kalergi called 'chauvinism', or Pan-Europe: and only concerted action by Pan-Europeans would defeat Franco-German chauvinism.

The problem of chauvinism provoked Coudenhove-Kalergi to a strong attack on contemporary forms of nationalism. Especially he denied that the nations of Europe were communities of blood. On the contrary, nations were communities of the spirit, which grew out of the action and reaction between gifted people and their great men. Further, these national cultures were closely interwoven parts of a great and homogeneous European culture. Education was a vital process in sustaining and spreading the realisation of this diversity-within-unity of European culture.

This redefinition of nationalism as cultural, not racial, and European as well as national, had great implications for the question of frontiers—a question vital to East-Central Europe, and which, he argued, West Europeans under-rated. For if nations were communities of spirit, they could not be delineated by frontiers, whereas states could be, and indeed were, so delimited, usually arbitrarily, by might, as in the recent peace settlement. Coudenhove-Kalergi argued that implied in his definition of nationalism was, therefore, a radical disassociation of nation and state. Further, what he called the Pan-European edict of liberation, arising from his cultural definition of nationalism, deprived state frontiers of their national meaning; the Pan-European customs union deprived them of economic meaning; and the Pan-European security pact deprived them of strategic meaning. Thus, he argued, if and when the economic and national causes of political hatred between neighbouring states were removed, this hatred would automatically cease. Coudenhove-Kalergi denounced the artificial fostering of the national and racial hatreds between people, and pledged that Pan-Europeans would work for national reconciliation through education and propaganda, including exchanges of teachers, students and children internationally.

Only at the very end of his work, and in the baldest terms, did Coudenhove Kalergi consider how Pan-Europe was to be achieved. It would be done in stages. First came the calling of a Pan-European conference which he proclaimed 'would produce an enthusiastic echo throughout the world'. Intriguingly he thought Italy the most obvious state to take this step, as the power living in friendly relations with all the states of the continent. An enthusiastic open letter to Mussolini followed; his search for patrons led him in strange directions. The programme of this first conference must be firmly outlined: territorial questions would be excluded and committees formed to deal with a court of arbitration, a court of guarantees, disarmament, minorities, communications, customs, currency, debts and culture. Resolutions would also be passed to commit the member states to meet regularly, and to found a Pan-European bureau, on the lines of the Pan-American model, 'as the central organ of the movement for unification'.

Thus a great programme of Pan-European work would, in this first stage, be set in train. Stage two would see results, in the form of the conclusion of compulsory treaties of arbitration and of security pacts between all the democratic states of the continent. The treaties and pacts would be backed up by the establishment of a court of arbitration, plus reciprocal frontier guarantees for those who wished to forge a 'peace alliance'. The advantages of this would be so great that soon all European states would want to join.

The work of stage two was therefore essentially political and strategic; that of stage three was economic. This would begin work on a Pan-European customs union, that is, the federation of Europe into a coherent economic entity. Coudenhove-Kalergi did concede that this would take time, but work on the abolition of existing customs barriers must be energetically pursued. An obvious starting point was the successor states of the old Austro-Hungarian empire: they would lead the way in creating regional customs or monetary unions, which would later amalgamate.

Finally, in stage four, a Pan-European constitution would be hammered out. There would be two chambers: a house of peoples and a house of states, the former of three hundred representatives, the latter of twenty-six representatives of the eligible European states. Equality of language in these chambers must prevail, but English should be made the compulsory language in all primary and secondary schools. This was because English was a world language, a 'natural Esperanto'.

Coudenhove-Kalergi then spelt out that all the states of Pan-Europe would gain more than they would lose from a federal union: although those of Eastern Europe had most to gain together with national minorities and European overseas territory.

He appealed to all democratic parties to support the Pan-European movement because Pan-Europe was the only sure guarantee against Bolshevism.

He recognised that neither the communist parties, being pro-Soviet, nor the parties of the far right, being strongly nationalist and militarist, could be expected to show anything but hostility. The non-communist socialist parties were mainly interested in a united socialist Europe and their position was ambiguous. The position of the mainly bourgeois parties in between was unclear, and Coudenhove-Kalergi believed that it was vital that they committed themselves to a viable foreign policy—such as Pan-Europe—that was neither pro-Soviet nor extreme nationalist.

Coudenhove-Kalergi then characterised Pan-Europe's opponents. The 'national chauvinists', as he called them, would be the noisiest; the communists would demand the inclusion of the Soviet Union; and the militarists would hope to do well from another war. Most of all, however, he feared those with vested interests in industries and agriculture protected by monopolies and national tariff barriers: these would be the most dangerous and powerful opponents of the Pan-European idea, with the resources to mobilise opinion in their cause. It was vital to get economic interests which favoured continental free trade to come out in favour of Pan-Europe against the protectionist lobby.

Finally, Pan-Europe could not get off the ground politically before taking root in the hearts and minds of all Europeans. A sense of Pan-European solidarity must be created and mobilised, for which a Pan-European movement was being established throughout Europe in the form of the Pan-European Union. Coudenhove-Kalergi appealed to the youth of Europe to lead this movement: he appealed to people of all classes, calling on women and intellectuals in particular. He looked to 'European Carnegies' to do for the movement what the American Carnegies had done for Pan-America. He concluded his book by defining the emblem of the movement: a white cross on a golden sun.

What, in sum, are we to make of Coudenhove-Kalergi's conception of Pan-Europe? It was a visionary structure rooted in a distinctive coupling of Europe's present weakness and her external vulnerability. It was this fusion that gave his Europeanism its urgency and its mixture of pessimism and hope. For Europe's plight after the First World War was so serious that the radical solution of federal union, however impractical or irrelevant it seemed, had to be considered, and, if only through necessity, adopted. His Pan-European movement would augment and facilitate a process, and determine the form, in Europe, of a historical development already in train over much of the globe.

The purpose of the book was to contrast the evils of the unreformed, degenerate, anarchic European status quo with the virtues of an organised, regenerate, federal continent: the contrast being deepened when Europe's prospects were placed against those of the continental federations that were coming to dominate the rest of the world. Further, *Pan-Europe*, like other works of prophecy whose point lies in depicting the evil of things as they are and the good of things as they ought to, or must be, assumed that the very act of depiction would suffice to achieve the goal in view. Coudenhove-Kalergi had shown *why* a federal union of Europe was so desirable, even necessary; his Pan-European movement, by publicity and propaganda, would spread the good news and mobilise public opinion and pressure. But beyond this, little attention was really paid to the great question: *how* was Pan-Europe to be accomplished? Certainly, Coudenhove-Kalergi set out the pattern of conferences, together with their agendas, which would supposedly achieve the goals of Pan-Europe, but little was said as to how to get states to attend or cooperate as required. One of the reasons for indifference to this matter of *means* lay in Coudenhove-Kalergi's ambiguity as to whether federal union was to be achieved as a result of necessity, inevitability or voluntary human policy and action.

Yet Coudenhove-Kalergi was sharply aware of the identity of the enemies of his form of Europeanism. His belief in the necessity for psychological warfare, education and propaganda as key roles for the Pan-European movement was based on the need to break down existing forms of nationalist prejudice. However, his own instincts and values led him to assume that nationalism was in decline, and that his movement was working with, not against, the tide of history; with the help of a great patron, his cause would triumph. Hence his confidence that a potentially favourable public opinion was there to be inspired, that the panoply of legal-institutional devices through which a federal Europe would guarantee its members peace, security and prosperity would actually work, and above all that governments themselves would respond to the imperatives of his Pan-Europeanism.

Professional diplomats of the time found it hard to take Coudenhove-Kalergi's Europeanism seriously. Tyrrell, then Permanent Under-Secretary of State at the British Foreign Office, wrote in 1926: 'I know Count Coudenhove: he is a thoroughly impractical theorist';[14] he could not have been more damning. Historians can take a longer and more charitable view. Coudenhove-Kalergi's Europeanism *was* idealistic and, in some respects, impractical, but as a radical critique of existing European order, it had to be.

As a blueprint for a federal Europe it was imprecise, naïve and overly optimistic, but again, in the nature of the exercise, this was inevitable. What matters more is that in the light of what we now know of the extensive developments of various forms of Europeanism in the interwar period, of the failures of the established systems of European and world polity in the same period and since, and of the growth of Europeanist movements and institutions since 1945, we can see that *Pan-Europe* had an original and prophetic quality. It authenticated the case for a form of federal union, however ill defined, as the prerequisite for the survival, identity, peace and prosperity of liberal Europe.

Notes

1. R.N. Coudenhove-Kalergi, *An Idea Conquers the World* (London, Hutchinson, 1953), introduction by Rt. Hon. Sir Winston S. Churchill, ix.
2. R. Wohl, *The Generation of 1914* (London, Weidenfeld and Nicolson, 1980).
3. R.N. Coudenhove-Kalergi, *Crusade for Pan-Europe* (New York, G.P. Putnam's Sons, 1943), p. 8.
4. ibid., p. 21.
5. ibid., p. 24.
6. ibid., p. 54.
7. ibid., p. 55.
8. ibid., pp. 5–6.
9. R.N. Coudenhove-Kalergi, *Pan-Europe* (New York, Alfred Knopf, 1926), Foreword, xiv.
10. ibid., p. 11.
11. ibid., p. 33.
12. ibid., p. 71.
13. ibid., p. 105.
14. Minute by Tyrrell, 2 October 1926, on a report from the British minister in Vienna on the first Pan-European Congress; FO 371/11246: C10417/10417/62, PRO, Kew.

3 Marxism and European Unity

R.N. Berki

For the purposes of this chapter 'Marxism' will be defined rather narrowly and concretely, whereas the term 'European unity' will be given a broader, less precise signification. 'European unity' thus should be conceived as embracing a great deal more than various endeavours which in our own days might be retrospectively looked upon as 'forerunners' of the European Community, namely federalist, functionalist and similar movements and aspirations, and attempts designed to harmonize European economies (e.g. customs unions). These, laudable as they might have been themselves, were pushed out of focus by more basic bread-and-butter issues, and by a series of conflicts between various economic and political interests. The most fundamental point about the interwar period is that it bore on itself the immediate legacy of the First World War, the most drastic and conspicuous specimen of European *disunity* encountered in modern times. Moves towards European unity took place under the heavy shadow of Petrograd and Versailles, in the context of bitter antagonisms, and—surely a relevant point to make here— led at the end to the even darker shadows of Guérnica, Munich, Katyn, Auschwitz and Dresden. Thus in order properly to understand the problem (or rather self-evident failure) of European unity in the interwar period, we must pay equal, and even more, regard to the Ruhr occupation, Locarno, the Dawes and Young Plans, the Anschluss and the Sudetenland, than to Pan-Europe and Briand's scheme. An effort must be made to confront the bare, ungarnished political reality of Europe, before, and possibly in preference to, surveying its more pleasing embellishments. And this, as we shall argue later on, is precisely where the value of an approach like Marxism to political reality can be seen to lie: in its hard, hostile, critical endeavour to cut through pious rhetoric and impotent 'good will' to the endemic conflicts hidden below. That Marxism contains its own pious rhetoric, which likewise requires to be critically confronted, is of course not to be denied; at the end of the chapter we shall have something to say on that score, too.

The 'Marxism', then, with which this chapter will be mainly preoccupied is the variety that is usually called 'revolutionary'. In effect this refers, in the context of the historical period which is our concern here, to the doctrines of Lenin, Trotsky, Bukharin, Stalin and their followers, and the political movements inspired by the same, i.e. the Soviet Union and communist parties adhering to the Comintern. This is the Marxism which, by virtue of its shrill critical stance, can most poignantly place European unity aspirations into a broader and deeper perspective, and also, by virtue of its occupying a veritable political power-base, can be seen to be playing an active, even principal, role in the world which contains these aspirations. In Marxism–Leninism (and movements closely allied) we have a well-nigh perfect coincidence of high theory and actual politics. Here furthermore, it might be argued, lies the *specificity* of the interwar period, both in relation to Marxism and in regard to the problem of European unity. This is the era which sees Marxism entering the world of power politics for the first time in a really big way.[1] And the same era sees European unity aspirations surging, and being thwarted, by political forces of which Marxist politics itself is an integral part. Thus revolutionary Marxism is both (politically) important and (theoretically) interesting. In the ensuing brief survey of the major stances and developments of Marxism in relation to the issue of European unity, we shall attempt to pinpoint the close interplay between high theory and actual politics. For the sake of convenience (as well as following crude historical commonsense) the chapter will be organized into three major substantive parts, to be followed by a short and (possibly– speculative–polemical conclusion. These three are first the 'background', where our concern will be predominantly with Marxist theory; then the volatile and truly 'revolution-ary' period of the 1920s, which sees Marxism being active and positive in regard to European unity aspirations; and finally the 1930s leading to the débâcle of the war, with Marxism now firmly settled as state power concerned primarily with the maintenance of the status quo, and the cause of 'European unity' submerging under the waves of renewed international conflict. Two things about Marxism will be highlighted. The first is what might be called the underlying paradox of Marxism, its being fundamentally both 'for' and 'against' European unity, generally and in the period in question; to which paradox we have to add the historical drama (tragedy, if you like) that the more Marxism becomes effective in the world the more its position *vis-à-vis* European unity has to be characterized as *negative*. The second concern is also with the negative significance of Marxism, now in relation to an *understanding* of the problem of European unity, with pointed reference to the interwar period; as already mentioned in passing, Marxism might be found useful in suggesting reasons why European unity was *not* achieved at the time.

It would scarcely be an exaggeration to say that Marxist doctrine and politics, as originally conceived, contain a built-in bias in favour of European unity. There are several points to be made in this connection. Firstly, on the negative or critical side, Marxism, following closely the direction of classical liberalism, contains a square condemnation of the modern 'sovereign' state, including the nation-state, which it assigns among super-structural and historically determined social phenomena and which it seeks to transcend in a (not to remote) future. The state, with its vaunted legal sovereignty and seeming political independence, is an emanation or 'expression' of the conflict of social classes. Secondly, Marxism has no theoretical regard for nationality, or more precisely for the political relevance and expression of nationality. The bourgeoisie is already international and 'cosmopolitan', embarked on a course intended to conquer the whole world for capital, except that (a point which becomes extremely important later) bourgeois internationalism is fundamentally conflictual and self-contradictory: as capitalist rule requires the state for its *internal* consolidation, so this same stabilizing agency accentuates the *external* instability of the global capitalist system. International capital needs the 'national' state; individual profit-seeking is (necessarily) cloaked in the guise of political nationalism. The internal and underlying conflict of the two great classes has therefore as its inevitable external reflection the conflict of states. To put it more precisely: it is in the nature of capitalist production and capitalist rule to be competitive, antagonistic, conflictual, not just in the big arena locking in combat the bourgeoisie and the proletariat, but *by the same token* in the smaller arena where members of the capitalist ruling class are internecinely fighting one another; it is this latter conflict which is primarily played out in the form of international wars.

The proletariat, in the perspective of Marxism, is also international or in the process of becoming international; its predicament, its class interest and its destiny are all pushing it in the direction of realizing 'human' (i.e. universal) freedom, happiness, peace, perfect cooperation in production. The Marxist goal or ultimate historical scenario, 'communism', contains no conflict of classes or indeed classes themselves, and consequently no states with their entrenched power concentrations and trappings of legal sovereignty. The 'government of people', in Engels' renowned phrase, is now transformed into the 'administration of things' and, it may be remarked at this point, on this level of historical elevation it scarcely matters (as it obviously did not matter much to Marx and Engels) whether you have one vast global 'administrative' organization or several, existing peacefully side by side. Two points on nationality, however, require a somewhat more extended and highlighted comment right here. In the first place, while Marx and Engels squarely place *political* nationalism (with state chauvinism, aggression, claims to racial superiority, etc.) into the historical—i.e. finite—context of the capitalist epoch, it does not follow that nationality itself, i.e. diverse *cultural* identity, is also envisaged to disappear completely in the great whirlpool of universal communist 'humanity'. It is at least an open question whether or not Marx and Engels looked forward to an amicable 'world of nations' under communism—a Marxist direction resolutely followed by some writers, notably Bauer, Stalin and Mao, while just as resolutely denied by others, including Luxemburg, Lenin (as we shall see) and Trotsky. This is obviously an important ambivalence of Marxist doctrine in any discussion concerning 'European unity'. And the second point is of even greater significance in the present context. It is this: while Marxism, as we put it earlier, has no 'theoretical' regard for nationality (i.e. not entertaining its claim to be a potent determining force in history), it has always acknowledged, indeed emphasized, the strategic or *political* role of nationality in the actual waging of class conflict in modern times. The proletarian revolution is to take place, initially, in the 'form' of national proletariats overthrowing *their* respective capitalist oppressors and taking over their state. And even closer to the ground, in the perspective of Marx's and Engels' understanding of European politics in the mid-nineteenth century, there is a paramount role assigned to the liberation of oppressed nations (in particular, Poland and Ireland) as an indispensable step on the road leading to the universal emancipation of the working class. Thus, just as the underlying 'internationalism' of capital goes hand in hand with the destructive conflict of nations and states, so the internationalist or universal destiny of the proletariat involves fighting the historical class war *also* on the state and national level. We shall see later what this point signifies in the European politics of the interwar period.

Still concerning the original conception of Marxist doctrine, however, we have yet to say a few words in respect of what could be taken as a *positive* aspect regarding this 'built-in bias' of Marxism in favour of European unity. Here it is important to take cognisance of Marx's and Engels' unstated cultural assumptions as well as certain relevant implications of the Marxist theory of capitalist production and its future trajectory. There is ample evidence to show that Marx and Engels, following on the German radical tradition (e.g. Moses Hess's *Die europäische Triarchie*), regarded Europe as one integrated cultural whole, with French political theory, English political economy and German philosophy dovetailing and converging to create the cultural prerequisite of the coming ascendancy of the universal proletariat. The existing division of Europe into several conflicting sovereign states (reflecting the conflictual essence of capitalist production) is already in the process of being superseded, partly by the developmental demands of the productive system itself and partly by awakening universal proletarian–humanistic consciousness. Steeped in the Greco-Roman tradition and the hubris of the European Enlightenment, Marx and Engels have a scarcely disguised condescending view of the penumbral parts of Europe (Slavs, Jews, Balkan peoples), not to mention their paternalistic attitude to the indigenous culture and economy of non-European lands. The Marxist theory of capitalism is of course itself ethnocentrically skewed: the most 'advanced' state of capitalist production has been reached in Europe and the coming proletarian revolution is also expected to occur in 'the most advanced' (i.e. European) countries initially, acting 'all at once' (as it is said in the *German Ideology*). In the light of all these considerations, the fact that Marx and Engels scarcely, if ever, talk about 'European unity' or 'federalism' as such does not seem to matter a great deal: Europe, its cultural unity, distinctness and leading role in the world, and the absence of state sovereignty in the envisioned communist future, are all taken for granted and they point in the same direction.

But at this point we must note another important ambivalence in the original Marxist position. This has, it might be argued, far-reaching repercussions in the debates encountered in the interwar period, while at the same time supplying the key (or at least one key) for their adequate comprehension. This ambivalence concerns the nature of the 'proletariat' *qua* the leading revolutionary force in the modern world. What, precisely, makes the proletariat fit for this exalted role? There are two—seemingly coherent but in truth diverging—answers in the basic texts. On the one hand, the proletariat is destined to lead because it is the *oppressed* class, 'nothing' that aspires to be 'everything'. On the other hand, the proletariat is appointed to leadership on account of its being centrally involved in, the substantive mainstay of, *advanced* production, i.e. it is already 'everything'. Whatever other theoretical ramifications and subtleties might be involved here, it is easy to see how this basic duality influences and indeed confounds the Marxist stance on European unity. If it is the latter quality of the proletariat that is stressed, Europe inevitably comes to the forefront: this is the continent which is distinctive in having the most 'class-conscious' industrial workers, highest revolutionary tradition and experience, its advanced party and trade union organizations, etc. Stressing the former quality, however, Europe just as inevitably recedes from the horizon and there is now an opening to the 'East', with the penumbral and colonial masses emerging as the real 'toilers' of the world destined to lead the way. The Kautsky–Lenin wrangle and, on a different (but here more relevant) level, the Trotsky–Stalin controversy have in this ambivalence as it were their doctrinal embryo. But more about this later.

Here our next task is to fill in further developments in the Marxist background. Two points appear to be deserving of primary attention, respectively highlighting Marxist progression in the 'negative' critique of capitalism and the 'positive' endeavour of constructing, preparing for, the great historical transformation. As regards the former, undoubtedly the theory of imperialism is the most significant. The main features of the theory, as found in the writings of Lenin, Bukharin and others, are too well known to require any elaboration here; it purports to deal with capitalism in its 'last phase', a phase not actually observed by Marx and Engels, and one which is chiefly characterized by the increasing predominance of finance capital, the accentuated role of the bourgeois state in preserving capitalist class rule, and the emergence of a working class 'aristocracy' in the most advanced capitalist countries, thereby shifting the focus of revolution to the penumbra and colonial dependencies. What is of paramount importance here, however, is the special stress laid within this 'hard' theory of imperialism on the ubiquitous presence, and indeed virulence, of inter-imperialist conflict necessarily accompanying this ultimate phase of capitalist development. Imperialism means war, or at least constant war preparation and war readiness, and of course war means imperialism. As in Bukharin's *Imperialism and World Economy*, published in 1917:

> War in capitalist society is only one of the methods of capitalist competition, when the latter extends to the sphere of world economy. This is why war is an immanent law of a society producing goods under the pressure of the blind laws of a spontaneously developing world market, but it cannot be the law of a society that consciously regulates the process of production and distribution.[2]

As Bukharin points out, under imperialism 'the internationalization of economic life is by no means identical with the process of the internationalization of capital interests'.[3] Finance capital cannot but constantly attempt to expand, to conquer; the bourgeois interests of one country, one state, one region, will necessarily clash with those of another. 'Partial agreements are, of course, possible here and there . . . Every agreement or fusion, however, will only reproduce the bloody struggle on a new scale . . . were even *all* of Europe to unite it would not yet signify "disarmament" '.[4] It is relevant to note that this revolutionary Marxist perspective on imperialism was sharply contrasted, then and later, to the view held by moderate social democratic writers, notably Kautsky. For Kautsky, who essentially followed the line taken in Hilferding's *Finance Capital*, imperialism was not a substantive 'phase' of capitalism but simply a 'policy' of finance capital, to be pursued or abandoned by capitalist interests almost at will. Hence Kautsky foresaw a period of 'ultra-imperialism' after the First World War, i.e. capitalist interests peacefully uniting on a world scale; 'it is not excluded,' he wrote in 1915, 'that capitalism may live through another new phase, the transference of the policy of cartels to foreign policy, a phase of ultra-imperialism, which of course we must fight against just as energetically as we fought imperialism.'[5] In this latter perspective, therefore, European unity under capitalism appears possible and even progressive and desirable (though not the ultimate goal); at the same time it is not difficult to see, as Lenin and Bukharin saw clearly, that the ultra-imperialist view tends to gnaw away at the very foundations of Marxist doctrine: if capitalism can be an integrating agency and can ensure peace, then the case for an immediate proletarian-led revolution is considerably weakened, if it does not disappear altogether.

Lenin's celebrated 1915 article, 'On the slogan for a United States of Europe', a short and insubstantial piece, though of decisive long-term influence on the revolutionary Marxist view, should be seen in the context of this polemic, an application of the 'hard' theory of imperialism and related attack on the theory of ultra-imperialism. The point should not be missed that Lenin is quite happy to entertain the 'slogan' on a political, strategic level (similarly to Marx's embracing of the issue of national liberation), as a way forward towards political democracy, republicanism and destabilizing the entrenched European dynastic monarchies, a step towards the proletarian revolution. But on the level of high Marxist theory his rejection of the scenario is total and categorical. A United States of Europe 'under capitalism is either impossible or reactionary'. Imperialists could agree, temporarily and in a limited regional context but, Lenin asks, to what end?

> Only for the purpose of jointly suppressing socialism in Europe, of jointly protecting colonial booty *against* Japan and America, who have been done badly out of their share by the present partition of colonies, and the increase of whose might during the last fifty years has been immeasurably more rapid than that of backward and monarchist Europe, now turning senile . . . On the present economic basis, i.e. under capitalism, a United States of Europe would signify an organisation of reaction to retard America's more rapid development.[6]

For Lenin obviously the 'impossibility' and 'reactionary' character of European unity are not sharply contrasted fundamental alternatives but two sides of the same coin, since he clearly regards 'reaction', i.e. the consolidation of imperialism, as also 'impossible' in the (only slightly) longer run: imperialism will be consumed, destroyed *jointly* through its own self-destructive nature and the onslaught of socialism. But, projecting forward, it is fascinating to note how these two sides of the one coin come later to be manifested in the revolutionary Marxist perspective as *alternative* dominant arguments. Roughly, as we shall see, in the 1920s it is the 'impossibility' of European unity that is stressed more, i.e. its conflictual, inter-imperialist character, while in the 1930s it is the 'reactionary' nature of the same politico-economic tendency that comes to the fore in the Marxist view, i.e. as an aspect of the capitalist counter-offensive against the socialist Soviet Union.

One more point, however, as properly belonging to the Marxist background and indispensable for an understanding of the interwar period, should be highlighted here. This concerns the 'positive' side of Marxism in relation to European unity. The revolutionary Marxist view concerning European unity under socialism remains, until the 1920s, basically ambivalent, or if you like *indifferent*. It is not excluded but neither is it given special urgency or significance (except for Trotsky). Lenin continued to be cool and dismissive although the 'slogan' was included in the 1914 Programme of the Bolshevik RSDLP and confirmed at the Berne conference of its foreign section a year later. Lenin's view, on the more rarefied level, is certainly conducive to, or at least compatible with, aspirations towards larger units, the transcendence of national sovereign states, towards federalism and beyond. 'The aim of socialism,' he writes in 1914, 'is not only to end the division of mankind into tiny states and the isolation of nations in all its forms, it is not only the rapprochement of nations but also their fusion.'[7] And: 'The Marxists are, of course, hostile to federation and decentralization, for the simple reason that capitalism requires the biggest and most centralized possible states for its development. *Other conditions being equal*, the class-conscious proletariat will always stand for the larger state.'[8] While championing the right of self-determination for 'oppressed nations', he is emphatic and confident in expecting national liberation to lead to the 'more widespread formation of very big states and federations of states, which are more beneficial for the masses and more fully in keeping with economic development.'[9] And, of course, to make this point in concluding on the Marxist background, there is nothing to suggest that the original Leninist design for a 'union of soviet socialist republics' is anything but the first practical step towards world community; in point of high Marxist theory at any rate, the Soviet Union is an incipient world federation, not a nationally dominated 'great power', and hence as such by no means inimical to European unity aspirations. The Second Congress of the Comintern in 1920, in its 'Theses on the National and Colonial Question', declares: 'Federation is a transitional form towards the complete union of the working people of all nations'.[10] And distantly but clearly echoing the *German Ideology* (as quoted above), the 'Theses' envisage an 'international' proletarian dictatorship which means in the first instance dictatorship of the proletariat 'in at least a few advanced countries, which is capable of exercising decisive influence in the political affairs of the entire world'.[11]

The Marxist perspective on European unity in the 1920s, to turn now from the theoretical background to a most interesting unfolding interplay of high theory and hard politics, is predominantly determined by two factors. One is absolute and venomous opposition to the Versailles settlement which is seen by Marxists as a temporary but dangerous victory of imperialism, a 'peace' which is based on intensified exploitation of the European working class, together with (and as we have seen earlier, the two things are necessarily, logically related) continuing inter-imperialist rivalry and conflict. The other is a genuine expectation, certainly strong until 1923 but present throughout the period, of the spreading of the flame of proletarian revolution from its power-base in Russia to the advanced capitalist countries of Western Europe, with special reference to Germany, its imperialism lying prostrate after Versailles. There is no nonsense, therefore, about building on the foundations of a world 'made safe for democracy', with its formal international organization, the League of Nations, its burgeoning 'Pan-European' designs, disarmament schemes, pacifist movements, customs unions, social democratic parties seeking accommodation in the prevailing socio-economic structure and rejecting the Leninist revolutionary model. The basic fact in Europe is *conflict* under the veil of international peace, of class oppression coupled with the 'injustice' of the terms meted out to the vanquished nations.

In the 1920s Marxist attention is focused on inter-imperialist conflict, of which European governmental cooperation as well as various non-governmental departures are seen as so many secondary effects, as distinguished from a potential imperialist *league* directed primarily against the Soviet Union (though this contrapuntal melody also goes with the main theme). 'European unity' is primarily a weapon in the struggle among rivalling imperialist interests. Of these the Marxist perspective distinguished between several interlocking layers. On one level Versailles signified the triumph and resulting hegemony of 'Anglo-French' imperialism (with its vassals, the Little Entente states) over Germany. On another level it was noted that British and French interests also diverged and conflicted, as for example on the issue of German war reparations. But by far the most significant and novel factor, as seen by Marxists (who were of course not alone in observing this, though perhaps they should be credited with putting overwhelming emphasis on it, ahead of others), was the unfolding imperialist conflict between *America* on the one hand and British as well as French interests on the other. Versailles, as the Comintern declared as early as 1919, was essentially the 'peace programme of American finance capital';[12] the US imperialists could not make direct annexations in Europe, so they proceeded to enslave their nominal allies through peaceful economic and financial infiltration. In the Marxist view the Dawes and the Young plans represented a clear victory of American (and temporarily allied German) over French imperialism, whereas the Locarno Treaties signified a concerted, though in the event short-lived, European attempt to stand up to the United States.

And the Pan-European movement? As reported from the discussions of the Executive Committee of the Comintern in 1926:

> Bela Kun dealt with the Pan-Europa movement, which he described as an attempt to restore the destroyed European market and prepare an offensive against the United States . . . America wanted class peace in Europe to guarantee the profits on its loans; this meant greater exploitation and mass unemployment; in the international field this policy was reflected in pacifism and the disarmament conference.[13]

The limelight here, however, should mainly fall on Trotsky whose intellectual influence on the Marxist revolutionary perspective in this first part of the interwar period was decisive, second only to Lenin's. Trotsky's masterful and impassioned analysis of the imperialist conflict between Europe and America is also of first-rate significance because it is directly linked to his single-minded advocacy of a 'Soviet United States of Europe', in the 1920s among the chief propaganda 'slogans' of the Comintern. Trotsky looks upon the United States as 'the central figure in the modern history of mankind'. The European scene is incapable of being comprehended without bringing in the US presence: 'For the master of the capitalist world—and let us firmly understand this!—is New York, with Washington as its state department'.[14] Having taken over the job of 'conductor' from England, America is now embarking on a policy of 'pacification' resulting in 'Balkan-ized' Europe being on 'rations'. The 'vile fiction' of American pacifism is to be dispelled: 'American imperialism is in essence ruthlessly rude, predatory, in the full sense of the word, and criminal.'[15] The power of the United States, of course, is to be measured in the first instance in substantive economic terms, and Trotsky in various speeches and articles in the 1920s goes to great factual lengths in describing the predominance of American gold reserves, manufacturing capacity, etc., *vis-à-vis* European capitalist economies. *Qua* capitalist productive system, the United States is progressive and expanding, whereas capitalism in Europe is a totally spent force. But, as Trotsky points out, ingeniously bringing together the revolutionary Marxist polemic against social democracy and the analysis of the inter-imperialist conflict between Europe and America, the US onslaught also relies on the treacherous espousal by European social democracy of a 'religion of Americanism'. Social democrats are not just traitors to the working class but also to European capitalism, being now the subservient agents of the 'most powerful bourgeoisie'[16] of the world, and of the parasitic American labour aristocracy. Trotsky, of course, does not expect traditional European capitalist interests to give in meekly but envisages a 'rotten equilibrium' in Europe 'resting on the remnants of ancient power and on the elements of a new and lean existence upon standardized American rations'. And he concludes:

'It is hard to imagine anything more repulsive and obscene than this perspective.'[17]

It is Trotsky's conviction that the European bourgeoisie cannot save Europe from the clutches of American imperialism. Only the revolutionary proletariat, under the leadership of the communist party, is equal to this task. And European revolution for Trotsky goes hand in hand with European unity: the two things are inseparably linked in a means–end–end–means relationship. The more Europe suffers under the American yoke, 'all the more urgent, all the more practical and warlike will the slogan of the all-European revolution and its state-form — *the Soviet United States of Europe* — become for the European workers'. 'Nothing compels us to remain in an atomized Europe. It is precisely the revolutionary proletariat that can unify Europe, by transforming it into the proletarian United States of Europe.'[18] Now concerning the Trotskyist stand two important points have to be borne in mind. In the first place, Trotsky's Europe-oriented revolutionary perspective long predates the interwar period and Trotsky's own concentration on the Europe-American conflict. With him the pro-European theoretical bias built into original Marxism comes to the fore in a number of prewar writings. In 1914 Trotsky sees the first task of the proletariat to lie in the creation of a 'powerful fatherland;, 'the republican United States of Europe, as the foundation of the United States of the World'.[19] In 1916 he argues that a stable proletarian dictatorship is conceivable only 'for all of Europe, organized in the form of a European Republican Federation'.[20] For him clearly, as for Marx and Engels, Europe is a cultural unity distinguished from the rest of the world and destined for revolutionary leadership. The uneven development of world capitalism contains unevenesses within Europe too but nevertheless 'compared with Africa and Asia' capitalist Europe still presents a unity and it alone 'has grown ripe for socialist revolution'. Europe is not just a geographical expression but an 'economic term, something incomparably more concrete . . . than the world market'.[21]

Is it to be concluded, therefore, that with the Trotskyist perspective what we called earlier the basic ambivalence of Marxist doctrine concerning the world leadership of the proletariat is clearly decided one way? The matter is not so simple, however. In fact — which is the crucial and fascinating point to grasp — Trotsky's perspective just about manages to hold the incipient self-contradiction of Marxism on this issue together. Europe, for Trotsky, legitimately aspires to unity and global revolutionary leadership *partly* on account of its 'advanced' status, both in cultural and economic terms. But this positive revolutionary role of Europe is finally given perfect Marxist rationale only by bringing in the negative factor of Europe's subservient and exploited status *vis-à-vis* America. Europe in relation to America hence appears as being both 'nothing' and 'everything', all at the same time. Europe is now *the* Marxist revolutionary working class, in a global extension, distinguished on the one hand from the retarded and historically unimportant masses outside Europe, in the penumbra and the colonies (equivalent perhaps to the European peasantry in the original Marxist perspective), and on the other hand from the brash, uncouth, semi-civilized hordes representing trans-Atlantic imperialism (surely equivalent to the despised parvenu 'eminent sausage-makers' in Marx's own description of the European bourgeoisie). America, with its purely material and 'huckstering' skills, its rapacious imperialism and its pampered, corrupted working class, is the bourgeoisie writ large; Europe is poor in the flesh but infinitely richer in the spirit, the true embodiment of the Enlightenment, the foreshadowing of universal humanity, the sole immediate constituency of the coming proletarian revolution. America is in the process of uniting the world forces of imperialism and reaction; to meet this foe Europe must unite too.

It would not, we submit, be very easy to find a more intellectually pleasing scenario than this on European unity from the Marxist point of view. Yet Trotskyism all but disappeared from the Marxist political scene still in the course of the interwar period. Not completely and not for good, we might add. Although after the débâcle of the Spanish Civil War the international Trotskyist movement declined in importance, Trotskyist ideas continued to exert a wide-ranging influence, and not least on the issue of European unity under socialism. Deleted from the slogans of the Comintern in 1928, the title, 'United Socialist States of Europe', kept on appearing in left-wing propagandist literature right up to the war and beyond. For example, the British ILP which proudly professed to be a 'Marxist' party (though not a Trotskyist party) in the interwar period, proclaimed USSE as one of its principal aims at all appropriate occasions. Eminent party leaders F.A. Ridley and Bob Edwards jointly published in 1942 an extended pamphlet with the same title, in which it is said ruefully:

> The Russian Revolution went abroad with Trotsky. The establishment of European socialism on the basis of an advanced industrial and political technique would infallibly mean that Russia would, again as before 1917, become a (relatively) backward country, as both Lenin and Trotsky predicted would happen if and when the European Revolution triumphed. This state of things spells inexorably the end of the narrow nationalism of the Stalinist regime.[22]

And we may also remark here briefly in passing that USSE has remained an important aspect of the programme of West European Trotskyism in the postwar era too, with its most renowned theoretician, Ernest Mandel, still building on Trotsky's analysis of the conflict between Europe and America in the 1920s. An interesting point to note, however, is that having to account for the success of the EC and doing it without recourse to 'Stalinism', Mandel focuses on the secular global *decline* of American finance capital and imperialism. It is no longer the case, as it was with Trotsky himself, that European unity had to be fought for, by the bourgeoisie or the proletariat, in the face of a hostile and economically progressive United States: now 'European unity' is directly in the American global interest.[23]

Back to the interwar period, it is of course self-evident that Trotsky's fall and the decline of the idea of USSE are closely and inextricably linked, not only on the level of power politics but in point of Marxist doctrine, too. As we have seen, Lenin was quite cold to the idea of European unity under socialism. The main point is that Lenin quite confidently expected the revolution to catch on in Western Europe; if that had happened, the tangle of the USSE and the Soviet Union would have been solved (or at least placed in a different context altogether). But it did not and surely this is the basic fact explaining *both* Trotsky's fall from grace and the virtual disappearance of USSE from the mainstream Marxist armoury. The march of Marxism in Europe was halted at the Curzon line: with Europe no longer in the centre of revolutionary activities Marxism in power in Russia had scarcely another choice but to consolidate itself and seriously avail itself of the 'Eastern' opening, already implied in the Leninist theory of imperialism. On the doctrinal level this came to the fore as the conflict between Stalin's 'socialism in one country' and Trotsky's 'permanent revolution', the latter carrying the idea of USSE with it.

The USSE continued to figure quite prominently in the Trotsky–Stalin wrangle, following Trotsky's branded 'heresy'—and Stalin's condemned 'betrayal'. Trotsky in his *The Third International After Lenin* quite emphatically brings in the USSE slogan as a weapon with which to beat his antagonist. The slogan is still vitally important for the success of the international Marxist movement in the late 1920s, as he argues, 'because there is lodged in it the condemnation of the idea of an isolated socialist development'.[24] Stalin had no interest whatever in USSE and, apparently, only once in his life, in a speech in 1926, did he pronounce favourably on the primacy of Europe in the forward march of socialism. The reference is to a remark, as reported by E.R. Goodman in *The Soviet Design for a World State*, that the defeat of international capitalism would be possible only by the united action of the revolutionary working class of all countries 'or at least, of the principal countries of Europe'.[25] But this remark, again faintly echoing the European bias of the *German Ideology*, should not be taken to reflect any genuine preferences or strategic designs on Stalin's part. As early as 1917 Stalin argued that Russia might pave the way towards the achievement of socialism in the world, and he then flatly declared: 'We must reject the outworn conception that only Europe can show us the way.'[26] It is this latter position which is directly in line with Stalin's policy in the interwar period of building socialism in one country, and indeed Stalin repeatedly charged Trotsky with adducing the 'anti-Leninist' USSE slogan in order to thwart the efforts of the Soviet Union in going ahead with socialist construction. With the exit of Trotskyism from the scene, therefore, we come to an end of the 'revolutionary' first half of the interwar period and therewith the only serious attempt, combining high theory and political strategy, made by Marxism *positively* to contribute to the cause of European unity. The story of the 1930s, to which we shall now turn, shows the role of Marxism in this particular drama mainly in a *negative* light—as indeed the cause of European unity itself subsides under the surging waves of power-political and ideological conflict.

It is commonly agreed by historians that the end of the 1920s meant a watershed in European politics. The Ruhr occupation and an abortive Marxist uprising in Germany had been followed by a short phase of economic recovery and political consolidation, marked by the acceptance of the Dawes plan and the 'spirit of Locarno'. That is to say, in this brief period a kind of effective 'European unity' prevailed, with Briand and Stresemann cooperating in an atmosphere which easily spawned various optimistic schemes of further European integration, such as Coudenhove-Kalergi's which had considerable support in various governmental (including French and German) and private economic circles. But, it seems obvious in retrospect, European peace, cooperation and unity rested on the expectation of continuing economic stability and that came dramatically to an end in 1929. The crisis, as the historian R.A.C. Parker puts it,

> meant the end of the hopes of the 1920s for a restoration of a liberal world economy. Then it had been hoped that general prosperity could be based on a growing international trade fostered by stable currencies with fixed values, freely interchangeable one with another and that free movements of capital between countries would automatically produce sound and productive investment and steady economic growth. Now the failure of liberal international economic policies seemed complete and individual countries sought their salvation by national policies without much regard to their wider impact.[27]

We inserted this seemingly digressive quote to make the important point—which Marxists at the time never tired of making—that questions of high politics are decided not by the idealistic 'good will' of individuals but by the configurations of power and the interplay of entrenched interests. So it was at this time, and it is hardly a sensational remark to make that European unity—inter-govermental as well as business cooperation—became shipwrecked as a result of a fast-surfacing conflict of power and interest, itself issuing out of economic instability and insecurity. But to this we need immediately to add the other observation that while Marxism *in general terms* validly pointed—right through the interwar period—to the underlying and ongoing conflict of interest between classes and nations, to the hegemonic designs, injustice and basic instability emanating from the Versailles settlement and not resolved by 1939 (nor, may we add, to this day?), Marxists or the most influential among them were singularly slow in making the necessary adjustments concerning the unfolding nature of the European power conflict in *particular* terms. The 'Marxism' we are talking about now obviously refers to the Soviet 'power-base', under the total political (and doctrinal) leadership of Stalin, commanding the Comintern and through this 'international' agency the radical Marxist parties of Europe. Stalinist Marxism did not entirely cease to be 'revolutionary' (as alleged by Trotskyists and other 'left-wing' opponents, like Karl Korsch [28] and a section of the German communist party), but in its particular 'statist' or power-political perspective—as the author of this chapter had occasion to argue elsewhere— revolution was seen to proceed exclusively from the power-base. The first task of Marxists in power was to consolidate at home and to make the international movement subservient. And as international Marxist politics became an instrument in the furtherance of Soviet state interests, so 'Soviet' Marxism itself came more and more to reflect (as it had already started with Lenin's Bolshevism) the traditional power-political interests of the Russian state and to assume a Russian cultural character (bureaucratism, militarism, personal dog-fights at the top, etc.). But we must not overplay the cultural aspect and fall into the trap of ethnocentric arrogance, displayed by Coudenhove-Kalergi at one end of the spectrum and by Trotsky at the other, drawing a sharp and adverse distinction between 'Europe' and Russia. The developing situation of the 1930s is capable of an adequate explanation in terms of power-political 'realism' alone. Since Russia, or the Soviet Union, was a *great power* and in the 1930s was beginning to see itself as such, it had *necessarily* to demote any abstract 'European' interest and to regard the question of European unity coolly in instrumental terms (not unlike British foreign policy in modern times); in effect this meant suspicion, negative hostility at its worst and guarded support at its best.

What we have above referred to as the failure of Marxism to effect the necessary adjustments in its power-political stance in the 1930s stems from the historic (and, if anything, over-documented) error concerning the understanding of the nature of the fascist menace to the peace of Europe. We need not go too deeply into the causes of this failure. One relevant factor, however, and this has a lot to do with the developing Marxist attitude towards European unity, was undoubtedly the deep Marxist hostility to the Versailles Treaty, evident in the flirtation and, even more, going on between Marxists and national socialists in Germany in the early part of the 1920s, both sharing an objective interest in the undoing of Versailles and the disruption of Anglo-French hegemony on the continent. Soviet state foreign policy, parallel to this, tended to support German interests *vis-à-vis* the victorious Western Allies, dramatically at the time of the Rapallo Treaty but lingering on long afterwards. The Soviet Union, as any great power, aspired to protect itself by preventing the concentration of potential enemies. Consequently, while Germany appeared *both* weak and resentful of its status in Western Europe, the main—and logical—aim of Soviet foreign policy was to keep this resentment alive and Germany away from a Western *rapprochement*. In this perspective, therefore, any attempt to 'unite Europe', from Locarno to Pan-Europa, appeared to the Soviet Union anathema, to be strenuously opposed. However, once Germany was becoming strong and at the same time virulently anti-Marxist in its ruling ideology (and openly anti-Russian in its geopolitical designs), then it became rational for Soviet policy to foster and participate in a wide anti-German alliance, and hence also to support aspirations to European unity with an anti-Nazi edge.

But things were not as simple as that. Stalin, apparently, did not come to accept until 1934–5 that continental fascism was a greater threat to the Soviet Union than Anglo-French imperialism; at least to some extent his attitude seems to have been influenced by traditional Marxist reductionism (prevalent in the interwar period) in subsuming fascism under imperialism and expecting it to be a 'passing phase' before the next wave of proletarian revolutions in Europe. The general remark might be inserted here that for orthodox Marxist doctrine, including Leninism, there is strictly speaking *nothing* between imperialism (the 'highest phase of capitalism') and socialism. The main question therefore is where imperialism is strongest, and not what sort of ideology it is disguised under. Hence what we see developing in this period is a *rift* between Marxist high theory and shorter-range political strategy: theory demands that German fascist imperialism and Anglo-French liberal imperialism be subsumed under the one category, while political interest increasingly requires their separation. Hence, furthermore, the spectacle of a more or less simultaneous playing out by Soviet foreign policy of the two—logically speaking—alternative perspectives: predominantly anti-Nazi and predominantly anti-Western. In chronological terms there is a shifting emphasis but nothing more. Again the point can be illuminated from another angle: the hard theory of imperialism (of Lenin and Bukharin) places, as we have seen, overwhelming stress on inter-imperialist conflict, and the resultant 'impossibility'—or virtual impossibility—of durable supra-state union under capitalism. This stance, *ceteris paribus*, tallies with what we have identified above as the first alternative Soviet foreign policy perspective in the 1930s, i.e. the *prevention* of European unity, coupled with the hope that German aspirations would continue to lie in the West. But this same hard theory of imperialism—in a veritable Catch-22 situation—becomes considerably weakened, if not wholly confounded, by the very success of the Marxist power-base in presenting a threat to general imperialist interests. These interests, so it came to be recognized as the 1930s wore on, achieved a particular power-concentration of their own in the form of Nazi German military–political might. This emerging political situation, in turn, facilitated the growth of a *revised* hard theory of imperialism, espoused by Stalin and his successors.

As regards the first perspective, plenty of documentation can be supplied to show the Soviet attitude to European unity to be predominantly negative and hostile. It will suffice to refer here to two illustrations. In March 1931 the editor of the British Marxist *Labour Monthly*, Rajani Palme Dutt, set out to explain the European scene from the Marxist angle. The emphasis at this juncture is still exclusively on Anglo-French imperialism. French ruling circles, as Palme Dutt argues, have become aware of the long-term untenability of the Versailles settlement. In order to maintain French supremacy in Europe in the fast-changing political situation, they are now obliged to adapt their policies. The adoption of a 'Pan-European' stance is no more than a reflection of this awareness, the French government 'attempting in new forms to fix the existing statutory position in Europe' [29] and, significantly, to draw Germany into a new kind of Franco-German understanding. The Pan-European idea, in Palme Dutt's analysis, has three main aspects. First and foremost it is simply a means to secure continued French imperialist domination on the Continent, to be dubbed therefore 'Pan-Versailles'. Secondly, it has or rather had originally an anti-American edge, designed to promote the interests of European capitalist concerns in the face of trans-atlantic imperialist rivalry (i.e. harking back to the earlier, 'Trotskyist' theme). Thirdly, however, and obviously this is the aspect regarded by Palme Dutt as the most important and menacing, Pan-European aspirations are now mainly intended to isolate the Soviet Union and forge an anti-revolutionary European front. He refers, not unreasonably, to the evident reluctance of West European governments to involve the Soviet union in Continent-wide discussions. This leads us to the second example. In September 1930 the European member-states of the League of Nations established a commission to study the outstanding problems of European unity (concentrating on economic affairs) and to work out constructive proposals. The Soviet Union did receive an invitation to attend in 1931, which Foreign Commissar Litvinov accepted with reservations. However, his later successor Molotov said in a speech to the 6th Congress of Soviets in March 1931: 'The chief part in creating the anti-Soviet front is played by the so-called European Committee formed on the initiative of the French Foreign Minister, Briand, for the purpose of creating a bloc of European states against the Soviet Union.' [30]

The League commission gradually petered out and in the worsening international situation the Soviet Union had to adapt its policies. The rise of Germany led to the Franco-Soviet Pact of 1934 and to Soviet accession to the League of Nations. From being the scourge of Versailles and the instigator of revolutionary subversion, the Soviet Union became a champion of 'collective security' in Europe and generally a force of stability, now espousing cooperation with once reviled social democrats and even liberal democratic groups in the Popular Fronts. With that came almost of necessity a more benign attitude towards European unity, including the Pan-European idea. As K. Törnudd suggests, the change in the Soviet position (or at least in Litvinov's position) in this regard may to some extent have been influenced also by initial Nazi hostility to Coudenhove-Kalergi's ideas and movement.[31] At any rate it was Litvinov himself who, in a debate in the League Assembly in September 1935, shortly after the Soviet Union had become a member, made direct references in a positive vein to European unity aspirations. A European regional agreement, he then argued, would be warranted in the current international situation where 'the voice of European countries' would otherwise be 'drowned in the universal chorus of the League'.[32]

In closing this survey a brief reference has to be made to the twilight period of 1939–41 which, of course, from the Soviet point of view still belongs to the interwar period. In an oft-quoted and important article in the *Communist International*, reprinted in the *Labour Monthly* in the December 1940 issue, the Marxist theoretician Jozsef Revai addressed himself to the issue of a 'New Order' in Europe. The perspective and arguments in this article are significant in that, firstly, they combine the anti-German and anti-Western position (which then befitted the situation of the Soviet Union as a non-belligerent), and secondly, they project the dominant Soviet attitude to European unity in the period of the Cold War. Revai begins by associating the idea of European unity with the treacherous path of European social democracy, with special reference to the British Labour and French socialist parties who in the Manifesto of February 1940 adopted European federalism as their common platform, followed soon by the entire Second International. European federation, as Revai sees it, has three basic elements: economic integration, the limitation of state sovereignty, and as its core the wartime Anglo-French alliance. 'In actual fact,' federation was 'a question of creating a *European empire* of England and France, of the establishment of their joint rule over Europe.'[33] Revai here makes the striking point that this Western social democratic notion of European unity is on a par with the Nazi design of a New Order: the German banker Schacht and the French socialist leader Severac speak the same language. Both designs are based on the hegemonic domination of one imperialist centre, Germany in one case, France and England in the other. Revai adds that as a demonstration of the underlying identity of the two designs one can observe the tendency of continental social democrats to go over to the Nazis, mentioning the Belgian Henri de Man as an example. Federal Europe, including here Trotsky's USSE, for Revai means the intended perpetuation of European 'parasitism' at the expense of the rest of the world, a desire 'that bourgeois Europe should assume the leadership of the capitalist world'.[34] Like Pan-America, this means subservience to the leading regional imperialist power. Revai concedes that an international system of small states might be outmoded but this for him does not signify the supersession of the right of national self-determination. Social democratic ideas on federation, therefore, 'are ideas of national subservience and national betrayal now, and of the renunciation of the struggle for national liberation in the future'.[35] Finally he makes the point that although ostensibly designed to ensure peace, European federation in fact means 'organizing for war in permanence', 'to secure the rear of this or that imperialism in its struggle for world domination'.[36]

The last sentence quoted, of course, echoes the older Leninist theory of imperialism. But this for Revai and Marxists of his persuasion goes in tandem with what we have called above the 'revised' version, i.e. the acceptance of the prospect that imperialist interests *can* unite, peaceably and on a longer-term basis. The rationale of this is the presence and power of the Soviet Union on the world scene. As C.A.P. Binns writes, with direct reference to the later acquiescence of the Soviet Union in the existence and viability of the Common Market, 'when Lenin had written of the inevitability of inter-imperialist war imperialism was dominant, whereas now it had gone onto the defensive'.[37] Leaving aside the rather involved question of the coherence or otherwise of the two stages of this hard Marxist theory of imperialism, two points in Revai's analysis deserve special emphasis. The two are connected and indicative of the dominant Soviet line on European unity in the postwar era. Firstly, returning in a tortuous way to the view expressed in the 1920s (most forcefully by Trotsky), the idea of a single dominant imperialist centre has enabled Soviet commentators to connect all kinds of unity aspirations, not just in Western Europe, to the expansive interests of American capital. We can add that—in respect of Europe at any rate—this sounds more credible in the context of the 1940s and 1950s than in the 1920s. Secondly and more interestingly, the Soviet Marxist perspective has involved an increasingly open and emphatic espousal of the idea of state *sovereignty*. This is definitely a step beyond the notion of 'national self-determination', and its Marxist, or indeed original Leninist, orthodoxy is certainly questionable. The more state sovereignty is stressed, obviously, the further away one is getting from the original theoretical 'bias', as we termed it, built into Marxist doctrine favourable to European unity. Sovereignty, whichever way you look at it, is a stumbling-block in the path to integration. On a strategic level the

Soviet view undoubtedly makes exminent sense: the defence of state sovereignty is one way in which to prevent the successful unification of interests
under the domination of the strongest imperialist power.[38] But over and
above this, and on a more rarefied level, one can perhaps surmise that there is
also a natural affinity between a Marxism that has historically solidified into a
state, and which maintains and justifies itself as a sovereign great power, and
more traditional 'bourgeois' state interests and identities. It is certainly
remarkable (and cannot be explained in strategic terms alone) that Eastern
Europe under Soviet leadership has been lagging far behind Western Europe
in the field of integration. There are no purely 'Marxist' reasons why this
should have been so.

Let us then draw the various threads together and endeavour to advance a
few general observations on the subjects discussed, to serve as a kind of
concluding section of this chapter. That European unity, in spite of
strenuous efforts by a lot of people, did not come about in the interwar period
is a simple fact. Marxism, we are suggesting, was (and is) not too far out in
pointing to the underlying causes of this failure. In order to appreciate this, it
is of course necessary to reduce the Marxist perspective itself to its 'rational
kernel' and ignore, for the time being, its own futuristic and messianic
framework. Surely this rational kernel within Marxism is its attention
focused on the role of *interest* in politics, and interest defined primarily in
terms of power accruing to groups in society by virtue of their substantive
position in the system of production and distribution. This 'class' interest is
by no means the only thing that counts but it does count for quite a great deal
and it is easy to see, when surveying the interwar period in Europe for
example, that interest almost always overrides abstract ideals and isolated
individual departures.

A system of production and distribution based essentially on private
ownership and enterprise inevitably places class interest in the forefront. It is
here that class interest becomes self-evidently a major determinant of political
relationships. Nations do not emerge out of classes and are not defined in
terms of interest but national *states* do and are, in an important way. States, in
their external and institutional aspect, as concentrated repositories of *power*,
do become the bearers of the dominant class interest within them and as such
they come to act simultaneously as vehicles for the expansion of class power
and arrests on the way to this expansion. Capital cannot but endeavour to
expand and capitalist interests are both served by their respective state
organizations and hampered by them. Hence the chronic instability of inter-
state relations and the *tendency* to conflict which Marxists call 'imperialism'.
Now what is relevant here to note, given this basic character of a society and
polity based on interest—interest being built up from below, starting with

the individual entrepreneur and aggregated to become the national interest—
is that in this situation there is always a premium on staying *independent* as
long as possible, to pursue one's interest independently of others and against
them if necessary. This goes for the individual enterprise as well as for the
sovereign state. The transcendence of interest is *also* a function of interest: it
becomes worthwhile and rational only when interest is seen to be best served
this way. Regional capitalist cooperation, with or without supra-state organ-
izational forms, is not 'impossible' as Lenin and Bukharin thought but it is
certainly *difficult*; it 'goes against the grain' of private enterprise, we might
say. In a converse expression the point becomes even clearer: there is no
point, in this situation, in transcending immediate interests as long as there is
a reasonable chance of successfully promoting them in the concrete,
independently. Larger aggregation therefore is always a last resort.

Now looked at in this way, the failure to achieve unity and lasting peace in
Europe in the period under discussion becomes understandable; though at
this point we might want to dilute a little bit the Marxist 'language' employed
hitherto. The First World War left Europe in a condition where group
interests were in a potential *balance* and where, consequently, larger-scale
cooperation and integration were not—indeed, could not be—seen as overriding power-political imperatives. The Versailles peace settlement, while
intentionally harsh, unjust, vindictive, divisive and designed to ensure the
continued domination of the victors, paradoxically did not go far enough in
destroying potential opposition. Anglo-French and even American 'imperialism' were too weak to ensure their complete hegemony. And while on the one
hand European states were, or became as time went on, more or less equally
balanced in relation to one another (meaning primarily, but not exclusively,
Britain, France, Germany and Italy), together—or more precisely side by
side—they presented still such an overwhelming concentration of power as to
make it unnecessary in the short run to keep looking over their shoulders,
mindful of threats from without. Britain and France still had their overseas
'empires', sitting on great wealth jealously guarded and economically expanding; there was no overriding obstacle why Italy could not also carve a place
out for itself 'in the sun' and even less why Germany, with its enormous
productive potential and demographic resources, could not move to enlarge
its *Lebensraum*. In retrospect it appears obvious that as long as Europe was
globally dominant it had to be internally disunited, pushed on to internecine
conflict. It took a bloody war to change all that. This, surely, is the one
paramountly important point of *differentia* between the interwar period and
the postwar period, with European disunity defining the former and (at least
some measure of) European unity defining the latter.

All this, of course, is sheer commonplace and has been so for a long time,
not worth remarking *per se*, except that the commonplace acquires special

significance and interest in the context of this chapter, for it is *precisely* this outcome in the postwar world that is noted, and projected, in the Marxist analyses we come across in the interwar years. Both the revolutionary Trotskyist and the power-political Stalinist scenarios have become reality together, in a peculiar way and with history, as usual, procrastinating. What in the 1920s and 1930s were merely straws in the wind became solid edifices later. On the one hand, in 1945 certainly American 'imperialism' (and there is no need to attach a pejorative connotation to the term here) achieved its overall and indisputable global hegemony, making it this time really imperative for European interests to unite and create a 'common market'.[39] Note that the EC, irrespective of its tentative (and laudable) efforts at 'nation-building', is still essentially an *interest* organization of *states* representing dominant economic concerns. Its internal and external 'trade-wars', concerning French lamb, American wheat and Japanese cars, are not altogether a different phenomenon from what used to be described by Marxists as the tendency to 'inter-imperialist' conflict. But of course this conflict is now muted, and that again is not an accident. Here we turn to 'on the other hand', leaving as it were Trotsky behind and into the Stalinist universe. Super-imposed on inter-imperialist conflict and altering its character there has been since 1945 an imperative political and economic necessity to achieve European unity in a defensive posture against the other extant 'imperialism', that of the Soviet Union. Marxism *qua* great power more or less succeeded where Marxism *qua* revolution failed conspicuously. Lenin failed to unite the workers of the world under the Marxist banner and Trotsky's USSE lies in the historical scrap-yard; but Stalin's Soviet Union certainly managed to unite Europe against itself. And again, whatever emotional label we choose to attach to terms here, there is no denying that European unity in its aspect of anti-Soviet defence is also a matter of *interests*, negative rather than positive in its essence.

This raises the much more interesting question, but alas one we can deal with here only fleetingly—in an endeavour to 'close the circle'—of whether or not the state-like development ('degeneration' in another parlance) of Marxism in the Europe of the interwar period was itself historically necessary. In other words: why did Marxism *qua* international revolutionary movement fail to achieve European unity—let alone the worldwide unity and victory of the working class? We would be strongly tempted to respond to the former formulation of this question with an unqualified affirmative: yes, the consolidation of a nationally based power-base was the *only way* in which Marxism could take on a historical role in the interwar period and thereafter. Stalinism may be disappointing from the pure revolutionary point of view but it works. And as regards the latter, more pointed, formulation of the question, our response could proceed something like this: effective unity, proper, genuine and enduring cooperation among individuals, including the group level, cannot be based on 'interest' alone. Interest plays a very important and *external* part in social relationships and in politics but it does not go all the way; it is aggregative, defensive and destructive. Classes, and only classes, engage in conflict but they do not construct as such.[40] Unity follows only from what here we might like to call the 'national' principle (not meant in a strict ethnic sense), i.e. a form of group identity which by definition supersedes and logically precedes individual interest. This principle was ignored by international revolutionary Marxism in the interwar period at its direst peril. Trotsky's perspective, and the idea of a United Socialist States of Europe, came as we argued close to what would have been required: in conceptualizing Europe *vis-à-vis* America it came within earshot of identifying Europe as a potential *nation*, defined constructively, culturally *as well as* in terms of interest. But in so far as international revolutionary Marxism chose to rely on the vacuous myth of 'class solidarity' it not only effectively destroyed itself but through its impotence allowed Europe to go under in the flames of mutual destruction in 1939–45. The price to be paid for eventual integration was a very heavy one indeed and it could perhaps have been avoided.

Notes

1. cf. the author's paper, 'Revolution, power, alliance: Marxist politics in the interwar period' (Political Studies Association Conference, Aberdeen, 1987).
2. N. Bukharin, *Imperialism and World Economy* (1917) (London, Merlin Press, 1972), p. 54.
3. ibid., p. 61.
4. ibid., p. 139.
5. K. Kautsky, *Selected Political Writings*, transl. and ed. by P. Goode, (London, Macmillan, 1983), p. 88.
6. V.I. Lenin, 'On the slogan for a United States of Europa' (23 August 1915) (Moscow, Progress Publ., 1966), p. 5.
7. V.I. Lenin, 'The socialist revolution and the right of nations to self-determination' (1916), in *Questions of National Policy and Proletarian Internationalism* (Moscow, F.L.P.H., n.d. p. 139).
8. V.I. Lenin, 'Critical remarks on the national question' (1913), ibid., p. 53.
9. V.I. Lenin, 'Socialism and war' (1915), in *Lenin on War and Peace: Three Articles* (Peking, F.L.P., 1966), p. 27.
10. *The Communist International 1919–1943: Documents*, sel. and ed. by J. Degras (London, Cass, 1971), Vol. I, p. 141.
11. ibid., p. 142.
12. ibid., p. 33.
13. Degras, *Communist International 1919–1943*, op. cit., Vol. II, p. 250.

14. L.D. Trotsky, *Europe and America: Two speeches on Imperialism* (1926), (New York, Pathfinder Press, 1971), p. 12.
15. ibid., p. 15.
16. ibid., p. 19.
17. ibid., p. 29.
18. ibid., p. 31.
19. Quoted in E.R. Goodman, *The Soviet Design for a World State* (New York, Columbia University Press, 1960), p. 28.
20. ibid., p. 153.
21. ibid., p. 156.
22. F.A. Ridley and Bob Edwards, *The United Socialist States of Europe*, (London, National Labour Press, 1942), p. 47.
23. E. Mandel, *Europe versus America? Contradictions of Imperialism* (1968), (London, NLB, 1970).
24. L.D. Trotsky, *The Third International after Lenin* (1929–30) (London, New Park Publishers, 1974), p. 13.
25. Goodman, *The Soviet Design*, op. cit., p. 156.
26. ibid., p. 162.
27. R.A.C. Parker, *Europe, 1919–45* (London, Weidenfeld and Nicolson, 1969), p. 101.
28. See H. Gruber, *Soviet Russia masters the Comintern* (New York, Doubleday, 1974), pp. 58–9.
29. R. Palme Dutt, 'Notes of the month', *Labour Monthly*, Vol. 13, No. 3 (March 1931), p. 141.
30. Quoted in K. Törnudd, *Soviet Attitudes Towards Non-Military Regional Co-operation* (Helsingfors, Centraltryckeriet, 1961), p. 79.
31. ibid., p. 81.
32. ibid., p. 80.
33. J. Revai, 'A "New Order" in Europe?', *Labour Monthly*, Vol. 22, No. 12 (December 1940), p. 628.
34. ibid., p. 634.
35. ibid., p. 633.
36. ibid., p. 634.
37. C.A.P. Binns, 'From USE to EEC: the Soviet analysis of European integration under capitalism', *Soviet Studies*, Vol. 30, No. 2 April (1978), p. 251.
38. cf. Advocates of federal union 'are actually preparing the ground for the actual sovereignty of Anglo-French imperialism in a Europe from which sovereignty has formally been banished', R. Goodman, 'The meaning of federal union', *Labour Monthly*, Vol. 22, No. 1 (January 1940), p. 42.
39. cf. 'The experience of the 1930s, combined with the new role of the United States as a hegemonic power, provided the impetus for European integration after the Second World War', P. Cocks, 'Towards a Marxist theory of European integration', *International Organization*, Vol. 34, No. 1 (Winter 1980), p. 39.
40. cf. the author's inaugural lecture (1986), 'State, class, nation' (Hull, The University Press, 1986).

4 British Capitalism and the Idea of European Unity Between the Wars

Robert Boyce

To judge by the standard published accounts, the idea of European unity scarcely figured in the shaping of British history between the wars.[1] Europe, these accounts emphasise, remained severely divided by nationalism, revanchism, and the numerous unresolved problems arising from the First World War. British statesmen did what they could to appease Germany and stabilise Europe. In the Rhineland Pact signed at Locarno in October 1925, for instance, Britain went so far as to join Belgium and Italy in guaranteeing both France and Germany from unprovoked aggression by the other power. But the results of British efforts were modest and short-lived. In 1929 Aristide Briand, the French premier, spoke vaguely of his hopes for European federation—he evidently meant confederation—at the Tenth Assembly of the League of Nations. But by May 1930, when he circulated a memorandum outlining his proposal to interested countries, the world slump was under way creating conditions for renewed political extremism, and the memorandum received a cool reception in most quarters.[2] Hence, the claim is implicitly made, Britain was a good citizen in the European context: nationalism, not unity, was the main issue confronting British statesmen throughout the interwar period.

It must be acknowledged at once that this conventional picture, while requiring qualification, is by no means completely wrong. There is no question that nationalist rivalry and conflict were chronic in Europe throughout the interwar years, that British foreign relations were devoted largely to the adjustment of differences on the Continent in an effort to restore a stable balance of power, and that at the official level Britain ignored the European idea for all but a very brief period midway between the world wars. This much is confirmed by the Foreign Office records.

Among the dispatches in the Foreign Office archives are two letters from Viscount Chilston, minister in Vienna, to the Foreign Secretary, reporting on

65

the Pan-Europa Congress being held in that city in October 1926. In his first letter Chilston dismissively described the objective of the congress as 'fantastic'.[3] His interest was, however, aroused when he learned that countries including France, Belgium and Germany were sending high-powered delegations, and in his second letter he acknowledged, 'The movement has certainly made great strides'.[4]

About a year later a junior member of the Foreign Office affirmed that the British public would be 'astonished' at the degree of interest in the Pan-Europa idea on the Continent.[5] But neither he nor Viscount Chilston succeeded in persuading colleagues in London to take the European movement seriously. Sir William Tyrrell, the Permanent Under-Secretary, summed up the prevailing attitude in a reference to Count Richard Coudenhove-Kalergi, founder and moving spirit behind the Pan-Europa Society: 'I know Coudenhove: he is a thoroughly impractical theorist.'[6] The only official of any standing in London who took Coudenhove's efforts seriously was Alan Leeper, First Secretary in the League of Nations and Western Department from 1929. Perhaps it was his Australian origins that enabled him to place them in a broader perspective. At any event he was sure that the day was bound to come when Europe, yielding to global pressures for larger economic units, organised itself into a bloc. Britain would be forced to choose between going 'into' Europe or staying out, and at the same time and for the same reasons the constituent parts of the British Empire would be drawn into the orbit of other blocs.[7] Eventually, of course, Leeper was to be proved right. But his Foreign Office colleagues found this prospect unrealistic or simply too remote to contemplate.

The Foreign Office was therefore unprepared for Briand's initiative in the summer of 1929, which it learned of only through press reports from Paris. When Arthur Henderson, the Foreign Secretary in the recently formed Labour government, requested more information from his advisers, the Office library could only piece together reports on the Pan-Europa Society and certain other more obscure organisations, which encouraged the impression that the European movement was little more than a one-man crusade by Coudenhove himself.[8] Henderson, sharing the common British suspicion of French ambitions for hegemony on the Continent, indeed refused to take Briand's initiative at face value and instead looked for disguised motives behind it. Nor was British ignorance quickly remedied. By a nice irony Tyrrell, having become ambassador to France in 1929, soon discarded his sceptical view of the European idea and encouraged British sympathy for Briand's attempts to consolidate France's efforts at *rapprochement* with Germany. During the autumn of 1929 and early months of 1930 Tyrrell repeatedly affirmed that France was serious about solving the German 'problem' by absorbing it within a European confederation of some kind, and moreover that numerous signs pointed to Germany's readiness to participate in such a venture.[9] Despite his repeated appeals, however, London treated his reports with marked scepticism. As Leeper pointed out with some impatience in May 1930, his colleagues had done precious little to find out about the European movement: even now the Foreign Office library had not acquired any of Coudenhove's published works.[10]

The inadequacy of intelligence on the European movement, which was at variance with the normal professionalism of the Foreign Office and diplomatic service, was symptomatic of the problems of policy management created by the remarkable transformation of international relations since 1914. The outbreak of the First World War had permanently shattered the existing liberal world order in which the state, and particularly the British state, performed a modest and essentially passive role in the economic affairs of the nation. Henceforth, both domestically and externally policy-makers actively pursued objectives and employed a variety of instruments. The economist J.M. Keynes published an essay on *The End of Laissez Faire* in 1923 describing the deeprooted and irreversible character of this transformation, but the Foreign Office along with most other departments of state displayed little willingness to acknowledge it before events forced changes in 1931. During the First World War a few far-sighted members of the Foreign Office had sought to anticipate this brave new world by proposing the creation of a new politico-economic intelligence department.[11] But most of their senior colleagues were thoroughly indifferent to the proposal or downright hostile on the grounds that they would end up as a species of official commercial traveller; they wanted as little as possible to do with trade.[12] As a result, the Treasury, the Board of Trade, and the Bank of England assumed responsibility for international negotiations on such issues as reparations, war debts, tariffs, quotas, trade finance, capital lending, and currency stabilisation, and thus came to occupy a central place in the management of external relations, while the Foreign Office was left unequipped to deal with these issues and unable to coordinate the activities of the various departments or institutions involved.

From the outset of the interwar period the marginalisation of the Foreign Office became apparent. In 1921, 1922 and again in 1927 the Foreign Office protested to the Treasury at being kept in the dark on reparations policy, which left Britain's diplomatic relations with France and Germany virtually incoherent—to no avail.[13] In 1928 the Foreign Office sought to initiate changes in foreign lending policy in order to assist British exporters and sustain British commercial interests in South America.[14] But the Treasury would not allow this encroachment upon its bureaucratic preserve and pressured the Foreign Secretary into withdrawing the Office's brief to the Cabinet.[15] The Foreign Office had to be satisfied with a lecture from the

Governor of the Bank of England on the practical difficulties of altering policy.[16] In 1929 it was the Chancellor of the Exchequer, not the Foreign Secretary, who headed the British delegation to The Hague conference called to deal with both the New or Young Plan on reparations and the withdrawal of allied troops from the Rhineland. In 1930, after a series of unsuccessful attempts to collaborate with the Bank of England, E.H. Carr of the Foreign Office complained that the Treasury went to 'absurd lengths' to protect the Bank from political interference.[17] The following year the Foreign Office came into sharp conflict with the Board of Trade, the Treasury and the Dominions Office when it advocated support for a French scheme of intra-European preferences.[18]

In September 1931 the gold standard collapsed, and shortly afterwards Britain abandoned free trade; *laissez-faire* was now manifestly supplanted by an actively managed economy. Nevertheless the Foreign Office's marginalisation became if anything greater than before. In April 1932 the Foreign Secretary was little more than an onlooker when negotiations took place in London at a four-power conference on Danubian reconstruction. In June negotiations on the settlement of the reparations problem at Lausanne was handled by the Prime Minister and Chancellor of the Exchequer. A few weeks later the Foreign Office was represented merely by observers at the Ottawa conference where negotiations led to the adoption of an ambitious and extremely provocative scheme for organising the British Empire into a protective economic bloc.[19] Again in 1933 the Foreign Office played virtually no part when the World Economic Conference, the last attempt to devise an internationally negotiated solution to the economic crisis that so gravely affected international relations, was convened in London. The extraordinary instability of the international exchanges after the breakdown of the gold standard led the Treasury to assign financial attachés to the three major foreign capitals. In principle their function was to advise their respective ambassadors, but in practice they served only the Treasury and their communications usually bypassed the Foreign Office altogether.[20] In 1936 the Foreign Office was left in almost complete ignorance about the negotiation of the vitally important tripartite agreement, restoring a semblance of stability to British, French and American currency relations. In 1938 Neville Chamberlain, the former Chancellor of the Exchequer and now Prime Minister, assumed control of negotiations with Hitler over the destruction of Czechoslovakia.

The foregoing examples may suffice to demonstrate the loss of Foreign Office control over external relations as the result of the overlap of political and economic policies. The importance for the present account derives from the fact that most accounts of British external relations are based upon Foreign Office records. These, as indicated above, reveal little interest in the idea of European unity. In contrast, the records of British business opinion confirm that the idea acquired a compelling quality during the 1920s for most serious observers of economic developments. For them it was obvious that the growth of the large corporation was making obsolete the modest domestic markets of the European nation-state. The Foreign Office, while only half alive to this challenge, was only too well aware of the political impediments to European unity. British industrialists and spokesmen for corporate capitalism were therefore prepared to take the European movement far more seriously. They were not necessarily better informed about it than their country's diplomatic representatives. But they faced a particularly hostile economic environment in the 1920s, and in recognising global economic changes they also tended to take the European idea seriously, perhaps too seriously. Indeed, so plausible was it from their standpoint that by 1929 many of them spoke as if a European bloc was a virtual reality. In doing so they reacted all the more vigorously to existing British policies and thus altered the course of history.

From 1918 until 1931 successive British governments pursued a broadly internationalist strategy for restoring a strategic equilibrium and economic prosperity. Politically Britain supported the League of Nations and promoted its various activities. It allowed its wartime alliances to lapse, assisted the restoration of Germany and more cautiously the Soviet Union to full membership in the community of nations. It also pursued, albeit with some reluctance, a special relationship with the United States in order to draw America into world affairs and augment Britain's own influence. On the economic front, postwar British governments made few concessions to nationalists or imperial protectionists in their adherence to internationalist policies. Instead they exploited their control over access to the world's largest commodity import and financial markets in order to promote what was commonly termed economic disarmament. Through the auspices of the Economic and Financial Section of the League of Nations, Britain in 1922 took the lead in rescuing Austria from the brink of financial collapse and social breakdown. That same year Britain formally declared its hopes for a comprehensive write-off of all war debts and reparations. Early the next year Britain became the first country to negotiate a war debt repayment schedule with the United States. Later in 1923 British experts played a central role in the drafting and implementing of the Dawes Plan, an interim solution of the reparations problem which enabled German hyper-inflation to be brought under control and capital investment in central Europe to be revived.

In April 1925 Britain returned to the gold standard. Aside from the United States, which had never formally left it, this made Britain the first major country to resume its commitment to exchange its currency for gold and the only one to do so at or near its prewar parity. Thereafter the Bank of England assisted Belgium, Italy and Poland to return to the gold standard, and devised similar schemes for several other countries including Romania and Yugoslavia. With the international exchanges again functioning smoothly, British business leaders actively promoted trade liberalisation, using the League of Nations as their principal agency.

But there was a price to be paid for such vigorous and sustained international leadership. While deflationary fiscal and monetary policies implemented in 1919–21 succeeded in bringing domestic inflation under control and starting the recovery of the pound sterling, the same policies also helped to transform the postwar restocking boom into a precipitous slump. Unemployment, which had remained negligible during the period of demobilisation, was pushed to grotesque levels, and industrial unrest, triggered initially by efforts to keep wages in line with inflation, continued in the face of falling prices and employers' efforts to force down money wages. The situation was helped for Britain's hard-pressed coal miners when the Ruhr crisis in 1923 reduced German production and sent wholesale prices sharply higher. But the resumption of German production the following year brought renewed pressure on Britain's miners, which reached crisis point in the summer of 1925 when mine-owners began a lock-out that threatened to end in a nation-wide general strike. For the next nine months Britain remained in a state of suspended crisis, with a temporary government subsidy to the owners due to end in April 1926. At this point the expected happened and a brief but dismaying general strike occurred.

The older industries such as mining, heavy engineering and textiles, which already faced acute problems of secular decline, suffered most from the policy of putting financial prestige before domestic recovery. But the new industries based upon chemicals, electricity and the internal combustion engine also suffered severely from the effects of high interest rates and the extraordinary rise in international value of the pound sterling, which nearly doubled in five years to reach its prewar parity of $4.86 in April 1925. The economists and bankers who supported these internationalist policies justified them on the grounds that in revising global commerce they benefited all sectors of the economy and not only the City and its mercantile supporters such as the shipbuilders, shipowners and munitions makers. Only through fixed exchange rates secured by adherence to the gold standard, they claimed, could confidence be restored and international trade revived. But their words failed to carry conviction, and the closer they came to realising their internationalist dream of returning to the policies of the pre-1914 world the more sceptical British industrialists became of the benefits in store for them. The older industries remained seriously depressed through the latter part of the 1920s. Yet significantly it was spokesmen for the newer industries, which fared relatively well at this time, who took the lead in criticism of economic internationalism.

One reason for their dissatisfaction was that many of them, like their counterparts in the cotton industry, had borrowed heavily from the banks to facilitate the conversion to peacetime production only to find themselves dangerously burdened with short-term debt when interest rates rose and price levels fell. Another was that the newer industries, in contrast to the old, were very capital-intensive and required large, affluent and relatively homogeneous markets. Their spokesmen thus placed greater value upon the preservation of the domestic and Commonwealth markets than the markets of continental Europe or elsewhere, and generally favoured some form of protection to safeguard their market share. Businessmen in the newer industries were also, despite their relative success within the domestic economy, acutely aware of being overtaken and squeezed out of world markets by their vastly larger and more dynamic American competitors.

Several times over the previous hundred years America's burgeoning economy had attracted widespread comment in Britain. In the early 1900s Joseph Chamberlain had promoted Tariff Reform by exploiting anxieties about Britain's industrial decline *vis-à-vis* the United States and Germany: hardly a speech during his campaign in 1903–6 failed to mention these two powers. Later, during the First World War, Britain was made gratefully aware of America's industrial strength when it became dependent upon American production for its physical survival. In the aftermath of the war political estrangement and boom/slump conditions deflected attention to problems nearer home. But by the mid-1920s, with Britain ostensibly depressed and economically in decline while the United States enjoyed unprecedented prosperity, attention again turned westwards. Thousands of Britons visited the United States to see at first hand its industrial advances, and nearly all returned impressed. Most of them recognised that the mass-production techniques, as epitomised in the Ford Motor Car operation in Detroit, had inaugurated a new industrial age. The large corporation, such as Ford, General Electric, Standard Oil and Dupont, had a vastly greater reach than the factories of the previous age, and imposed new imperatives upon the political system similarly to extend its range of control. There seemed little doubt that Britain and other competitors must come to terms with this new scale of operations if they were to survive. What remained a matter of dispute were the appropriate means of emulating the 'American system'.[21]

Among right-wing commentators many predictably emphasised differences between the organisation of British and American labour. On the eve of the general strike the *Daily Mail* sponsored a trade union mission to the United States in a well-publicised attempt to highlight the rewards of docility on the shop floor.[22] A few months later the Ministry of Labour organised a similar mission involving both employers and trade union leaders.[23] The Federation of British Industries, the largest of the 'peak' organisations, had sent its own mission to tour American industrial centres in 1925.[24] Meanwhile the *Morning Post* carried a series on the United States which affirmed that socialism was not an issue in America because nearly all the workers there were themselves capitalists.[25] Left-wing observers, on the other hand, chose to emphasise the role of high wages in sustaining demand in the American market, and free traders emphasised the absence of barriers between the forty-eight states of the Union, while protectionist opponents pointed instead to the United States' massive external tariff wall which offered its manufacturers a privileged place in their domestic market. These differences notwithstanding, there was nevertheless agreement on the basic proposition that the new scale of industrial production demanded markets on a comparably large scale. The continent-wide domestic market of the United States more than met this condition; the British domestic market as clearly did not. This was the issue addressed by Sir Alfred Mond, Britain's leading industrialist, and Leo Amery, a leading Conservative politician, who led the way in promoting public awareness of the changing shape of international economic relations, the American threat and the seriousness of the European idea.

Mond in the mid-1920s wore three hats, as Chairman of the chemical company Brunner Mond, Chairman of Amalgamated Anthracite, the largest mining trust in South Wales, and as a Liberal MP and front-bench spokesman on economic affairs for the Liberal party. He had been a leading figure in the Free Trade union and opponent of any retreat from free trade by his party.[26] But by 1924 he was complaining of the deflationary impact of British monetary policy, which in his view favoured financial interests at the expense of industry, and spoke of the awesome strides that American industry was making in the expansionary monetary conditions created by the Federal Reserve System.[27] By 1925 he had given abundant indications that he was disillusioned with Britain's internationalist economic policies, in particular the return to the gold standard at the prewar parity.[28] Early the following year he resigned from the Liberal Party, crossed the floor, and almost immediately became one of the Conservatives' most strident advocates of organising the British Empire into an economic bloc capable of competing with the United States on an equal footing.

In September 1926 Mond travelled to New York in the hope of negotiating a place for his firm in a global cartel scheme being arranged between Dupont and the German I.G. Farben. When his efforts failed he returned to England and swiftly set about amalgamating the country's major heavy chemical manufacturers into a new firm, Imperial Chemical Industries (ICI), which instantly became Britain's largest industrial firm. Mond announced its formation in a burst of publicity which he used to promote his new vision. As he and colleagues explained, they believed their example should be followed by other sectors of British industry in order to stand up to the foreign combines which were threatening to divide the world.[29] The global phenomenon of 'continuously growing concentrations of interests and of industry', he warned on another occasion, threatened to leave Britain isolated between the United States, an empire of forty-eight states, and a countervailing European bloc. Britain must therefore take steps to create a 'United Economic Empire', if it was not to see the rest of the Empire drawn into the larger markets offered by the other blocs.[30] On yet another occasion he set out the stark choice of isolation for Britain or a united empire organised into a bloc of such enormous territory, population and resources that it could effectively confront the other superpowers: 'It would not be a question of negotiation, but of stating our terms.'[31]

An examination of the Foreign Office, Board of Trade or Cabinet records, or the columns of Hansard for the years 1925–30 reveals scarcely a reference to Sir Alfred Mond or first baron Melchett, as he became in 1927. The political battle he waged took place almost wholly in public meetings, in the columns of the press, or at meetings of businessmen's organisations such as the National Union of Manufacturers, the Federation of British Industries, the British Empire Producers' Organisation, and the Empire Industries Association. Leo Amery's efforts were a different matter. As Secretary of State for the Dominions and Colonies in the Conservative Cabinet between November 1924 and May 1929, he occupied a place at the very centre of the political system. But like Melchett from 1925 he turned practically every occasion into an opportunity to promote the vision of a united British Empire, larger and more populous than the United States, while haranguing colleagues to support an imperial industrial strategy.

Amery found himself vigorously opposed by Winston Churchill, the Chancellor of the Exchequer who had the advantage of being able to point to the political blunder of 1923 when the Conservatives had allowed Labour into office by going to the country on a platform of tariff reform before any serious attempt had been made to mobilise public opinion. Amery failed to persuade his other Cabinet colleagues that imperial protectionism was now politically practicable, and judged solely by the immediate practical results one would be bound to conclude that his efforts were fruitless, for the government baulked at large-scale protectionist or imperialist economic policies. Yet seen from a wider angle there are grounds for claiming that his proselytising efforts had very considerable results. By the latter part of the decade British interest in American industrial development amounted almost to a fixation: if anything, more intense than Europe's preoccupation with the 'American challenge' in the 1960s or the current preoccupation throughout the western world with the Japanese 'economic miracle'. Britain's relative industrial decline predisposed the public to take an interest in the subject. Nevertheless Amery may be credited with stimulating this interest and reviving support for the geopolitical conceptualisations of Chamberlain's Tariff Reform campaign, which largely governed the framework of debate on Britain's future once the world slump began.[32]

Until 1925 speculation about Britain's future as an industrial power focused almost exclusively upon the United States. Europe, impoverished and more divided than ever as a result of the war, seemed to be simply a problem to be overcome rather than a source of serious economic competition. But once the Reichsmark, the pound sterling, the Belgian and French francs, the lira and other lesser currencies were stabilised, efforts began to reduce the trade barriers that 'balkanised' the economy of the continent. At this point discussion of geopolitics in Britain took on a new dimension: account was now taken of the obvious attractions of a unified European market.

The first clear sign that Europe would participate in efforts to reduce protectionism appeared at the third congress of the International Chamber of Commerce held in Brussels in June 1925, when delegates from most of the continental countries enthusiastically endorsed British-drafted resolutions on trade liberalisation.[33] Shortly afterwards another sign appeared when France called upon the League to organise an international conference to deal with the trade problem. Hitherto France had actively opposed British attempts to use the League as an agency for trade liberalisation, claiming that commercial policy was a matter strictly for national decision. This was therefore a noteworthy development, and in due course a World Economic Conference was scheduled for May 1927 in Geneva.[34]

The British bankers and publicists who had been leading the campaign to restore economic internationalism seized upon news of the Geneva conference in order to discourage the British government from entering into any prior economic commitments to the Dominions at the 1926 imperial conference.[35] As Walter Layton, editor of the *Economist* and one of the most influential free traders of the day, repeatedly warned, Europe was at the crossroads. If encouraged, the continental countries could be expected to move decisively in the direction of expanded multilateral trade. But if Britain failed to provide leadership or, worse, signalled its intention of moving towards exclusive or preferential trade relations with the rest of the Empire, the opportunity would be lost and the continental countries would similarly resort to further 'balkanising' policies or form an exclusive European bloc based on rigid cartel arrangements.[36]

Layton, who attended the World Economic Conference as head of the semi-official British delegation, was more than pleased with the outcome. It had been widely expected that France would use the occasion to promote a policy of cartels designed to regulate trade and maintain France's relatively strong position on the Continent while safeguarding it against further

American economic encroachments. In the event, however, French delegates made little effort to promote cartels or defend their policy of tariff reciprocity, and joined other European delegations in giving nearly unanimous endorsement to a series of resolutions, drafted by British experts, in defence of freer trade. Layton declared it a historic victory for European liberalism. But other observers described it more narrowly as a victory for British commercial principles over those of France, which, as events were soon to show, came closer to the truth.[37]

In the immediate aftermath of the World Economic Conference, commercial relations in Europe were with a few exceptions marked by goodwill and a readiness to examine ways of reducing trade barriers. However, little actual progress was made, partly on account of opposition from industries benefiting from protection, but also on account of serious disagreement over the appropriate course of action to take. Countries such as the Netherlands and Denmark, with strong liberal traditions, favoured the application of the most-favoured-nation clause in its most unconditional form, while others, including France, Belgium and Switzerland, advocated the conditional form of the clause in order to strengthen Europe's hand *vis-à-vis* the United States and other economic powers seeking to benefit from reduced tariffs in Europe without conceding increased access to their own markets. Numerous attempts were made to follow up the World Economic Conference resolutions through the agency of the League of Nations, but the most-favoured-nation issue remained the stumbling-block, and the stalemate continued through the final two and a half years of the decade, amidst growing anxiety over the future of the world economy.[38]

For Europe as a whole the 1920s were a time of impressive economic growth. Most of the belligerent countries regained prewar levels of production by 1924, and by the end of the decade many reached levels of output that they barely surpassed until well after the Second World War. Like Britain, however, most of them also became unsettled by the impact of American economic expansion in the later 1920s. US exports took a rapidly increasing share of the European market for manufactures and created a worryingly large current account deficit for the Continent as a whole. For the time being the deficit was offset by receipts from tourism and short- and long-term American lending. But the influx of high-spending American tourists tended to cause resentment, as did the fact of Europe's increasing dependence upon American money markets and vulnerability to banking decisions taken in New York. Resentment was also aroused by the impact of American foreign direct investment, either through the take-over of European firms or through branch plant construction, which increased almost exponentially towards the end of the decade along with the value of securities on the Wall Street markets. Most of the US direct investment, moreover, was concentrated in the new or, as they would be called today, 'sunrise' industries, whose products—such as cars, communications equipment and office machines—were visible reminders of the extent of American economic penetration. The main target for US direct investment in Europe at this time (as in other decades before and since) was Britain; here the City, which was hostile to any restrictions on international investment, tended to subdue criticism of the 'invasion'. But the financial sectors of the continental countries were smaller and less influential in shaping domestic opinion. Hence anxiety over American investment found increasingly strident expression. France, despite burgeoning prosperity and full employment, raised the loudest objections. Claims were made that the United States was extorting war debts in order to obtain the wherewithal to buy up the country's industrial base and turn it into an economic colony.[39] The French government sought to offset American advantages by imposing fiscal penalties on foreign-owned firms and withholding most-favoured-nation treatment on imports. This led to US retaliation and extreme strain in Franco-American relations by the latter part of the decade.[40]

Other factors also played their part in shaping European opinion, including the new direction of Soviet economic policy and uncertainties over the direction of British commercial policy. Since 1917 observers in the West had watched anxiously for signs that the Bolsheviks would apply their revolutionary zeal and organisational skills to transform the Russian empire into a modern industrial superpower. The New Economic Policy in 1921 appeared to mark a step in this direction, and the introduction of the first Five-Year Plan in 1928 was taken as a signal that the transformation was well and truly under way. By this time well-informed European observers had also become acutely aware that British opinion was veering away from free trade and that the Conservative government which had taken office in November 1924 was acutely divided over policy. During the World Economic Conference in 1927 Layton had used the threat of British abandonment of free trade to promote support for liberal resolutions.[41] Shortly afterwards the seriousness of the threat was underlined when the continental countries, having endorsed the resolutions on freer trade, found the British government unwilling to authorise the League of Nations to give them its wholehearted endorsement.[42]

But once again in the autumn of 1928 it was developments in the United States that dominated attention. The presidential elections in November resulted in a landslide victory for Herbert Hoover. For the previous six years Hoover had shone as Commerce Secretary in the lacklustre administrations of Harding and Coolidge. Americans, who had come to associate him with the current prosperity, regarded him as a reassuring figure, but British and European observers regarded him very differently, as the personification of American economic nationalism and aggressive expansion.[43] By now many observers believed that mass-production techniques had led to the 'saturation' of the American domestic market for manufactured goods.[44] They therefore expected that once in office Hoover would intensify America's search for overseas markets. Accordingly, when he used the period between the election and his inauguration to tour Latin America, they took this as a sign of his intention to organise the Americas into a single economic bloc.

Throughout the winter of 1928–9 European business conditions were adversely affected by the Wall Street boom, which drove up interest rates to frightening levels, discouraged further American lending abroad, drew in foreign funds to New York, and threatened to plunge Europe into the currency chaos that had nearly resulted in revolution earlier in the decade. Reactions were thus intense when it became apparent in the spring of 1929 that the United States was prepared to compound the injury by increasing its trade protection.[45] In 1922 the United States had introduced the Fordney-McCumber tariff, the so-called 60-per-cent tariff, which raised duties to their highest level in US history and higher than almost anywhere else in the developed world. This had occurred at the tail-end of the severe postwar slump. But now, despite prosperity and a strong balance of payments, another Republican administration was prepared to acquiesce in a further tightening of the screw. In the summer of 1929 virtually every government in Europe formally protested to Washington against the proposed tariff revision. At the same time chambers of commerce and other business and political organisations called for Europe to organise itself in order to resist American economic aggression.[46]

British observers such as Melchett and Amery readily accepted the necessity for a European economic bloc. Amery, indeed, had gone so far as to participate in the Pan-Europa Society in order to promote a separate continental bloc. In 1927 he criticised the report on world affairs that Sir Austen Chamberlain, the Foreign Secretary, presented to the Commonwealth Conference for leaving out all mention of the Congress of the Pan-Europa Society, which Amery described as the most important event of the year.[47] That same year Mond told a gathering of Tory MPs that he had just returned from a tour of European capitals where he had spoken to leading politicians and businessmen.

> It was quite remarkable, and I should not have believed it had I not come so closely into contact with it. The idea that you must form some economic union of European countries, some form of joint action in industry . . . in taxation, in tariffs, and even further steps than that, in order to enable Europe to go on existing against the Continent of North America, is becoming almost axiomatic, almost a passionate faith.[48]

Mond's claims were made on the eve of the World Economic Conference and were accompanied by criticism of the 'European' minds in Britain who were more interested in promoting multilateralism in Europe than the unity of the British Empire. Inevitably they invited the suspicion that he was overstating the strength of 'European' sentiment on the Continent in order to persuade his colleagues that the die was cast and that economic internationalism had no future. But Mond and Amery were not alone. Expectations that the world would eventually devolve into vast blocs in response to the imperatives of mass-production industry predisposed many British industrialists to regard agitation in Europe as evidence that unity was already on the political agenda. Thus Sir William Larke, Director of the National Federation of Iron and Steel Manufacturers, spoke of an eventual European economic bloc as a virtual certainty.[49] So too did Sir Hugo Cunliffe-Owen of British-Americam Tobacco, Sir Hugo Hirst of the General Electric Corporation, and Alfred Hacking, Secretary of the Society of Motor Manufacturers and Traders.[50] As Harold Butler, a British official in Geneva, asserted before an audience of Manchester businessmen in February 1927: 'There can hardly be any doubt that the example of the unrivalled prosperity of the United States during the last five years has furnished a powerful stimulus to the idea of European co-operation.' The European powers were pressing ahead with industrial ententes or cartels, he affirmed, and warned that British industry must quickly adapt if it was not to be isolated between the United States and an organised European bloc.[51]

Labour as well as management in British industry gave evidence of concern. Ernest Bevin, the transport workers' leader and one of the trade unionists on the Ministry of Labour mission to the United States in 1926, acknowledged before the annual Trades Union Congress in 1927 that he had been extremely impressed by the level of prosperity attained in the United States and spoke in favour of associating Britain with a United States of Europe in order to replicate the conditions that favoured industrial progress in the United States.[52] Some time during the next three years he turned away from Europe and towards the British Empire in his search for a solution to Britain's dilemma. But it is clear from the first report of the TUC's Economic Committee, of which he was the leading member, which was published in 1930, that it was the same assumption of a global trend towards economically comparable blocs that informed the trade unionists' outlook.[53]

By the latter part of the 1920s numerous politicians were also beginning to express their belief in the inevitable transformation of the world economy into a handful of continent-sized blocs. The young Tory hopefuls Robert Boothby, John Loder, Harold Macmillan and Oliver Stanley published a book that accepted the inevitability of this trend.[54] Oswald Mosley, the ambitious young Labour politician, took a similar view.[55] The *Round Table*, the leading journal of liberal imperialism, expressed the same view.[56] Ramsay MacDonald, the leader of the Labour Party, briefly joined in the chorus, and in 1929 so too did the Conservative minister and Birmingham MP, Neville Chamberlain. As Chamberlain put it,

> Alone, the United States of America are vast enough, and contain sufficient resources within their own limits, to stand on their own feet, and to tower somewhat menacingly over smaller units. It is the recognition of these facts, and the need for self-preservation, that has raised the idea of a United States of Europe, and has turned the eyes of the British Empire towards the old conception of an economic unity between its members . . . To-day, the alternatives are being pressed upon us with increasing urgency. We, in these islands, cannot stand by ourselves alone. If we do not think imperially, we shall have to think continentally.[57]

The Conservative Party, unsure of the practicability of imperial protectionism or its electoral popularity, chose to avoid the issue during the 1929 general election, a decision the Liberal and Labour Parties were pleased to accept. But hardly was the new minority Labour government formed than Briand announced his intention to speak at the forthcoming League Assembly in favour of European federation. Briand's plan, it soon became evident, was vague and politically unfeasible. Yet in the circumstances it was scarcely surprising that spokesmen for British industry should generally have taken the proposal seriously. Thus the *Statist* referred to Briand as 'a far-sighted realist' whose support for the European idea confirmed that it was no longer 'the plaything of visionaries'.[58] Similarly, *The Economist* affirmed that 'material and social forces are inevitably' leading towards European unity, and welcomed Briand's initiative as a practical effort to create a United States of Europe in emulation of the United States.[59]

Equally significant was the fact that once Lord Beaverbrook, the press baron, challenged the Tory leadership in July 1929 by demanding support for Empire Free Trade and debate over the future of British commercial relations began in earnest, virtually every contribution was formulated in terms of an emerging constellation of economic blocs comprising an American-dominated Western hemisphere, a united British Empire, a European bloc, and perhaps a Soviet dominated Asian bloc as well. Beaverbrook himself almost invariably based his own argument on this assumption. In July 1929 his *Daily Express* warned:

> Europe, in spite of its age-long antagonisms, is turning more and more towards some sort of fiscal co-operation as its one chance of not being crushed by the overwelming might of America. The United States of Europe will become the reality of the twentieth century, not from reasons of sentiment, but as the only way

of equalising the odds against Transatlantic competition. [For Britain] it is the choice between (1) Europe and deterioration; (2) America and subservience; (3) the British Empire made once and everlastingly properous by the unbreakable link of free trade between all its parts.[60]

So of course did the ever-active Amery [61] and Melchett [62], but so too did the *Manchester Guardian Commercial* which accepted that a European bloc might be created if Britain did not take steps to forestall it;[63] Stanley Baldwin, the leader of the Conservative Party, who took the brunt of Beaverbrook's prodding;[64] Sir Gilbert Vyle and Sir Walter Raine, the senior officers of the British Chamber of Commerce;[65] and even Sir Arthur Salter, head of the Economic Section of the League of Nations and a prominent Liberal free trader.[66] Indeed, practically everyone involved spoke as if Britain had to make an immediate choice between joining Europe or organising the Empire into an alternative bloc, or, in the case of free traders, actively resisting the emergence of a European bloc.

By July 1930 opinion throughout the British business community favoured the attempt to organise the Empire economically. The actual decisions that marked an end to economic internationalism—the abandonment of the gold standard, introduction of foreign lending controls, anti-dumping legislation and a general tariff, and the granting of increased preferences for Empire products—were implemented over a ten-month period starting in September 1931. By this time Britain was well and truly immersed in the world slump, which invites the conclusion that it was the slump that caused disillusionment with internationalism. But careful examination of the evidence confirms that the disillusionment was widespread *before* the slump began, since the new consensus within the business community, at least to the extent of abandoning free trade, was already apparent before the slump was more than a few months old.

The sources of this dissatisfaction were numerous: the secular decline of the older industries, the excessive zeal with which post-war governments promoted a return to the prewar gold parity for sterling and other internationalist policies, the decline in the British share of Empire markets, difficulties in restoring satisfactory economic and political relations with continental Europe, and the disturbing challenge from American industry working in close alliance with a succession of narrowly nationalistic Republican administrations in Washington. The efforts of Coudenhove and others to promote a united Europe played only a modest role in encouraging Britain's retreat into an exclusive Empire bloc. Nevertheless the assumption that Europe *must* eventually unite into an economic bloc in order to survive in face of threats from the East and the West was so widely held in Britain by 1929 that the most preliminary schemes for promoting this goal were treated as evidence that this development was actually under way. In short, it was the *idea* of European unity more than the movement itself that affected the course of British history. Politicians and permanent officials had little to say about it, but as evidence of interest this is by itself very misleading. British capitalist interests had a good deal to say about it, and eventually reacted to it in such an overwhelming way that the course of Britain's external relations was affected for a decade.

Notes

1. See, for instance, W.N. Medlicott, *British Foreign Policy since Versailles, 1919–1939* (London, Methuen, 1968); Arnold Wolfers *Britain and France between the Two Wars* (New Haven, Yale University Press, 1940); C.L. Mowat (1968), *Britain between the Wars, 1918–1940* (London, Methuen, 1966).
2. League of Nations, *Documents Relating to the Organisation of a System of European Federal Union*, L.N. A.46.1930.VII.
3. R.W.D. Boyce, 'Britain's first "no" to Europe: Britain and the Briand plan, 1929–30', *European Studies Review*, Vol. 10 (1980), p. 18.
4. ibid.
5. ibid.
6. F0371/11246, C10417/10417/62, Tyrrell minute, 2 October 1926.
7. F0371/14365, C1570/230/18, A.W.A. Leeper minute, 24 February 1930; F014366, C3439/230/18, A.W.A. Leeper minute, 8 May 1930.
8. F0371/14234, W7294/6739/98, memorandum, 24 July 1929.
9. F0800/284, Tyrrell to Henderson, 30 October 1930; F0371/14365, C230/230/18, Tyrrell to Henderson, No. 3, 8 January 1930; ibid., C1002/230/18, Tyrrell to Vansittart, 28 January 1930.
10. F0371/14366, C3439/230/18, A.W.A. Leeper, 8 May 1930.
11. Sir Victor Wellesley, then controller of commercial and consular affairs, took the lead. In his words, 'A new epoch of economic life lies before us and all the signs of the time point to the economic factor becoming the dominant one in our future foreign relations', F0368/2036, 62458/f.14578, Wellesley memorandum, 9 March 1918. See also F0368/1855m 141670/f.2049, Wellesley memorandum, 28 June 1917; Memorandum by the Board of Trade and the Foreign Office with respect to the Future Organisation of Commercial Intelligence, Cd.8715, 1917, Foreign Office Committee report, pp. 17–30.
12. G.M. Trevelyan, *Grey of Fallodon* (London, Longmans, 1948), pp. 158, 359. Lord Balfour, Grey's successor, encouraged little change of attitude. As he wrote in reference to tariff reform and Imperial preference during the war, 'It is certainly not the business of this Office to deal with international economics, nor is it qualified to do so', F0800/207, Balfour to Long, 2 August 1917. According to Frank Ashton-Gwatkin, who later collaborated with Wellesley, 'The Foreign Office did not understand or support him' in his reform efforts, Ashton-Gwatkin, *The British Foreign Service* (Syracuse, NY, Syracuse University Press, 1951), p. 20.

13. T160/122, F4566, Curzon letter to Horne, 19 November 1921; ibid., Gaselee letter to Treasury, 26 April 1922; ibid, Gaselee letter to Treasury, 12 November 1927.
14. F0371/14094, W1846/1846/50, 'Foreign Trade, Finance, and the Foreign Office', memorandum by Sir Austen Chamberlain, 16 February 1929.
15. T175/34, Leith Ross minute, 1 March 1929; F0371/14094, W1846/1846/50, Sargent minute, 1 March 1929.
16. T175/34, Lindsay memorandum to Hopkins, 22 March 1929.
17. F0371/14346, C3974/658/2, Carr minute, 23 May 1930. See also F0371/17676, C749/1/18, Sargent, Vansittart minutes, 2 February 1934; F0371/18451, R3922/3922/37, Vansittart minute, 7 July 1934; T175/86, Vansittart to Fisher, 15 August 1934.
18. F0371/15159, C2149/673/3, Fountain memorandum, 24 March 1931; F0371/15160, C2790/673/3, Leith-Ross minute, 23 April 1931; PREM 1/105, Thomas minute to MacDonald, 16 May 1931; PREM 1/106, Vansittart to Selby, No. 38, 19 May 1931.
19. F0371/16409, W9649/1167/50, Gwatkin letter to Wellesley, 19 August 1932.
20. F0371/17318, W3986/278/50, Wigram minute, 28 March 1933; F0371/16604, A2972/59/45, Mounsey minute, 27 April 1933.
21. Robert Boyce, *British Capitalism at the Crossroads 1919–1932: a study in Politics, Economics and International Relations* (Cambridge, Cambridge University Press, 1987), chs. 1–4.
22. *The National Review*, March 1926, p. 27; ibid., May 1926, pp. 351–3.
23. CAB 23/53, 4(26)3, minutes, 16 June 1926.
24. Boyce, *British Capitalism*, op. cit., p. 102.
25. *The Morning Post*, 25 May 1925, p. 13.
26. Boyce, *British Capitalism*, op. cit., p. 102.
27. ibid., pp. 46, 48, 102.
28. ibid., pp. 77–8.
29. *The Morning Post*, 13 October 1926, p. 12; ibid., 23 October 1926, p. 12; ibid., 23 December 1926, p. 12.
30. *The Spectator*, 30 October 1926, p. 729; *The Times*, 30 October 1926.
31. *The National Review*, January 1927, p. 672. See also *The Morning Post*, 19 February 1927, p. 8.
32. Boyce, *British Capitalism*, op. cit., pp. 111–12.
33. *The Times*, 22 June 1926, p. 13; ibid., 23 June 1926; ibid., 24 June 1926, p. 13.
34. League of Nations, *Official Journal*, 6th Assembly 1925, p. 81; William E. Rappard, *Post-War Efforts for Freer Trade*, Geneva Studies, ix, 2, (Geneva, 1938), p. 26.
35. *The Economist*, 23 October 1926, pp. 659–60, 668–70.
36. *The Liberal Magazine*, January 1926, pp. 32–3; ibid., September 1926, p. 521.
37. Boyce, *British Capitalism*, op. cit., pp. 119–22.
38. Boyce, ibid., pp. 130–3.
39. André Siegfried, 'European reactions to American tariff proposals', *Foreign Affairs* (October 1929), pp. 13–19; Lucien Romier, *Who Will Be Master, Europe or America?*, trans. Matthew Josephson (London, John Hamilton, 1929); Edouard Herriot, *The United States of Europe*, trans. Reginald Dingle (London,

G.G. Harrup & Co, 1930).
40. Frank A. Southard, *American Industry in Europe* (New York, Houghton Mifflin, 1931), pp. 121–2.
41. League of Nations, *Report and Proceedings of the World Economic Conference held at Geneva, 4–23 May 1927*, 1917.II.521.4 (Geneva, 1927), 72, 107, 112.
42. League of Nations, *World Economic Conference, 1927*, 1927.II.50 (Geneva, 1927); *The Free Trader*, August–September 1927, p. 166.
43. J.B.C. Kershaw, 'The American presidential election and the future of British and European trade', *Financial Review of Reviews*, January–March 1929, pp. 51–60.
44. See, for instance, statements by Sir Robert Horne, Anthony Eden and William Graham in Hansard, House of Commons, H.C. Deb. 5s, vol. 209, col. 802, 913; ibid., vol. 214, col. 1949.
45. J.M. Jones, Jr., *Tariff Retaliation. Repercussions of the Hawley-Smoot Bill* (Philadelphia, University of Philadelphia Press, 1934).
46. Boyce, *British Capitalism*, op. cit., pp. 199–201.
47. ibid., p. 111.
48. Sir Alfred Mond, *Industry and Politics* (London, Macmillan, 1927), p. 276.
49. *United Empire*, May 1926, p. 274.
50. Sir Hugo Cunliffe-Owen, 'Industry and the Empire crusade: a statement to manufacturers', London, n.d.; Sir Hugo Hirst, preface to J.E. Barker, *America's Secret. The Causes of Her Economic Success* (London, John Murray, 1927); Alfred Hacking in *United Empire*, January 1927, pp. 43–4.
51. H.B. Butler, 'The International Economic Conference', paper read before the Manchester Statistical Society, 24 February 1927 (Manchester, 1927).
52. *Report of the Proceedings at the 59th Annual Trades Union Congress, 1927*, pp. 387–96.
53. Trades Union Congress, 'Commonwealth trade: a new policy' (London, 1930).
54. Labour Party, *Report of the 30th Annual Conference, 1930*, pp. 200–204.
55. *Industry and the State: A Conservative View* (London, Macmillan, 1927).
56. *The Round Table*, March 1926, p. 249; ibid., June 1926, pp. 476–501.
57. *The Free Trader*, December 1925, p. 265; *Empire Review*, August 1929, pp. 91–4.
58. *The Statist*, 27 July 1929, p. 125.
59. *The Economist*, 14 September 1929, p. 463.
60. *Daily Express*, 26 July 1929, p. 8. See also Lord Beaverbrook, *Empire Free Trade* (London, *Daily Express* 1929), p. 5; Hansard, House of Lords, 75 H.L. Deb. 5s., 19 November 1929, col. 548–50.
61. See for, instance, *Sunday Express*, 28 July 1929, p. 10; *The Times*, 25 October 1929, p. 8; *The Times*, 1 November 1929; *The Times*, 15 February 1930, p. 14.
62. *Sunday Express*, 14 July 1929, p. 12; *The Times*, 13 November 1929, p. 16; *The Times*, 15 November 1929, p. 11; *The Times*, 20 November 1929, p. 9.
63. *Manchester Guardian Commercial*, 31 October 1929, p. 507.
64. *The Times*, 22 November 1929, p. 19.
65. *The Times*, 4 October 1929, p. 16; ibid., 23 November 1929, p. 18; *Manchester Guardian Commercial*, 10 October 1929, p. 411.
66. *Manchester Guardian Commercial*, 28 November 1929, p. 635.

5 European Ideology and European Reality: European Unity and German Foreign Policy in the 1920s

Peter Krüger

One of the fundamental questions in the history of European unity seems to be simple: how did those who wanted to unite or to integrate this rather curious, irregular continent proceed, what ways and methods did they apply to achieve unity? In the course of European history, the goal in itself seemed to be, more often than not, highly questionable, and if it was pursued at all, the method applied was quite rough: hegemony or dominance of a leading power. The most brutal version of this practice was put into effect by Adolf Hitler. As it is handed down in his table talks, for him it was an incontestable fact that 'this welding together of Europe has not been made possible by the efforts of a number of statesmen devoted to the cause of unification, but by force of arms.'[1] This was the most uncompromising denial of any kind of cooperation or federal procedure of European unification, based on compromise and on the equality of rights of all states. It is absolutely consistent with such a denial that Hitler hated and scoffed at the small nations. This contemptuous mentality is not unusual, especially with those who think they have discovered the clue to the laws of history. In 1848, Karl Marx mocked the 'tiny-wee' nations; he was convinced of the superior right of great, progressive nations and condemned as nonsense the idea of international fraternization.[2]

The attitude towards small nations is a good indicator of how seriously are taken declarations which stress as fundamental the principle of equality in any effort to construct some kind of European community. Even if there is agreement in principle, it is well known that great powers are always tempted to pass over the rights and needs of small countries. After all, it had taken a long and difficult historical process before it was accepted that the only way consistent with equal rights and political freedom to unite Europe is the thorny way of conciliating conflicting interests, finding compromises, and establishing a sound basis of common principles, interests and goals. From

84

the European states system and the German Confederation of 1815 to the European Community, historical experience seems to demonstrate that such a stable international organization, based on principles of equality and independence, gives effective guarantees to the existence of smaller states. Moreover, it presents the best framework for them to secure a certain influence in international affairs.

Instead, however, more or less enlightened advocates of a united Europe in the 1920s offered plans which were derived from abstract and lofty principles. These principles were to substantiate and to legitimize the bid for unity, and they reached from the defence of European culture and tradition, and Europe's allegedly endangered independence, to the universal goals of peace, harmony and prosperity. Although the benign purpose was to end European conflicts and quarrelling, such ideas again included an element of subtle pressure, an obligation to strive for higher values, demanding adherence and allegiance.

There may have been countries, however, with other priorities, other problems, and other ways to solve them. Obviously, the different plans for European unification suffered from the same weaknesses, a certain lack of convincing and realistic connections between European ideas and the existing acute conflicts, interests and difficulties. It was not easy to demonstrate exactly why such an extended scheme like European unity might become a practical solution to actual problems. This wide gap made Pan-European movements vulnerable to ideological formulae: the oversimplification of reality, the concentration on a general principle, sometimes with a pseudo-religious gloss, the belief in the uniqueness of Europe and the occident, and the conviction of fighting for a superior idea, a higher-level civilization. A more imminent danger in the gap between the general idea of European unity and the actual problems in Europe lay in the fact that particular political or economic interests of nations—as, for instance, Germany—or powerful social classes might take advantage of that idea in order to cover and promote their own purposes. Moreover, it also proved to be a doubtful venture to attempt to establish European unity on the shaky grounds of transient economic problems. Since the nineteenth century, some kind of European integration has been proclaimed again and again as the preferred solution to certain difficulties which might have been dealt with as well, or even better, by other means. Such advocacies of the European idea have been criticized, in most cases immediately, by down-to-earth opponents, in particular by distinguished economists.

Finally, there is a phenomenon which tends to complicate things even further. Even among those who had a genuine and practical interest in some kind of European integration—above all in the economic sphere—there were people who used comprehensive European schemes and ideologies to support their more restricted aims. There was a fluid, variable relationship and sometimes mutual penetration between ideals, ideologies and pragmatic politics regarding European unification, and this state of affairs was the background of every practical approach to that question in the 1920s in Germany. Both spheres, however—the ideological and the practical—should be separated more strictly in historical analysis than has been done up to now. Even the answer to the question, what came first, Pan-European propaganda or practical needs, is not as easy as it once appeared to be.

Almost all historical research regarding Germany has been concentrated on ideas, ideologies, plans and the efforts of groups, organisations and movements to promote European unity, on their motives and on the reasons for their failure. Sometimes, scholars tend to deal with the European question in the interwar period as a—miscarried—prelude to European integration after 1945 and to emphasize the development of political ideas, of public debate, and of a growing cooperative movement. Such studies are important, but they cover only part of that great and ramified subject. To complement this approach, I would suggest examining the other side of the coin; structures and interests and their possible interrelation with the idea of European unity. A few attempts have been made to concentrate on this problem, but have soon reached the deadlock of the inadequate question: Pan-Europe or Central Europe? As a more receptive starting point and a focus of investigations, the politics of government appear quite appropriate, because government after all is the place for decisions on needs and interests. Hence, German foreign policy after the First World War may provide an interesting case study of the role of European ideas and solutions in actual planning as well as rhetoric. I will, therefore, concentrate on the area of German foreign policy where European integration was discussed seriously: international economics and especially the plans for a European customs union. The substantial discussions on European initiatives did not take place as part of a dialogue between the German government and the Pan-European movements, but took place within certain government circles. They were conducted in the context of actual interests, economic needs, and—most interesting— diplomatic planning.

Obviously, the year 1925 marked a new phase in the widespread political discussion of schemes for European unification. What happened before 1925 was a rather disparate development in several stages. What followed after 1925 was characterized in the first place by the fact that the discussion became more concentrated, more purposeful. A certain focus emerged in the preparation, starting in autumn 1925, of the World Economic Conference of the League of Nations, this conference itself (4–23 May 1927), and the subsequent efforts to secure not only permanent results but permanent institutions and meetings. This new form of international consultation was supposed to prepare the ground for the joint action of all countries and for a minimum consensus about important aspects of the world economy, namely commerce, industrial production and agriculture. In the second place, political and economic conditions had improved considerably due to the politics of understanding, the Dawes Plan and, above all, Locarno.

As to the first period before 1925, it seems reasonable to follow the different, sometimes dramatic, stages of Germany's attitude towards Europe. For it was this period that paved the way for a more consistent German attitude towards Europe in the second half of the 1920s, and it revealed driving forces and constellations typical not only of this initial phase of efforts to build a European community. Thus it is possible to get at the same time a general idea of the historical development as well as some substitute for a systematic discussion of the facts which influenced a European orientation in German foreign policy.

A basic decision about the deeply controversial problem of Germany's international position had become inevitable by the end of the First World War. The issue was old and had provoked public debates since the 1890s. It was part of the comprehensive controversy about whether or not Germany should proceed in her breath-taking industrialization, leaving behind her agrarian basis and traditional structure. Within this framework and aggravated considerably during the war, a fundamental question arose: should Germany try to regain a certain degree of self-sufficiency and to become as independent as possible while avoiding what was called 'over-industrialization'? The terrible experience of the Allied blockade seemed to provide impressive evidence for a positive answer and to justify extensive war aims in order to win a sphere of dominance large enough for that purpose. The alternative was that Germany should proceed along the path of industrial modernization, seek an increasing share in the world economy, and strengthen her ties with other countries. After the devastating defeat at the end of the war, the German government took a firm decision in favour of international cooperation and an open, liberal world market. It is hard to see what else they could have done to improve the situation and to avoid the crushing conditions contained in the peace treaty, though this certainly was not the way the victors considered that issue. However this may be, the pragmatic internationalists in Germany prevailed, and the conservatives and nationalists grudgingly acquiesced—for the time being.[3]

Moreover, during the Paris Peace Conference in 1919, the Germans tried to act as champions of political and economic understanding. Their draft of a League of Nations charter was distinctly more radical than that put into effect later. They made reasonable and in part progressive proposals for a liberal world market with a programme to reconstruct international trade, production, credit, and currencies and plans for the supply and distribution of raw materials and food. These proposals, however useful they might have been in general, served of course to secure vital German interests. They clashed with the intentions of the victors and were in vain.[4] But under these circumstances it was not surprising that European solutions also became attractive to German minds. The economist Professor W. Lotz told British emissaries in March 1919, 'that there should be a United States of Europe, otherwise he prognosticated a great decline in Europe'.[5] This became the guide-line of arguments followed by German politicians and officials. They tried firmly to establish the priority and the necessity of European economic cooperation as an alternative to the impending catastrophe. Reconstruction after the war as a common European task and responsibility; that was the motto. It is worth noting, however, that such views and intentions went beyond mere tactics in a desperate situation. The emphasis on liberal principles was the result of a long tradition of international business and experience, and was strengthened by the outcome of the First World War and the dark aspects of the future.

The immediate aftermath of the war was the first stage; the second was the struggle about the right way to cope with the huge and far-reaching economic consequences of the war in 1920–1, above all with reparations, the incomparably high indebtedness, inflated currencies, shortage of foreign exchange and low purchasing power, the decay of international trade, a wave of protectionism and the new boundaries and restrictions. The German government made continued efforts to convince the other countries of the urgent requirement to take joint action and to rebuild the European economy. In addition to this, the solution to European misery obtained a strong German emphasis. Europe could only recover if Germany and her economy were restored; so ran the message which belonged to the permanent chorus of almost every German statement regarding the situation in Europe. Germany, it was said, was indispensable for 'the well-ordered economic life of Europe'.[6]

This emphasis engendered mixed feelings in other countries, the more so when German nationalists narrowed this view and combined it with renewed ideas of German predominance in Central Europe. Nearly all experts agreed that the European countries desperately needed common arrangements on debts, credits, currencies and trade, as well as a considerable increase in the exchange of goods and in the movement of capital. But the prospect of rapidly re-establishing German preponderance in this way caused a real dilemma. Nevertheless, during the period of the politics of fulfilment after May 1921, the option of close European cooperation spread in German government circles. The Minister of Reconstruction, W. Rathenau, in particular, was engaged in schemes of European economic cooperation. In his conference with the French minister Loucheur, one of the champions of industrial organisation, at Wiesbaden, 12–13 June 1921, he suggested a 'Société internationale de reconstruction'.[7]

Moreover, immediately after the war the French as well as the Germans started considering plans for a close cooperation or even interlocking of their heavy industries, along with those of Belgium and Luxembourg. Their views and political preconditions, however, differed too much. The French–German antagonism was too strong for an agreement.[8] But the idea remained alive throughout the years to come, discussions and negotiations from different points of departure took place again and again, and the project, though on the rather small scale of a cartel only, was successful as soon as the political atmosphere had improved in the Locarno era. Although it was not until 1951 that the European Coal and Steel Community brought about a decisive solution to the complicated strategic, political and economic problems involved, it is remarkable how persistently this project had been pursued for more than thirty years under totally changing conditions.

Some general conclusions concerning European integration may be drawn from this historical process and its deep and far-reaching political implications. It revealed the strength of structural and regional preconditions, the crucial importance of the network of heavy industries in north-west Europe, and their impact on all efforts at integration. Another essential point became obvious soon after the war. Any project of European integration depended on the relationship between France and Germany. Finally, once again historical events confirmed the well-known fact that economic and political problems could not be separated. A certain basis of European security, understanding and compromise was absolutely necessary before the widespread feelings in favour of European cooperation and unity could be transformed into cautious political action.

Prime Minister Lloyd George wanted to achieve just this, to have a plan agreed upon by the other European countries which would take into account the connection between political and economic questions. With his initiatives —Rathenau was involved from the beginning—Lloyd George opened the third stage, a rather ambiguous one, in the development of German policy towards Europe.[9] He tried to pave the way for a solution to Europe's post-war problems by a joint effort of the European countries in a well-prepared and comprehensive conference including Germany and Soviet Russia. This proved to be a huge task which required a new international atmosphere of compromise and practical proposals for European cooperation and conciliation in different fields, reaching from a general non-aggression pact and other measures securing peace to financial and trade arrangements. Above all, the reparations problem, a dangerous point of conflict, had to be neutralized.

One of the most interesting projects was a Central International Corporation Limited which was to be established by the governments of the major

European powers. Subject to their approval, the Central Corporation was supposed to coordinate the formation of national corporations according to the agreed guide-lines. In the protocol of 25 February 1922, which was signed by German government representatives too, it was agreed that

> the main object of the corporations will be to examine the opportunities for undertaking work in connection with European reconstruction and to assist in the financing of such undertakings. The policy of the corporations will be to co-operate where possible with other agencies and undertakings.[10]

The plan was similar to what Rathenau had in mind, when he suggested a 'Société internationale'. Soviet Russia was given priority for joint reconstruction efforts. Other areas with alarming economic weaknesses were to be dealt with later.

As part of the preparations for the Genoa Conference the Germans drew up a rough outline of a European customs union.[11] The basic idea was the setting-up of larger economic areas and the removal of a rather long list of trade barriers. Since it was unrealistic to establish a customs union at once, certain preliminary stages appeared to be useful: firstly, a reduction of customs and the termination of import and export prohibitions; secondly, customs communities; thirdly, a customs union. A Central European solution was considered too, although 'European free trade' was a clear preference. Nevertheless, scepticism prevailed regarding the feasibility of these plans, because most countries were expected to refuse to cede any part of their sovereignty or to reduce the protection of their domestic markets. The government experts doubted whether they would be able to get a customs union accepted in Germany, where the narrowing of foreign markets might fuel a growing protectionist mood.[12]

The last aspect of the European perspective which needs to be mentioned was a political problem, the serious lack of a new European order which came to the surface of public attention on the occasion of the Genoa Conference. Victors' alliances and a global organisation, the League of Nations, did not satisfy the urgent requirement of a more specific and precise European arrangement to establish a modern, durable European states system. A new European consciousness sprang up which supported such ideas and raised hopes that the conference might advance European cooperation. The huge conference in itself was seen as a demonstration that Europe existed and wanted to be alive. European feelings flared up on a common ground of shared problems and expectations.[13] Besides, the Genoa Conference and Europe's misery resulted in a new wave of publications on European unity. Furthermore, among the politicians disappointment grew with the weak performance of the League of Nations. Although criticism of the League was not fair, for it had existed for only two years and could not be held responsible for what the peace-makers had neglected, the disappointment was important because it furthered somewhat a return to the European idea. In Genoa, even Eduard Beneš, the Czechoslovak Foreign Minister, an adherent of the League of Nations and a sensitive and cautious politician, agreed with Rathenau that a kind of League restricted to Europe was necessary.[14]

But all hopes were in vain. Lloyd George and others had to bury their plans and visions when the Germans decided to conclude a separate treaty with the Soviets at Rapallo (although there were other events which contributed to the failure of Genoa). One of the reasons why this treaty created controversy, even within the German delegation, was that several German experts understood quite well the ill-effects this decision would have for European cooperation. Moreover, Rapallo revealed the ambiguity of German foreign policy, despite the serious interest in European projects and mutual understanding.[15]

The new phase in European affairs since 1925 cannot be understood without taking into account the severe setbacks and dangers of 1923 and the birth of a period of understanding in 1924. The failure of Genoa, the reparations crisis, the worsening political and economic situation and, finally, the almost war-like clash between France and Germany in the Ruhr disaster interrupted political efforts to promote European cooperation, but inspired political commentators and led to the formation of European movements, as well as to the consideration of cooperation among industrialists, particularly in the north-west European belt of heavy industries which were threatened by inacceptable business conditions and ruin. As early as winter 1920–1, Hugo Stinnes, the leading industrialist in the Ruhr area, perhaps even in Germany, advocated a customs union with France.[16] After autumn 1922, he worked hard to achieve an interlocking of German and French heavy industries, including, if possible, England, Belgium and Luxembourg. Moreover, he planned gigantic railroad systems in Central and Eastern Europe.[17] Of course, this had nothing to do with lofty European ideas, but it did reveal the trend towards international communities of interest which were trying to organise certain economic branches or sectors on a European level. Most of these plans were defensive strategies against the pressure of modernisation. Some government experts also continued to consider international economic combinations as a way forward.

In 1923, the idea of European integration gained a new dimension in public debate and in plans submitted to the German government. Integration was seen as the only way leading to a peaceful solution of European problems, above all the deadlock of reparations, and to an end of the devastating Franco-German confrontation. The crisis pushed forward such plans and also the ideologies which concentrated on the darker prospects of an old Europe in decay, powerless and helpless compared with the rising non-European world, especially the United States. Some of these proposals are of special interest. They were based on the deplorable and dangerous state of Europe in the absence of any renewed European states system and sought to put the reparations problem into the general context of economic and political decline in the postwar period. In some proposals, the Zollverein of 1834 served as a model for continental Europe, with France being expected to take the lead as Prussia did in the first half of the nineteenth century.[18] This customs union was to be completed by special industrial combines for different branches and regions, thus creating an atmosphere of security and peace on the basis of economic interests. An arrangement of that kind would enable Germany to pay reparations, and France to evacuate the occupied areas in the Ruhr and on the Rhine.

To negotiate on equal terms and to get rid of discriminating clauses in the Treaty of Versailles, such as the trade restrictions, was essential to the German government as a precondition of any European cooperation. As a basis of the proposed customs union, the European currencies were to be stabilised and credit made available. Of course, the more considered plans took into account the thorny problem of the English and American attitudes towards such a European community. In general, it was expected that England would finally give in if the European countries stood together. The United States might appreciate from the beginning, it was hoped, a stabilisation of Europe and the prospect of its huge market, although plans for European unification often tended to be seen as a defence against American economic superiority. None of these projects was really politically feasible but they provided a basis for discussion of practical problems.

When the Ruhr crisis was overcome, the first steps towards a policy of understanding were made. The most important event and the basis of all future progress in that direction was an arrangement about reparations, the agreement on the Dawes Plan. It was more than a mere reparations plan, for it contributed to financial stabilisation, and made possible a first stage of international cooperation. Based on the idea of recognising common principles and mutual interests, the Dawes Plan was supposed to become explicitly the 'means for assisting the economic recovery of all the European peoples' and to 'ensure the permanence of a new economic peace'. Peace, European cooperation, stability and prosperity—these were the aims. 'We have not concealed from ourselves the fact that the reconstruction of Germany is not an end in itself. It is only part of the larger problem of the reconstruction of Europe.' Thereby, an often repeated thesis of the Germans was confirmed: Germany's contribution was 'vital to the reconstruction of Europe'.[19]

In a speech of 13 November 1924,[20] Stresemann emphasised that for the first time since 1919 things had taken a turn for the better. The process of *détente* and peaceful settlement of conflicting interests, which was an indispensable precondition for European cooperation, was under way. At the same time the rearrangement of Germany's trade policy was at stake and, therefore, European economic cooperation was of an immediate importance. Stresemann pleaded for a liberal system, based on the most-favoured-nation clause, 'because this system alone could warrant an economic understanding and rapprochement between all countries of Europe'; otherwise, isolation and a struggle of all countries against each other would be inevitable and the resort to force a possibility. He also emphasised that an economic agreement with France was one of the most important instruments for achieving peace in Europe. Four points in this speech are important here: international cooperation was essential to the political and economic interests of Germany by reason of her industrial structure; a liberal trade system was the first stage for European cooperation; the Franco-German relationship was fundamental for the development of Europe; economic understanding would secure peace.

The German initiative for a security pact brought together the important countries of Europe and succeeded at Locarno. The final protocol itself summarised the European orientation as well as the interdependence between *détente* and economic recovery. Moreover, the close connection of the pact with the League of Nations and its Council facilitated an intensified Concert of Europe, particularly between the great powers, France, England and Germany.[21] A short period of a policy of understanding began, which stimulated considerably the continuing debate on European unity amongst parties—particularly the social democrats—trade unions, economic associations and scholars. So it is not surprising that this debate was more substantial and concrete than the discussions of the European movements which were welcomed mostly as propaganda. In his speech of 16 April 1925,[22] Stresemann emphasised the fact that Germany, more than ever, was interlocked with the other countries. Against the Balkanisation of Europe and the numerous new customs boundaries, he demanded the setting-up of larger economic units, and he suggested that only an abolition of customs duties might help Europe against the economic strength of the United States. Stresemann was, however, not very precise. It is therefore very important to know what steps were taken towards making European cooperation, or even integration, a reality.

There had been a noticeable development in German foreign policy concerning European questions since 1919. In the beginning, it could be characterised as a not very conclusive reaction to the day-to-day needs and problems. But gradually it became clearer and a long-range perspective reflecting German interests in Europe was developed. More and more,

Germany's European policy was clarified by experience, by familiarity with actual international problems and by the search for practical answers to European questions. Helping towards this were an eased atmosphere in European politics since 1924 and a new, if precarious, receptiveness to international debate and connections. In any case, the Germans were prepared to go ahead if it was expedient and if the circumstances were favourable. This happened when Louis Loucheur, then French representative to the League of Nations, on 15 September 1925, moved in the General Assembly for the convocation of a world economic conference. The initiative was rather like seeking refuge in attack. The motives of French foreign policy, the desire to maintain France's leading position, will not be discussed here, but it was well known that Loucheur was a strong advocate of European economic cooperation in the form of international combines, cartels and similar agreements, and, as he added in October 1925, of a European customs union.[23]

The responsible departments in Germany followed these and other statements closely. The German government supported Loucheur's proposals vigorously although, in view of the prevailing political uncertainty, they wanted to avoid figuring too prominently in either the preparations, the conference itself—from 4 to 23 May 1927—or the subsequent meetings. So they acted cautiously from the beginning. Behind the scenes, however, they became ardent supporters of the conference and of its basic idea of improving and facilitating the exchange of goods and capital, which was understood to be a vital task since trade lagged considerably behind production. They worked hard to make it a success and the international economy became the most effective area of the League of Nations policy of the German government.[24]

The German Foreign Office as well as the Ministry of Economics had decided that within the wider framework of that conference and its preparation they could pave the way for the idea of a European customs union and other forms of integration, for instance agreements between different branches of European industry, without coming to the forefront. As the Hamburg banker Max Warburg, who may almost be called an adviser of the government, put it in a letter to Stresemann on 10 November 1924: The Germans should deal with the problem of European unity as they did with the Dawes Plan, they should let the Americans discover the German ideas.[25] In any case German foreign policy had to be very cautious in order not to alienate the U.S.A. and England.

Although it was obvious that the government would have the backing of a majority of German business circles, trade unions and politicians, above all the social democrats, it was equally obvious that the difficulties and the clash of interests would be extraordinary. From the beginning in autumn 1925, the Foreign Office experts had analysed clearly the main obstacles and stages of a

European customs union, above all agriculture, currencies and heavy industry.[26] It was taken for granted that an immediate elimination of customs and other trade restrictions would be impracticable in view of the deep differences in the economic structures of Europe. The responsible director in the Ministry of Economics, Hans Posse, explained on 24 February 1927 to leading industrialists that mere tariff policy was not enough and that a new economic order in Europe required more than a customs union.[27]

Apart from the World Economic Conference, the long and difficult negotiations about a trade agreement between France and Germany, conceived as a major contribution to European solidarity, promoted the idea of a customs union. When on 17 August 1927 the agreement was signed, almost three years of intensive contacts had created an atmosphere in which even the long-term consequences of Franco-German and European economic cooperation were discussed.[28] This trade agreement was a European event which failed to develop its influence only because of the Great Depression and the domestic crisis in Germany after March 1930. Nevertheless, when Briand in September 1929, in the League of Nations, revealed in public his ideas about a European union, the German Foreign Office did not react with enthusiasm. A political union appeared premature. It would seriously impede any territorial revision of the eastern boundary and it would have been too heavy a burden for the government in a critical domestic situation. Stresemann, however, in his last speech, answering Briand, emphasised the importance of a future economic union of Europe. This became the working basis of the German Foreign Office until the summer of 1930 when Chancellor Brüning cut short this development.[29]

Some concluding remarks may indicate the background of the discrepancy between practical politics and the ideas of the European movement which has been unable to become the driving force of European unity. There has never been a powerful mass movement in favour of a united Europe, and, like similar great ideas, it depended on support from interests which were far more powerful and had far more immediate influence upon the life of the people. The driving forces have been the structural changes of modern societies, the political and economic interdependence of industrial countries, the rapidly growing interlocking of the European states, and the clearsighted wisdom of some of their politicians, diplomats and officials, who presented better and more realistic ideas. The European movements were important in offering a vision, in influencing public opinion and in supporting those governments which preferred European cooperation to more nationalistic efforts to solve their problems.

Finally, was a European customs union the most adequate and progressive solution? The question depends on another one: was there an approximately equal level of industrial development and modernisation in Europe? The case of Germany demonstrated the opposite. There were several important groups in German society—landowners, the middle classes, to some extent industrial circles, etc.—which rejected international competition and cooperation in favour of the ruthless nationalism which prevailed in the early 1930s.

Another problem lay in the ambivalent tradition of a European customs union which was promoted by protectionists as well as free traders. In the 1920s German economists with high reputations such as Eulenburg or Esslen warned against simply changing the small-scale protectionism and chauvinism of one country into the protectionism and chauvinism of Europe. Moreover, they reacted vigorously against the danger of European cartels and protectionism petrifying outmoded economic structures and traditional models of an international division of labour between industrialised and non-industrialised countries. They also warned of the new problems of control and social policy which would arise in a European version of 'organised capitalism'. In opposition to all that, these economists demanded global free trade and competition as far as possible (that meant, with a certain protection for young industries), global industrialisation, and above all a dynamic process of change and adjustment, so that all countries could make use of technical progress and increased purchasing power.[30]

Perhaps these economists underestimated the stimulation and flexibility of a European customs union, but their challenging and essential questions required discussion. The European movements, however, mostly refrained from the hard and painstaking consideration of practical problems of a European community. They did not really answer such intricate questions and hardly investigated the conflicts of interest and their origin, the interdependence of political and economic issues, the problem of regional structures and differences, the agricultural crisis and the imbalance of currencies. There were, it is true, many detailed studies but in most cases on a rather abstract level.

But more significant, I think, than anything else is the fact that the European movement did not cope with a fundamental European tradition, the nation and the nation-state. The modern nation-states remain the most important political factor in Europe, even though they thought it expedient to develop new forms of a modernised European states system based on close cooperation and partial integration, and to renounce certain rights in favour of supranational agencies. The nations and their diversity still embody Europe. This explains why further progress towards European unity is so extremely difficult today; and it is one of the greatest misunderstandings, due to an over-estimation of the so-called European idea, to believe that a gradual process might lead to the United States of Europe. This goal can be achieved only by a sequence of almost revolutionary political decisions and it is worthwhile to ask at what cost.

Notes

1. H.R. Trevor-Roper (ed.), *Hitlers Table Talk, 1941–1944* (London, Weidenfeld & Nicolson, 1973), p. 541.
2. Franz Mehring (ed.), *Aus dem literarischen Nachlass von Karl Marx und Friedrich Engels, 1841–1850* (Berlin, Dietz, 1923), Vol. III, pp. 146–64.
3. Peter Krüger, *Deutschland und die Reparationen 1918/19* (Stuttgart, Deutsche Verlagsanstalt, 1973), Parts II and III.
4. Peter Krüger, *Die Aussenpolitik der Republik von Weimar* (Darmstadt, Wissenschaftliche Buchgesellschaft, 1985), pp. 69–76.
5. *In Germany, March 1919. The Personal Diary of Frederic Wise*, privately printed, London, p. 24.
6. Köster to Rome, 9 May 1920, Politisches Archiv des Auswärtigen Amts, Bonn (= PA) (German Foreign Ministry Archives), U.St.S. W, W.A. 7, Vol. 1.
7. Loucheur Papers, Hoover Institution on War, Revolution and Peace, Stanford University, Box 12, Folder 13.
8. Krüger, *Deutschland und die Reparationen*, op. cit., pp. 133–7, 176–9; Henning Köhler, *Novemberrevolution und Frankreich* (Düsseldorf, Droste 1980); contacts in August 1919; PA, Deutsche Friedensdelegation Paris/Versailles, 25, Vol. 1; Georges Soutou, 'Une autre politique? Les tentatives françaises d'entente économique avec l'Allemagne, 1919–1921', *Revue d'Allemagne*, Vol. 8 (1976), pp. 21–34.
9. Carole Fink, *The Genoa Conference: European Diplomacy, 1921–1922* (Chapel Hill and London, University of North Carolina Press, 1984); Krüger, *Aussenpolitik der Republik*, op. cit., pp. 152–73.
10. *Sammlung von Material für die Konferenz in Genua am 10. April 1922*, Supplement No. 2, strictly confidential, Berlin, Reichsdruckerei, 1922, p. 9.
11. PA, Handakten Simson, Konferenz von Genua, Vol. 21: Stichworte; Vol. 22: Memo de Haas, 19 Jan. 1922.
12. *Sammlung*, op. cit., main volume, pp. 93–97.
13. A good survey of various kinds of European efforts, but neglecting the incentive of the Genoa Conference for the outburst of publications and proposals on European unity, 1922–30: Richard Vaughan, *Twentieth-Century Europe: Paths to Unity* (London, Croom Helm, 1979) pp. 25–43. See also Carl H. Pegg, *Evolution of the European Idea, 1914–1932* (Chapel Hill and London, University of North Carolina Press, 1983).
14. Beneš/Rathenau talk, 2 May 1922, PA, RM 5 h, adh. 2, Genoa.
15. Krüger, *Aussenpolitik der Republik*, op. cit., pp. 173–83.
16. Memo Trapp, 11 January 1921, PA, RM 6, Vol. 1; Memo Simons, 28 January 1921, PA, RM 7, Vol. 1.
17. PA, RM 5 secret, Vol. 1; Peter Wulf, *Hugo Stinnes: Wirtschaft und Politik, 1918–1924* (Stuttgart, Klett, 1979), pp. 329–43. At the same time, Chancellor Wirth suggested, in vain, a comprehensive European economic and political arrangement under pressure of reparations, hoping to prevent French dominance and to gain American support, Wirth to Washington, 3 October 1922, PA, RM 5, Vol. 9.

18. Unsigned Memorandum of 20 March 1923 ('Versuch einer europäischen Regelung des Reparationsproblems'), PA, Nachlass Maltzan, Englische und italienische Antworten.
19. *Die Sachverständigen-Gutachten* (French, English, and German texts), (Berlin, Deutsche Verlagsgesellschaft, 1924), II, pp. 6, 49.
20. PA, Nachlass Stresemann, Allg. Akten, Vol. 18.
21. *Reichsgesetzblatt 1925, Teil II*, pp. 976–77 (French and German texts of the Treaty of Locarno, 16 October 1925).
22. PA, Nachlass Stresemann, Allg. Akten, Vol. 23.
23. Louise Sommer, 'Die Vorgeschichte der Weltwirtschaftskonferenz (Genf 1927)', *Weltwirtschaftliches Archiv*, Vol. 28 (1928), pp. 340–418; Report Döhle's (Paris), 22 October 1925, PA, W, Wirtschaft 1 B, Vol. 1.
24. Karl Přibram, 'Die weltwirtschaftliche Lage im Spiegel des Schrifttums der Weltwirtschaftskonferenz', *Weltwirtschaftliches Archiv*, Vol. 26 (1927) pp. 305–438; E. Respondek, *Verlauf und Ergebnis der Internationalen Wirtschaftskonferenz des Volkerbundes zu Genf* (Berlin, Heymanns, 1927). For details of Germany policy, 1925–30, Peter Krüger, 'Die Ansätze zu einer europäischen Wirtschafts-gemeinschaft in Deutschland nach dem Ersten Weltkrieg', in Helmut Berding (ed.), *Wirtschaftliche und politische Integration in Europa im 19. und 20. Jahrhundert* (Göttingen, Vandenhoeck and Ruprecht, 1984), pp. 149–68.
25. PA, Nachlass Stresemann, Allg. Akten, Vol. 18.
26. Ritter to London, 28 December 1925, PA, St. S. WW.
27. Bayer-Archiv, Leverkusen, 62–10.
28. *Akten zur deutschen auswärtigen Politik, 1918–1945*, Series B, Vol. I/1, No. 68, Vol. VI, No. 120; *Reichsgesetzblatt 1927, Teil II*, pp. 524–876.
29. Krüger, *Aussenpolitik der Republik*, op. cit., pp. 490–92, 523–30. Circular of 14 November 1929, PA, W, Wirtschaft 1 Volkerbund-Zollfrieden, Vol. 1.
30. Krüger, 'Ansätze zu einer europäischen Wirtschaftsgemeinschaft', pp. 151–5.

6 Reflections on *Europa* (1935)

A.G. Lehmann

Introducing into the study of a quite recent past the evidence offered by works of fiction can give rise to severe methodological problems. The starting point of these remarks, *Europa*, is a work of fiction famous in its time, now forgotten.[1] It is furthermore the case that its author Robert Briffault, when he wrote it, was not at all a typical representative of the interwar years, being in fact 63 years old. Though a communist he was not exactly an orthodox Stalinist, nor was he seeking to be treated as spokesman of that movement like, for example, the young novelist Louis Aragon in the same years; and though *Europa* was for a short time a very successful novel indeed, it cannot be said to have marked a significant turning-point in history—not even, I regret to say, in the annals of literature—being in fact a sort of digression even in its author's career.

In short, if historians of the European Idea fail to refer to Robert Briffault and his novel *Europa*, or its sequel, *Europa in Limbo*,[2] one would not accuse them of serious negligence. Whether or not *Europa* is a great forgotten literary masterpiece is likewise irrelevant; though arguably it outranks anything by Compton Mackenzie or A. Powell in the same vein in the same period. It is almost (but not quite) in the same class as *Brideshead Revisted*, though *Brideshead* is the more professional, the more polished composition. My excuse for drawing this book to your attention rests on other grounds altogether.

First, I notice that, as its title advertises, this is meant to be a novel—carried out on a large scale too—actually *about* Europe, as a socio-political entity. And the sub-title *A Novel of the Age of Ignorance* is there to draw to our attention to something which we might or might not know on opening the book for the first time—namely that the author is a Marxist, charting the countdown to the Great War of 1914 and its inescapable concomitant of Revolution; just as the book's sequel *Europe in Limbo* designates the sequel of events occurring in an age not yet fully transfigured by that revolution.

Of course, socio-political entities may be the subject but cannot be the actors in fiction; the actors of a novel are imitation persons, male and female; and *Europa* is also an *Erziehungsroman*: a novel about growing up, placed in the last years of the nineteenth century and the first decade of the twentieth. As one would expect, it is centred upon a young hero of the same generation as Briffault himself, and having a strong resemblance to him. At any rate, young Julian Bern is the son of a retired diplomat; he grows up in a cosmopolitan and, as they say, cultured world, mostly outside England (though he is put through the ordeal of a philistine public school); he rejects the tutelage of faith and adopts the vocation of research scientist (in Briffault's case it was medicine); and he ends up applauding Rosa Luxemburg in Berlin in July 1914 and embracing revolutionary socialism in a general way. At one point in the book it is remarked that Julian has survived the war—the narrator has glimpsed him, worn and ageing, in New York in around the year 1922—but that is not important. What is important is the dialectic of a personal evolution, which is also of course an answer to the Marxist riddle, how the class-enemy can ever be converted to the revolutionary cause.

This personal evolution, as presented in the novel, begins with the contradictions of religion. Julian as a child confronts a pious Catholic mother and a superstitious priest who confiscates *The Origin of Species* when he catches the boy reading it; but these are set over and against a sceptical and amused father who eggs on the child to go his own way and 'find out for himself'. There comes to his parents' salon, also, a German philosopher who stoops over the child and, placing a hand on his head, utters the sybilline query, 'Thou mightest be he'. On that occasion too, Nietzsche (for it is he) is made to harangue his hosts about Europe; but it is the query which remains in the mind: later Julian wonders if it refers to his being destined to *understand* things about which everyone else is deluded. At all events, challenging the dogmatism of theology leads on to the development of a questioning—or, as we would say, critical—disposition and a thirst for positive knowledge; and it is in that frame of mind that Julian passes from a classical education, via Cambridge, to an apprenticeship in the modern evolutionary science of marine biology. So far there is nothing which might not come out of the life-story of an H.G. Wells or any other adept of scientism, except perhaps one thing—Julian has grown up in Rome *surrounded by* relics of the tremendous past, *under the shadow of* that institution which has dominated European civilisation for nearly two thousand years. It is all familiar, like yesterday; the Church is incarnate in that diabolically clever cardinal, the tempter, the collector of beautiful objects, who is such a friend of the family. But familiarity breeds contempt—or, at least, helps on demystification.

After theology, which Julian demolishes on logical positivist grounds, there comes the demystification of love and sex—that other great hypocritical 'lie'[3] imposed on mankind by the architects of this multimillenial civilisation. Julian passes through various entanglements—and, more interestingly, observes the prewar England of suffragettism and female literary liberation—before the inevitable encounter with a *grande passion*. In a novel, it is quite acceptable that the incomparable Princess Zena should have been first sighted as a child in a very Proustian seaside holiday scene; that she is talented, beautiful, lively, open-minded, married to a scoundrel; that fate and fortune eventually smile, and love (for the time being) triumphs over all. Zena, so far as one knows, is a less historically grounded person than young Julian; but to anyone reading this novel with care it must be noticeable that she is to be identified—no doubt symbolically—as the daughter of another Russian Princess, Darya, and that this mother—precisely—is on just one occasion referred to under her sobriquet, which is *Europa*. As a model for Europa, Darya has sat for the old sculptor friend of the family. There is thus a symmetry—a symmetry to do with Europe—in the confrontation of Zena and Julian, the hero, since Julian, for his part, is the *son* of the retired diplomat who also bears a message about Europe, which we shall come to presently.

But first, to complete what needs to be said about Julian's education. The decisive stage in his growing up is that by which he carries the lesson of science from the laboratory into the street, and becomes contemptuously dismissive of the ruling classes (whom he continues to live with on comfortably familiar terms) and enthusiastic for revolt by the common man. At the end of a learned treatise on biology, Julian wishes to add a chapter applying his findings to a new view of human societies; his academic supervisor dislikes this proposal, and his judges and—as it turns out—adversaries in the science establishment object to the introduction of analogical thinking into an otherwise orthodox scientific argument. Briffault never indicates clearly what Julian's argument was about. But Julian at least is clear that marine biology leads to materialism and a materialist solution of the body-mind problem, and that that position, in turn, leads to the necessity of socialism, in place of all the distorted social relations that mark an age of ignorance, privilege, malfunction and disintegration (it is as though he—or Briffault—has been reading Engels' *Anti-Dühring*). These conclusions are in the novel confirmed by a succession of encounters and conversations with the underprivileged classes, suitably graded in sophistication as Julian advances in maturity. A German *émigré*, early on, expounds to him a doctrine of 'thief societies'; later he hears the English socialist Tom Mann putting the case for socialism and calling for working-class solidarity; presently he is convinced of the 'blatant insolent injustice' that has gone on for 'three thousand years', the 'sullen war between master and slave'. Finally the spectacle of German socialism and its massive organisation convinces him that this long war may soon be brought to an end by the victory of Spartacus. Thus, although Julian ends on the same side as Rosa Luxemburg—and indeed with Lenin too, or at any rate one of Lenin's sinister followers—this occurs substantially without too much attention to the contradictions of capitalism as taught in 1914 or in 1935 by the followers of Marx and of Stalin respectively. Julian, at best, becomes a slightly *condescending* Marxist.

The other half of the novel *Europa* is the background in relation to which Julian grows up. This is neither more nor less than a highly ambitious canvas of pre-1914 society in its most cosmopolitan and 'European' form and flavour, together with the message that all this is on the point of collapse. The panorama is too elaborate to be fully described here; after an introductory dialogue in the Café Royal in 'our' time (fictional date 1922), flashbacks cover earlier happenings in Rome, London, the English counties, Viareggio, Florence, Cambridge, Mayfair, Paris, Naples and its surroundings, St Petersburg, Vienna, Italy again, Lancashire, various places on the Côte d'Azur, Munich and Bavaria, finally Berlin. There are scenes of stifling suburbia, airy academe, earnest coteries, grand receptions in town houses long since pulled down, baton charges against strikers in a mining village, mass rallies in Nice or in Berlin, scholarly conversaziones . . . But above all, Europe is represented through *la dolce vita*, the lives and leisures of a thoroughly dissolute 'upper crust'.

I may say that this gives scope for sensationalism of an order which, even for 1935, is very daring. An icily detached Julian organises a visit to a Lesbian brothel in Nice for a couple of dowdy English lady peepers—naturally there are complications in the sequel. More conventionally, a Russian princess is detected in Paris, trying out a piece of black magic on an effigy of her estranged husband; the monk Rasputin is displayed behaving very badly to a duchess; the wife of a Jewish merchant banker is strung up and flogged in front of the other guests at Prince Nevidof's curious Italian castle, for cheating at cards; a ruthless subaltern of Lenin, who happens to harbour an old grudge against that prince, is brought in to carry out an ingenious revenge; back in London Julian's aristocratic aunt is a fantastic prude, but when police raid a high-class property which she owns in Bloomsbury, she has to pay hush-money to the press. Ultimately, as earlier Proust, so here Briffault tends to offer a view of élite *moeurs* which is the contrary of edifying; though there is also a healthy scatter of crooks and charlatans *à la Balzac*, weaving in and out of the dramas that unfold.

In case a reader should miss the significance of all this, Briffault puts down plenty of markers. Both the narrator, and gradually also the character Julian, attest the cultural decay of Europe, *and its political ruin*.

The downfall of a civilisation is not, I suppose, to be directly inferred from the inversion of its élites. That may be a symptom of a more serious *social* malfunction, however; in the socialist tradition (at least down to 1939) an absence of high moral seriousness has commonly been seen as a crippling political fault. At all events, in *Europa* it is hard to imagine real political control when rulers have as their background the complacency and incompetence exhibited in their peer groups. Balfour at a ducal reception assures his hostess that war is impossible—'I see no prospect of such a calamity'[4]; but Russian nobles support Serbian conspiracies out of mere spite; you have only to look at Vesuvius for Lady Irene to tell you that we are *all* dancing on the edge of a volcano; an old gypsy 'delights' the Archduke Ferdinand 'by telling him that he would bring about the biggest war in history'; a lady guest of the naval commander visiting Naples suddenly interjects, 'oh wouldn't it be thrilling to see Constantinople bombarded'. In sum, there is a monumental irresponsibility in the air . . . Early on, the narrator tells us baldly: 'The mould was only just then, in those *fin de siècle* nineties, beginning to crack. The rifts which were then beginning to appear have become gaping fissures. But with the cracking of the mould, Western Civilization itself is cracking.'

I suppose there is nothing particularly new in a left-wing writer denouncing decadence and decline in the interwar years. Contemporary with Briffault's novel is the output of Aragon's communist novels: *Les Cloches de Bâle* ends with Clara Zetkin being brought on stage just as Rosa Luxemburg makes an appearance in the closing pages of *Europa*. And about the same time too, a young Christopher Caudwell is offering the world his Marxist revaluations under the title *Studies in a Dying Culture*. What I think is unique to Briffault is the intellectual basis of his Jeremiad.

Briffault's Marxism is a rather peculiar and personal doctrine. For purposes of this argument it is sufficient to remark that when the Great War ended he was left profoundly horrified by what he had seen and been through—Gallipoli, Flanders, as an officer in the British Army—and horrified by the complacencies of raw patriotism, especially the sort exhibited by the English, whom he presents invariably as philistines or worse. His reaction—or at any rate *one* of his reactions—was to embark on a gigantic programme of reading and research, first into the philosophy of history, then into anthropology. It is true that he owes a great deal to Engels' *Origin of the Family*, at least for introducing him to the ideas of Morgan. But in his largest work, the three fat volumes entitled *The Mothers*,[5] if there is no profound novelty there is at least a prodigious encompassing of all social anthropology published up to that time. Already he is demystifying. Thus if Westermarck has recently affirmed that primitive societies value premarital chastity, Briffault in a footnote lists not less than *fifteen hundred references*[6] to printed evidence to rebut that piece of bourgeois nonsense. In doing so, he is demolishing our tendency to judge our moral suppositions 'natural', or in some special manner sanctioned. This may warn us of a certain propensity to mania in the theories being hammered out. Sure enough, the general findings of *all* anthropology are taken by Briffault to confirm the thesis that sun worship and the supersession of matriarchy by patriarchical institutions mark the original foundation of civilisation; and that from the outset such civilisation, with the division of labour and the establishment of priestly orders and ruling élites, has entailed exploitation, injustice and systematic deception.

With these anthropology-based ideas firmly grasped, Briffault's particular message to the world is the prodigious simplification which he then expounds in his next book, *Breakdown: The Collapse of Traditional Civilisation.*[7] First published in America on the eve of the election of F.D. Roosevelt to the presidency, *Breakdown* is intended no doubt to appeal to an isolationist citizenry which might like to hear unpleasant things about Europe (though it was also published in England). It therefore antedates the publication both of the first volumes of A.J. Toynbee's *A Study of History* and of B. and S. Webb's *Soviet Communism: a new Civilization?*.

Briefly, its message is this. The present or 'western' phase of civilisation is a continuation of the Graeco-Roman world, and a prolongation of the Middle Ages; in it, authority and tradition may be less visible than formerly but they remain, as they have always been, tyrannical. It is simply that the privileged classes and groups, the rulers and the persuaders, the soldiers and the parasites, now enjoy the use of propaganda to repress and cripple human intelligence. This system is still what it was in Plato's time: 'not properly speaking a social organisation, but an organisation of profitable dominating power'. To be sure, the beneficiaries need to keep it unchanged, but unfortunately for them to immobilise it is actually the very way to destroy it. Inability to change is how organisms perish. Worst of all, in the condition of today, is the crippling of people's minds: 'the oldest civilisations . . . established by priests . . . had little occasion to use policemen and bombs. They used theology.' In our (second) European civilisation a secular legacy from Greece and Rome exists alongside religion, but the latter is still a great force: 'the English mind is becoming daily more illiterate, religious, imbecile'. And the same is true elsewhere: consider Spain, says Briffault, where 'a gifted people has for centuries lain in a death-Coma'. England and Europe, in short, live in the past.

> The ethical question of justice is at the present time bound up with what is sometimes called the class-war between the people who profit by existing arrangements and the workers or workless proletarians. The profiteers are much nicer people than the proletarians . . .

However, they—and the priests—hoodwink the masses: *all* traditional civilisations have done much the same, so 'to be morally indignant about *that* would be absurd'.

In sum, though, thinks Briffault, few people now regard western civilisation with feelings of devotion, loyalty and enthusiasm. At most they regard it with indifference, while to the great majority of intelligent people 'it is an object of horror . . . the incarnation of moral evil . . . intolerable, insensate and criminal'. The myth of wisdom and tradition is played out: 'the fruit of the accumulated experience and wisdom of mankind . . . should be understood to mean that it is the accumulated result of the greed, the savagery, the ignorance, the unscrupulousness, and the barbarism of mankind in its ruder phases.' There is no way in which, given the institutions of predation, 'the social world can be made good by making people good'. As for these states and governments 'which are obliged to fight against other governments to exist at all', taken all together they form 'the most criminal organisation known', one which is only tolerated because of modern thought control. If democracy is the form of government best adapted to the interests of a controlling middle class of 'predatory industrialists', and if the American government (up to, and including, the Hoover administration) is 'the worst, the most shamelessly corrupt, the most unprincipled and lawless government ever perpetrated', then likewise fascism is 'nationalism, predatory capitalism, and traditional civilisation at bay, with mask and gloves off'.

Fortunately, says Briffault, western traditional civilisation 'is in the last phases of its agony', and indeed has come to an end completely in 'one-sixth part of the world' (an expression shortly to be taken up in Hewlett Johnson's book, *The Socialist Sixth of the World*, 1939). The 'gigantic revolution' of the Russians has been produced not by 'amiable conversations' but by force; the dictatorship of Stalin (contrary to his critics' hostile views) appears to Briffault to consist of 'an invaluable firmness combined with singularly competent leadership . . .' and has 'accomplished more in a dozen years for the protection of human existence and the abolition of hunger and insecurity than traditional civilisation has accomplished in five thousand years'. With the revolution's abolition of religion, the human mind will soon be able to operate 'normally', without distortion; a new humanity is about to come into being. 'Man as studied by the modern psychologist, philosopher, and general provider of thought, is a pathological specimen. As well might the naturalist investigate the nature of birds by devoting himself to the study of Strasbourg geese.' But remove the poison, remove the 'artificial stupefaction', remove the doctrines purveyed by priests and tyrants and demagogues, and then, 'no limit can be set to the transformation which mind will undergo' . . . 'To bring into being supermen, nothing is needed but to put a stop to the mendacities which afford impunity to a traditional barbarism which terms itself civilisation.' To anticipate superman, in this way, is not Utopian: 'it is the result that must logically follow from the passing away of factors which have crippled the human mind.'

Such is the message of Briffault's book *Breakdown*, three years before *Europa*. And of course it goes far to explain the significance of a passage in *Europa*—a passage which occurs in the opening scene as a matter of fact, where Julian's antecedents are sketched out and in particular his *father* is described by the narrator's sculptor friend remembering him from long ago. Old Mr Bernard Bern, the retired diplomat living in Rome, was in those days a friend of the Prince of Wales and the confidant of kings, but, professionally, a failure:

> There was Bern, who should clearly have been at the Embassy, vegetating on some piddling pension. Of course, he was a bit queer. Not a real politician. Had curious notions far too original for the fellows in Downing Street. He had an idea that England ought to compel Europe to disarm and federate. Said she could have done it without striking a blow; that, had she insisted, no power on earth could have withstood. He actually went to Lord Salisbury with a plan—to revive the Roman Empire, as he put it—a united Europe with its capital in Rome. Said it was the only thing that could have permanently saved England. For when England was at the climax of power he maintained that she was in danger, doomed in fact unless something were done. Lord Salisbury had glanced at the door, uncertain whether he was quite safe closeted with a madman. 'What of Prince Bismarck and the German Empire?' he had asked, to put him off. 'Were England to declare her intention of standing by the side of France, Germany would be reduced to impotence,' Bern had declared. 'England ally herself with France! My dear sir, that is not within the realm of practical politics' . . . the Marquis, who disliked the French, had said. Bern alleged that the United States could have been induced to back a demand for a League of Nations. 'The United States,' Lord Salisbury had said, 'are not a power.'—I suppose Bern was a little mad. Who knows? After all, the idea may not have been as mad as Salisbury thought . . .

And so on.[8] The topic of federation, strikingly introduced in this passage, is never once referred to again in the course of the novel. Why? because—it must by now be clear—for Briffault Europe is something located in the past: whether as a Roman imperium, or a set of traditions reaching back to medieval Christendom and the successor states. Mr Bern sought to prolong something traditional, but which was on the point of collapse. Like his cardinal friend, if in a different way, he cherished at any rate the amenities of the old Europe, the Oecumene, which his son would observe and—finally—repudiate.

Though United Europe is dismissed in this way, and is not worth a second thought, there is a passage in Briffault's second novel, the sequel *Europa in Limbo*, where Julian is listening to a case for the League of Nations. The discussion causes him to think, involuntarily, of his father all those years back. The League too, in some way, is a device to bolster up the past and give the predators a few more years. Not a very effective way, says Julian, since whoever heard of a League of Bandits abolishing banditry or a League of Nations abolishing war? And he speculates (by anticipation of a remarkable kind) on how one should blame Japan for attacking China, or Italy for attacking Abyssinia or Spain.[9]

Whether or not a League of states is subject to the same kind of denunciation as a Federation, the underlying objection is the same: predators run the states and corrupt the people. It might be worth noting here the grounds upon which Nietzsche was made to add his voice to the denunciation of Europe—at least in Briffault's fictional account of his visit, mentioned above. "'The old Roman *virtus* [he explains] became translated by the Christian rabble into *virtue*, the morality of the feeble, the envious, herded by the priest who slunk into the mantle of the Roman *imperator*".' This is the particular disaster which has 'reduced Europe to a stupefied continent . . . robbed of all intelligence', a prey to every kind of 'swindler' who pretends to be a thinker. Crazed by the neurosis called Nationalism, and by the politics that go with it, European Man (in the words of this fictional Nietzsche) "'has before him the gigantic task of transvaluating the values handed over to him by degenerate Christianised Rome . . . Europe, as a political configuration, may have incidentally to be suppressed and destroyed in the process" '.[10]

The fact that Briffault came by an unusual route to his sweeping denunciation of Europe as a political or cultural *idea* gives his writing a certain interest which it is not now easy to feel for other Marxist polemics in English in the 1930s. Few admirers of Engels at that period had Briffault's wide and quite deep familiarity with social anthropology, let alone the contact with field data (in Australia) to which he lays claim in one or two places in *The Mothers*. In consequence, few Marxists in the 1930s give quite the same weight to tradition that he does, and none shares his peculiarly foreshortened perspective on western civilisation—a perspective for which there are clear parallels in the writings of A.J. Toynbee. Add to that Briffault's age, his background in an extinct prewar cosmopolitan world, and the rootlessness of which his Anglophobia is a symptom: as stated before, this man is in no sense a *representative* of the interwar generation, even if he keeps abreast of the world in an intellectual manner of speaking. His hero Julian eventually takes up writing to earn a living, and is made to say, in *Europa in Limbo*, that what he can produce is hampered by being stilted and out of date, not in tune with the new generations of bright young things. In the same way it is somewhat noticeable that in 1937, when younger men were turning their attention to Spain and the sharp confrontation there of Left and Right, Briffault kept straight on denouncing the perfidy and rottenness of the British; and in the year following *Europa in Limbo* published a new broadside under the title *Decline and Fall of the British Empire* (1937). One is tempted to refer to Toynbee, and the suggestive distinction he makes (in 1939) between 'cultural archaism' and 'cultural futurism' (in *A Study of History*, Vol. VI).[11] If the 'futurists', fascist and other, are perceived to talk in a new way, Briffault is certainly anchored in cultural archaism, even if only to denounce it.

So he remains a fish out of water, an oddity, an extremist, too, and no fit subject for generalisation. It *just happens* that when all is said his novel *Europa* was a best-seller, possibly—in part—because it is sensational and piquant, with a good range of exotic settings and not a little snob appeal, but claiming to be about Europe, and with a violently anti-European thesis. That this did not apparently harm sales *proves* of course nothing, but is, even so, a fact of history.

It is when one's attention strays from Briffault and his novel to the climate of the 1930s that *Europa* suggests a slightly different point, really to do with perspective. By '1930s' is here meant a slice of only a few years: admittedly a period packed with momentous and disturbing events, and leading up to August and September 1939. But when do these 1930s that one has in mind *begin*? Not, I believe, with the invasion of Manchuria—too remote; nor with the slump of 1931, though depression and slow recovery do colour the decade. Nor even perhaps with 30 January 1933 or the Reichstag fire, but certainly by 1935—with the invasion of Abyssinia and the subsequent failure of sanctions, and the much trumpeted German rearmament, and a British general election won by Baldwin on a platform of collective security (no less!). Maybe what we are attempting to recapture is an unduly British or Anglo-Saxon perspective. Even so, for at any rate something like half a decade, if we go back through the records of the time or summon up their remembrance, the concerns and fears widely shared every day really did make it hard even to imagine, let alone want to do anything about, any form of European unification. Forget Lord Salisbury and Prince Bismarck—who, after all, aimed to unify with Herr Hitler and his movement? I would even venture to suggest that the eloquent Pan-European call of Herriot and Briand was not even remembered two or three years after its utterance by anyone except specialists in international politics. *Et pour cause!* Or again, in the closing months of the 1930s, actually in 1938, the year of Munich, Mr Clarence Streit, over in the Mid-West, conceived and produced a stirring call, to *Union Now*—'a federal Union of the Democracies of the North Atlantic'—and a few liberally inclined persons spoke for it in England—H. N. Brailsford, Barbara Wootton—and a few MPs even professed to favour it. But all in their hearts knew that this was not really a starter. It could not be pretended by Streit or anyone else that Germany or Italy were 'democratic states', and by 1939 Austria and Czechoslovakia and Spain had ceased to be one also. Federal Union as an intended movement helps to give point to the general historical judgement that, with promptings by *Europa*, needs to be made: namely, that the course of European history in the 1930s has a character which excludes the possibility of meaningful new schemes for European unity being given serious consideration, while older meanings to 'Europe'—or 'Europa'—have been rudely consigned to the museum by strident nationalisms. If—as was visible by 1935 or 1936—the League of Nations Assembly was at best impotent, and all the beautiful earlier sentiments of Locarno or the Renunciation of War were derisory cobwebs; if a couple of dictators could raise their voices and shout about guns and their imperative demands in such a manner as to call into doubt any long continuance of the status quo or any very harmonious transformation of it: then how could a well-intentioned Federal Union be taken seriously except by a few underemployed publicists and public relations men? And how should matters be otherwise as regards visionary dreams of a united Europe in those darkening years?

Notes

1. R. Briffault, *Europa: A Novel of the Age of Ignorance* (New York, Scribner's, 1935). References and page numbers in what follows are taken from the English edition, issued some months later by Hale, 1936.
2. R. Briffault (1937), *Europa in Limbo* (London, Hale, 1937).
3. *Europa: A Novel . . .*, op. cit., p. 106.
4. ibid., p. 214. One of the piquant features of Briffault's evocation of *la belle époque* is the unusually large number of historical characters scattered throughout the huge dramatis personae. Nietzsche has already been mentioned; A.J. Balfour is another such.
5. R. Briffault, *The Mothers*, 3 Vols (London, Allen and Unwin, 1927).
6. ibid., Vol. II, pp. 16–63.
7. R. Briffault, *Breakdown: The Collapse of Traditional Civilisation* (New York, Brentano's, 1932; English ed., Gollancz, 1935).
8. *Europa: A Novel . . .*, op. cit., p. 9.
9. *Europa in Limbo*, op. cit., p. 284.
10. *Europa: A Novel . . .*, op. cit., pp. 18–19.
11. A.J. Toynbee, *A Study of History*, Vol. VI, (Oxford, Oxford University Press, 1939), pp. 111–17.

7 Nationalism and National Identity in the new states of Europe: The examples of Austria, Finland and Ireland

David Kirby

The term 'national identity' bristles with difficulties of definition, and I propose to treat it with some caution. We might, for example, spend much time discussing whether 'national identity' in the twentieth century can exist outside the framework of the state, or whether it is primarily conjured into being in order to give states a cohesion and self-justification which they would otherwise lack. Certain it is that there is an inherent conflict between what we might call the 'imposed' identity of the territorial sovereign state and the 'perceived' identity of those who are its citizens. In many instances, of course, there is a general consensus or acceptance of the authority and assumptions of the state. If its citizens feel aggrieved, their displeasure is more likely to be occasioned by the level of taxation or the state of the roads, and not directed at the presumptions of national identity stamped in their passports. But there are also times and circumstances in which significant sections of people living within a state feel deeply alienated, or endorse a view of identity very different to that propagated by those who govern.

My second point follows on from this. There is nothing static or eternally immutable about this relationship of the territorial state and its citizens. No longer valid are the sanctions of the dynastic state, which, in default of truly effective means of coercion, relied heavily upon God and the fatalistic disposition of the rulers' subjects. On the other hand, even though the modern state has at its disposal means to persuade and coerce its citizens which would have been the envy of any so-called absolutist ruler, its legitimacy and very *raison d'être* derive, not from higher, divine authority, but from the people. This means that there is always a potentially unstable symbiosis in the relationship of the ruled and those placed in authority.

At the same time as the modern state has sought a multiplicity of means of imposing an identity upon its citizens, the impositions and norms of the society of rank—obligations and duties, regulations and ordinances, all of

110

which strove to uphold a corporate social identity—have given way (though not entirely) to perceptions which presuppose that the individual is somehow endowed with an inalienable and natural right to determine his or her own destiny. The old adage *ubi bene, ibi patria* imperfectly expresses the assumption that man is free to choose his fatherland on the basis of perceived benefit, and the massive migration of peoples which has occurred over the past two hundred years is an even more forceful, though equally imprecise, affirmation of this assumed right. Technological developments—the steam engine, the rotary press, the internal combustion engine, the microchip—have also fostered the illusion that men are free to determine their lot, and no longer have to bend their backs to the plough, send their sons to the army, obey the dictates of the bailiff or of the parson.

In modern nationalism, a belief in the power of the individual *Willensakt* and of the will of the general community often become inextricably entangled. Herein lies another paradox. At the same time as it is compelled to come to terms with the changing circumstances of society in economic flux, nationalism seeks to conjure up a mythical community from the past. There was thus a strange double process going on throughout much of the nineteenth century: whilst the nationalists were seeking to resurrect or promote an ideal community which they dubbed the nation, huge numbers of people on the move were actually creating new communities, usually within an urban context. Newcomers to a strange city would seek out their kinsmen, would associate with those who spoke the same language, followed the same customs and religion, ate the same type of food. But they would also have to come to terms with a different environment—different work habits, routines, forms of behaviour (peasants spit a lot—city fathers, mindful of hygiene, put up large notices prohibiting this egregious habit)—and above all, an alien language. Thus, at the same time as this intermingling of the peoples of Europe, on a scale hitherto unprecedented, was taking place, doctrinaire nationalists everywhere were striving to promote a cause which claimed not only to identify people by virtue of their language, customs, history and 'destiny', but which also demanded their exclusive right to a separate national existence.

Nationalism may be regarded as a *revolutionary* force, which in many respects it was and still is. But it is also inherently *backward-looking* in many of its assumptions. This is particularly the case where it is necessary to revive or even create a national identity. Nationalism tends to stress organic ties, traditions, to conjure up a mythical community of the past, but it also needs to use the instruments of the modern state to enforce that identity. Left to their own devices 'the people' are incapable of realising their destiny; this was the lesson of 1848 for many German nationalists, who saw the only solution to the problem of German unity lying in the hands of a strong state leadership.

It is perhaps a truism to say that all states which achieve independence are something of a disappointment to the nationalist, for, in some way or other, the glorious destiny of the people seems to become encumbered with or ensnared in the machinations of a hostile environment—either malevolent external forces, which seek to mutilate or frustrate the goals of national unity through the imposition of unfair treaties or the downright theft of sacred national objectives, or unreconciled internal forces such as alien minorities, 'unpatriotic' or selfish interest groups. At another level, it may be said that once the dream becomes reality, when the nation-state becomes a free agent, so to speak, a host of problems arise which may sadly disillusion the ardent nationalist. For small states, such as those which came into existence in the eastern Baltic, winning credibility in the eyes of the outside world was of vital importance, as Anthony Powell's novel *Venusberg* amusingly demonstrates. The civil war prompted much gloomy speculation in Finland about the immaturity and backwardness of the Finnish people in the columns of the leading intellectual journals. The right-wing poet Bertel Gripenberg was in no doubt that the outcome of the civil war was a triumph for culture over barbarism, and many other Swedish-speakers saw a vindication for the historic role of their culture in the White victory. Berndt Estlander, for example, defending the ideal of a '*finländsk rättsstat*' against the asser- tions of a '*finsk nationalstat*', claimed that it was as a defender of western cultural values on the eastern frontier, not as a language state, that Finland attracted European sympathy.[1] Finnish nationalists, desperately striving to assert the claims of their own culture, found it difficult to overcome the Swedish inheritance. As the writer Jaakko Forsman admitted in 1923: 'Our older culture, Swedish through and through, is much more flexible, refined and assured: Finnishness is still to a large extent stiff and immature, just as our external appearance is clumsy and ungainly, and, dare I say, boorish.'[2]

Anxiety about how the nation presents itself to the outside world may also be complicated by internal centrifugal tendencies which in some way or other go against the ideal of national consensus and unanimity. The new states of Europe came into existence at a time of great social stress and conflict and economic hardship, at the end of the most brutal and destructive war the Continent had ever experienced. They came into existence, not so much as the result of any long-term, purposeful struggle for national independence, but because of the collapse and disintegration of the huge multinational dynastic empires which had dominated Europe throughout the nineteenth century. This process of disintegration in the midst of economic ruin went much further than national self-determination, for there were also many instances of regions or provinces seeking to secure their fortunes by association with other states, or by establishing some kind of regional autonomy, as in the case of the Tyroleans and Voralbergers, or the Ålanders and Swedish-speaking minority in Ostrobothnia.

The problem which thus faced what we may call the proponents of national unity was how to integrate and bind together the people who now found themselves citizens of an independent national state. In the cases of Finland and Ireland, that problem was made even more acute by the fact that civil war had marred the early days of independent statehood. There were, however, significant differences between the two countries in this respect. In the Finnish case, the civil war was not about territory, or even about independence. Social and economic distress provided the groundswell impetus for the social democratic party to attempt a seizure of power in January 1918, but at another level, the conflict was essentially caused by the collapse of state authority and the inability of the parties to reach consensus over what should take its place. The victorious Whites were of course unwilling to concede that the causes of civil war were primarily internal. In the White version of events, the war was one of liberation or independence, fought to free the country of the remnants of the Russian forces and, by implication, to rid the land of the Bolshevik disease which had afflicted certain elements of the Finnish working class. This belief, which first found expression in the Senate's proclamation to the Finnish people at the outbreak of civil war, was at best an uneasy one, for the fact that so many Finns had fought on the Red side could not easily be glossed over.

Civil war in Ireland broke out because an intransigent republican wing refused, as Cathal Bruga put it, to swallow the draught of poison which they perceived the Anglo-Irish treaty to be. Although defeated, the republicans could argue that they alone upheld the true cause of sovereign Irish independence, for which they had fought since 1918. Whereas the victorious Whites in Finland sought to downplay the civil war by insisting that their fight had been one for the independence and liberation of the country, it was the defeated party in Ireland which claimed to represent true Irish independence. There was also a social dimension to the civil war: the anti-treaty cause drew most of its support from the isolated and impoverished Gaeltacht, whereas the more prosperous elements tended to be pro-treaty, and the breaking-up of the third Sinn Fein party in 1926 tended to perpetuate this division. Fated with the crucial choice in 1927 of remaining loyal to principle, or electing to participate in parliamentary life, de Valera and his followers in Fianna Fail found an ingenious way of getting round the problem of swearing the oath. Subsequent participation in political life drew Fianna Fail further away from its radical programme of 1927, and from its western base. In the course of time, de Valera succeeded in eliminating the most obnoxious features of the 1921 treaty, without, however, uniting Ireland; and it is this issue which has most obviously bedevilled the history of the independent republic, though it has also tended to obscure many of the crucial social and political issues which posed an altogether different set of choices at the height of the troubles.[3]

A full-scale civil war is not the best way to start off along the road of independence, though we should remember that all the 'new states' of Europe which emerged after 1917–18 experienced considerable bouts of fighting and civil unrest. The brief civil war in Austria in 1934 was the culmination of over a decade of incipient conflict between the Red bastion of Vienna and the disparate right-wing forces, and was in a sense the most tragic of all three internecine clashes, since it demonstrated the utter bankruptcy of Austrian independent statehood. Like all other central European successor states, the fate of Austria ultimately was brutally determined by a resurgent and nationalistic Germany; but during the two decades of the first Austrian republic, what little there was of a sense of national political identity was eroded and undermined. The *Sanierungspolitik* may be seen as an attempt to liquidate the burden of the Imperial legacy, but it was generally perceived as a solution dictated to a defeated people by the victors, and it alienated large numbers of the middle class whose livelihoods were jeopardised. Furthermore, it was pushed through at the cost of lasting economic stagnation, which allowed no room for manœuvre with the onset of the Depression. Of course, Austria was by no means unique in this respect: other small countries, such as Latvia and Estonia, had to come to terms with the consequences of a loss of a vast and important internal market for their industrial goods. The Irish had to come to terms with the realities of economic dependence upon the United Kingdom, which imposed severe constraints upon attempts to develop native industries. What was lacking in Austria, however, was the political will and determination to put up with hardship if need be for the sake of sovereign independence.

None of the three major alternatives—imperial, Catholic, socialist—offered a viable basis for nation-building. With the demise of empire, all that was left were dreams and a fading loyalty to a dynasty whose leader's political ineptness did little to advance its cause. Catholicism as interpreted by Seipel and Dollfuss divided rather than brought together the disparate social and cultural strands of the industriäl areas and rural Alpine lands. The option of *Anschluß*, denied the rump state by the victors, became, as Norbert Leser has remarked, an excuse for failing to do anything.[4] In spite of the extreme disorientation brought about by the sudden collapse of empire in 1918, the idea of union with Germany was not universally popular during the immediate postwar months. Germany was feared and distrusted for a variety of reasons—by devout Catholics, anti-socialists, even businessmen worried about competition. The experience of the war years had in fact exposed the cracks which Bismarck's nation-building from above had papered over, and it might perhaps be fair to characterise the 1920s at least as a time of identity crisis for German-speakers in general.

The social democratic parties which found themselves bearing the main responsibility for the two German republics which emerged out of defeat were unable to offer a nationally binding policy, nor was there any powerful non-socialist republican bloc with which they could forge a working alliance. Attempts to break out of the impasse of class politics, and to reach out to a broader constituency, failed comprehensively. The Austrian social democrats were perhaps more fortunate than their German comrades in that they did not have to compete with a large communist party, but in the end they too were confined within their working-class bases, fighting an increasingly desperate rearguard action against hostile forces. In February 1934, one year after the parties of the left had been smashed in Germany, the Austrian social democrats were crushed by the Heimwehr and the security forces. The idea of independent Austrian statehood gained ground amongst the younger generation of socialist exiles during the war years, but many of the older leaders were never reconciled to the idea.

At first sight, it may seem remarkable that social democracy managed to survive and even to play an active role in the political life of the Finnish republic, in marked contrast to socialist parties elsewhere on the continent. This is sometimes attributed to 'Scandinavian' traditions of democracy, which over-estimates the strength of such traditions and fails to recognise more specifically Finnish reasons for the party's resilience. White propaganda notwithstanding, the troubles in Finland could not easily be attributed to a group of aliens who had usurped power. The Finnish labour movement was a powerful political force: the social democratic party had consistently emerged as the largest single party in democratic parliamentary elections after 1907, and its suppression would have been a major task, even had the victorious Allies not indicated that a full return to democracy was one of the preconditions for recognition of Finnish independence in 1919.

As Risto Alapuro and others have pointed out, the labour movement in Finland may be seen as part of the process of national mobilisation, encouraged rather than hindered by nationalists for whom the 'people' were the only allies against a largely Swedish-speaking upper class.[5] Now in my opinion, Alapuro has tended to downplay the element of class conflict within the labour movement, especially after 1905, and the degree to which significant numbers of Finns felt isolated and unintegrated in any meaningful sense into a national whole. Nevertheless, I would agree that there were strong integrational tendencies within the leadership of the labour movement, and that the civil war was as much as a shock on the Red side as it was on the White. Had the victors been the kind of single reactionary mass which the radicals on the Red side affected to believe, the outcome might well have been different. The fact is, however, that the Whites were split on a number of major issues, such as the constitutional structure of the new republic, and there was also considerable support for social and land reforms which were effected in the early years of the republic. Beneath the hysteria of certain sections of the White intelligentsia, there was also recognition of the need for national integration. Even the conservative Emil Schybergson admitted that socialists should not be treated as pariahs, and a number of other writers drew the same conclusion.[6] Suppression of the entire labour movement would not only have been a mammoth undertaking: it would also have flown in the face of decades of work by patriots of all persuasions to mobilise the people.

The social democratic party was in fact able to regain its level of support remarkably quickly after the débâcle of the civil war, winning eighty seats in the elections of 1919. The party split in 1919–20, and a dissident minority formed the socialist workers' party, which enjoyed a precarious existence until its suppression in 1923. The socialist workers' party is often seen as the legal front of the communist party, founded in Moscow in August 1918 by radical exiles. In my view, it is something rather different; it was the rallying point for the unintegrated elements in Finnish society, those living on the margins, such as the impoverished farmers and workers of the north who had to seek work in the forests during the winter, or for those at the cutting-edge of the post-civil war class conflict such as the skilled workers whose trade-union activities brought them under constant surveillance. In the old heartland of the pre-1918 social democratic party, the rural communes of southern and central Finland, the social democratic vote held up, and the socialist workers' party failed to make any inroads. On the other hand, active participation in the social democratic movement atrophied, which may be an indication of the waning appeal of organised labour as a means of expressing a distinctive identity, and a measure of the integration of the smallholders—as many of the party's former activists now became—into the mainstream of Finnish society. Rural workers' associations had to resort to non-political activities—renting premises out for dancing and other entertainments, even converting them to cinemas—in order to keep going. The socialist workers' party in the isolated and impoverished northern regions—where the intensive exploitation of the forests in the 1920s created class conflict—seems to have performed the same function which the old party had done a decade or so earlier in the areas where the problems of land tenure were most acute. The initial enthusiasm soon began to fade, as it had in rural areas after 1908. Even before the police stepped in, the fortunes of the socialist workers' party were beginning to decline. There remained isolated pockets of alienated communities, whose members refused to vote even for the social democratic party, and a number of individuals became involved in underground communist activity, which sought without much success to direct poor farmers' protest movements in the 1930s; but most lapsed into political inactivity.

It is hard to assess the strength of communist feeling amongst the population at large in the 1930s, and it is perhaps too easy to assume that the absence of any form of indigenous pro-Soviet movement in the Winter War indicates the frailty of communist or left-radical support. The moves made during that war to remove some of the obstacles to working-class participation in the affairs of the nation had an obvious propaganda value—which to some extent was directed abroad, where left-wing and labour opinion had long doubted whether Finland could be counted as a true democracy because of the denial of basic workers' rights. The Winter War certainly placed the question of national independence at the forefront of the agenda, but here is a danger of seeing it as a moment of historical transformation, as the German ruling class wished to see the *Augusterlebnis* of 1914. One must at the very least take into the reckoning the experiences of 1940–44, which show that the efforts of the Greater Finland nationalists to realise their dreams were by no means shared by much of the populace.

Committed communists and poor backwoodsmen thus stood at some distance from the ideal nation-state of the White nationalists. What of the Swedish-speaking minority? The problem of the Swedish-speaking minority in Finland is a twofold one. In the first instance, it is one of peripheral isolation, which led in the early 1920s to a strong particularism, seeking in effect to create a protective wall around the Ostrobothnian coastal strip. It was this which angered leaders of the southern cultural élite, who believed that the end result would be the gradual elimination of their influence and culture outside this narrow zone, far removed from the metropolitan centre. This was the second aspect of the problem: should the role of the Swedish-speaking minority simply be confined to defending its own interests, or should it continue to play a role in the building of the new state? For most of the cultural élite, many of whom had played key roles in the political and economic life of the Grand Duchy, to abandon this role was unthinkable. Withdrawal would be a betrayal of the historical task of the Swedish–Finnish element, that of defending western freedom and values. As a leading conservative argued, Swedish Finns had built up the foundations of the state, even to the extent of providing the Finnish nationalist movement with its leaders. Swedish-speakers were obliged for geographical and historical reasons to live side by side with Finnish-speakers, and they could not opt out.[7] It was this emphasis on the cultural role of the Swedish-speaker which eventually won the day. The Ostrobothnian opposition was too weak and isolated and lacked any true leadership to challenge the assumptions of the southern cultural élite. Their protest was essentially motivated by economic considerations: a desire to protect their native heath against alien (i.e.

Finnish) encroachment, as had already happened in the south, and a fear that a Finnish Finland offered little prospects for them or their children.

The Swedish-speaking upper class, which was located primarily in the linguistically mixed southern coastal region, had thus to deal with an isolationist movement in Swedish Ostrobothnia, as well as the separatist threat of the Åland islanders, a decade after parliamentary reform had effectively terminated their privileged political dominance of the estates. The advent of the new republic thus marked a serious crisis in upper-class Swedish–Finnish circles. Unlike the Anglo-Irish, they had only one home-land. In some respects, however, they did resemble their Unionist counterparts. Like the Southern Irish Unionists, they endeavoured to follow a policy of compromise and mediation within the new state, whereas the small farmers and tradesmen of the Ostrobothnian coastal strip and the Åland islands, like the Northern Irish Unionists, adopted a much tougher line, accusing the Swedish-speaking cultural élite/Southern Irish Unionists of selling out. Here, however, the resemblance ends. The agitation on the Swedish-speaking periphery died away, and did not revive during the Finnish nationalist campaigns to make the country virtually a one-language state in the 1930s. Furthermore, the Swedish-speaking minority has con-tinued to play a very active cultural and political role to the present day, whereas the Anglo-Irish have found themselves wanderers between two lands.[8]

I have used the word 'peripheral' to describe the main thrust of Swedish-speaking separatism in Finland, and I believe that the peripheral position of the country as a whole has meant that the status of the Swedish-speaking minority has never become a contentious problem. In the case of Ireland and Austria, the divisive factor has been imperial power. At one level, the prerequisites for a common identity above and beyond linguistic or religious divisions have obtained. Communities with distinct characteristics may nevertheless acquire common features óver a long period of time. As Karl Kautsky recognised in his critique of Otto Bauer's *Die Nationalitätenfrage und die Sozialdemokratie*, Germans living in Bohemia had more in common with their Czech neighbours than with German-speakers in Switzerland.[9] The syntax, morphology and even the vocabulary of Swedish spoken in present-day Finland owes a great deal to the influence of Finnish, which in its turn has been heavily influenced by Swedish. There has also been considerable interplay between the languages and cultures in Ireland. As Terence Brown has remarked, the antiquarian literary and cultural activities of the Ascend-ancy class in the nineteenth century 'offered Irishmen and women a range of modes of thought and feeling that could help confirm national identity and unity'.[10] But at another level, the experience of imperial rule, from at least the sixteenth century onwards, tended to perpetuate divisions. This was not so in Finland, for the connection with Sweden was broken in 1809, and the one area in which Russian imperial power sought to encroach, namely, in seeking to eliminate Finnish autonomy, served if anything to *strengthen* the attachment to the Swedish inheritance. The Anglo-Irish and the Protestants of Ulster, in their different ways, could and did play the British connection: the German minorities in Bohemia and Moravia could always appeal to *Deutschtum*, or at least, be consoled by the politicians in Vienna that they were a part of this magic family. The Swedish–Finnish minority, with the possible exception of the Ålanders, had no such option, for any possibility of a return to Sweden had already been firmly ruled out during the first half of the nineteenth century.

There can be little doubt that the efforts of the German–Austrians to create an ethnic state at the expense of Czechoslovakia did little to ease the future relations of the German minority with the Czech state, though, as Lajos Kerekes has suggested, this minority was significantly divided on social and political lines, with the social democrats looking for a political solution to 'Red' Berlin or Vienna, and the non-socialists entertaining grave doubts about the political or economic benefits of any such union.[11] The prerequisites for a distinctive German–Austrian state identity were also overshadowed by the sense of having lost an imperial role, and additionally by the frustration of not being able to unite with Germany. Austria was thus denied the opportunity for twenty years of experiencing peripheral, or subordinate, status, which arguably might well have created a sense of identity.

Independent statehood as a positive end in itself does not, however, end the connection with the former imperial power. In this sense again, Finland was more fortunate in that the influence of the former imperial power was minimal in comparison with that of Britain in the case of Ireland. The Finnish economy was able to build upon pre-independence export markets; trade with Soviet Russia declined to risible proportions. By contrast, the Irish economy was bound virtually hand and foot to that of Britain, which also continued to attract thousands of Irish workers. The British legacy was palpably evident in all aspects of public life in the Free State, and constituted a major problem for those concerned to create a new identity. On the other hand, Russia was perceived as a threat in ways which Britain was not—as a potential military enemy, and as the carrier of a revolutionary doctrine which had also affected elements of the Finnish working class. In Soviet Karelia, the defeated Red leaders were seeking to build a socialist Finnish state. Indeed, it might be argued that autonomous Finland has assumed a red mantle and decamped eastwards. There was thus an alternative 'socialist fatherland' across the border for the Finnish working class, though whether they perceived it as such is a matter of some doubt.

This is in fact the heart of the matter, namely, that everyday reality may preclude, or at the least make difficult, acceptance of images. The image of a state or social order promoted by nationalists or communists is total and all-embracing, in stark contrast to the inconsistencies of normal life. The basic assumptions may be shared, and the appeal may have its attractions under certain circumstances; but those to whom the appeal is directed have a distressing habit of making up their own minds what to accept and what to leave aside. It is what J.H. Whyte has called a 'compartmentalisation of loyalties' in the case of Irish Catholicism, which allows the Catholic to accept unquestioningly the Church's authority in one sphere whilst challenging it in another.[12] In other words, whereas there may be general acceptance of certain symbols of nationhood and identity, such as Catholicism, it is at best a passive one. The Church has perhaps been at its most influential in reinforcing conservative values appertaining to family life, though even here there will always be a discrepancy between the ideal and practice.

The image-makers of the new states were also faced with a double dilemma, for not only had they to reinforce or even revive those national values which they considered distinct, they also had to come to terms with the consequences of sovereign independence. Invariably, there was a deep sense of anti-climax and disillusion, as the 'people' seemed to be incapable of realising the urgency of their destiny. To protect the people from the baneful influences of the outside world, the shutters were put up. It was not only in Ireland that foreign books, plays and films were banned: right-wing and church opposition banned the staging of *God's Green Acres* in Helsinki, and the editor of an avant-garde journal was jailed for publishing translated sections of *The Good Soldier Švejk*. The Catholic hierarchy fulminated against the dance hall, the bad book, the indecent paper, the motion picture and the immodest fashion in female dress, 'all of which tend to destroy the virtues characteristic of our race',[13] and the parish priests lurked around the entrances of dance halls to pounce on the slightest sign of immoral behaviour. The legislation passed during the 1930s went some way to meeting the Church's desire for a Christian Irish nation; patriotic Christians in Finland were perhaps less successful, but they nonetheless constituted a powerful lobby, whose voice no government could afford to ignore.

Before the war, the temperance movement in Ireland had been linked with the struggle for independence: Ireland sober would be Ireland free. The cause of temperance had long been intimately associated with the Finnish nationalist movement, and it was one of the areas in which Red and White Finnish-speakers found common ground in 1919, when prohibition was introduced. The socialist Wäinö Wuolijoki claimed during a parliamentary debate on prohibition in 1921 that the representatives of the Swedish People's Party 'sought to improve the Swedish coastal race with alcohol, we seek to improve the Finnish race with temperance and the prohibition law'.[14] The cultural liberal Gunnar Castrén accused the agrarian party leader Santeri Alkio of seeing any abolition of prohibition as tantamount to surrendering Finland's independence.[15] In spite of their best endeavours, however, the priests failed to persuade their flock of the virtues of chastity, and the supporters of prohibition failed to stem the tide of illicit liquor. There was a steady increase in the rates of illegitimate births in the Irish Free State, and an evasion of the provisions of the prohibition law on a massive scale in Finland.

The efforts of moralists to rescue their poor and virtuous countrymen from the evils of the wicked world was part of the broader struggle to impose an identity based on an idealised world-view. The upholders of Finnish culture urged the Writers' Guild in 1935 to 'hearken to the whisperings of the spruce under which we dwell' and to draw upon 'the noble depths of our own Kalevalan spirit': an Irish writer asserted a year later that the idiom of Ireland's traditional music had 'in some subtle way the idiom of the Irish mind', and was capable of expressing 'deep things' which none of the great composers had ever done.[16] Fortunately for Irish culture, such preposterous nonsense did not go unchallenged. In a memorable phrase, 'we cannot see the man ploughing against the sky in an aura of antiquity', Sean O'Faolain challenged what he saw as a hopeless and deadening reliance on the past, which failed to recognise modern Irishmen for what they were: 'the descendants, English-speaking, in European dress, affected by European thought, part of the European economy, of the rags and tatters who rose with O'Connell to win with Mick Collins'. Meanwhile, George Bernard Shaw warned that if Ireland was incapable of responding to new ideas, 'if . . . she slips back into the Atlantic as a little grass patch in which a few million moral cowards cannot call their souls their own . . . then the world will let "these Irish" go their own way into insignificance without the smallest concern'.[17]

If there is a great deal of truth in F.S.L. Lyons' argument that the diversity of cultures in Ireland has made it difficult for the Irish people to have a coherent view of themselves in relation to each other and the outside world, if may also be the case that it has also inhibited stagnant introspection.[18] The young generation of artists and writers grouped around the short-lived periodical *Tulenkantajat* strove self-consciously to break out of what they saw as a mood of introspection, but as the Swedish-speaking modernist Hagar Olsson remarked, their Europeanism was a wooden horse smuggled into the Troy of Finnishness.[19] To pursue the Homeric metaphor, the young generation dared to listen to the siren song of decadent cosmopolitanism, condemned roundly by the upholders of official cultural values, but they remained firmly strapped to the mast. They were also obsessed, like their elders, with the creation of a *Kulturstaat*, the true vocation of the intelligentsia.

It may well be that the scope for diversity is in any case limited in a relatively homogeneous society which is also linguistically isolated. Diversity in the Irish and Austrian cases owes a good deal to the fact that intellectual and cultural debate is conducted in a major European language. In interwar Finland, the one option to a wider world, the Swedish language, was largely rejected by the national ethos of cultural self-sufficiency. Within this framework, there was also a powerful tendency towards national unanimity and integration, which was able to achieve a fair degree of success because there were also strong forces which helped mould communal consensus, and relatively few obstacles. There was, for example, a universal belief in the value of education as a means of advancement and enlightenment, and although the language conflict, the legacy of the civil war and the endeavours of fundamentalist Christians to have their say in determining the school curriculum caused some problems, these had a far less deleterious effect than did the efforts of Irish ministers of education to promote the teaching of Irish. The development of communications and the spread of cooperative associations and institutions undoubtedly fostered a closer awareness of the national whole. The same is true of the growth of a standardised popular culture, which provided easy access, which earlier popular movements had not, since these demanded active involvement whereas the wireless, cheap travel by the bus network, advertisements, consumer goods and popular magazines simply required spare cash and sufficient leisure time.

Here I come back to my main theme, that of 'imposed' and 'perceived' identity. The new nation-state acted as a kind of transmission belt between the two. It created and developed a framework of reference, and established the patterns of civic behaviour. In the case of Finland, the state was undoubtedly fortunate in that it could draw heavily upon a substantial inheritance; the rump Austrian republic was encumbered with its greater imperial past, the Irish Free State was ensnared in its chequered legacy. The 'embryonic state' which Johannes Gripenberg had perceived in the 1880s thus got off to a good start, in contrast to many others, and this may well have allowed those who exercised power greater scope for mediation between the conflicting groups seeking to impose a particular brand of national identity.[20] Though the state did defer to the demands of religious fundamentalists in certain respects, for example, the influence of the Church was considerably less in Finland than it was in de Valera's Ireland. Finland did not become the one-language state extreme nationalists wished it to be, and if little scope was allowed to left-wing radicalism, the extreme right had little success in imposing its full set of demands. In comparison with most other new states, it must be said that Finland managed to avoid potentially damaging problems by being sufficiently responsive to the need for change and for the preservation of a balanced policy.

Nevertheless, this is not the full story. 'National identity' springs just as much from the perceptions of society, and the norms and forms of behaviour which societies adopt, and this is an infinitely complex matter, since societies are by their very nature composite and the sum total is an aggregate of a great variety of strands. In a wicked moment, Karl Marx once suggested that it was a shortage of coffee, for which the French were blamed, which impelled the German people to turn against Napoleon, rather than any metaphysical sense of national solidarity. I would suggest that it may in the end be rather mundane things, such as cigarette brands, popular request programmes on the wireless, the outrageous doings of notorious people or victories on the athletics track, which create a sense of belonging, and rather more painlessly than the attempted impositions of the schoolmaster, the parish priest, temperance societies and others who seek to uplift the moral fibre of the nation.

Notes

1. B. Estlander, 'Finne och finländare', *Nya Argus*, Vol. 19 (1926), pp. 125–7; B. Gripenberg, 'Hvarförs egrade de hvita?', *Finsk Tidskrift*, Vol. 84 (1918), p. 150.
2. J. Forsman, 'Myöhästyneitä kansoja', *Valvoja*, Vol. 75 (1923).
3. F.S.L. Lyons, *Ireland Since the Famine* (London, Fontana/Collins, 1973), pp. 439ff; E. Rumpf and A.C. Hepburn, *Nationalism and Socialism in Twentieth-century Ireland* (Liverpool, University of Liverpool Press, 1977), pp. 33ff.
4. N. Lesser, *Zwischen Reformismus und Bolschewismus: Der Austromarxismus als Theorie und Praxis* (Vienna, Europa Verlag, 1967), p. 324.
5. R. Alapuro, 'De intellektuella, staten och nationen', *Historisk Tidskrift för Finland*, Vol. 72, No. 3 (1987), pp. 457–80. R. Alapuro and H. Stenius 'Kansanliikkeet loivat kansakunnan', in R. Alapuro *et al.*, *Kansa liikkeessä* (Helsinki, Kirjayhtymä, 1987), p. 40.
6. E. Schybergson, 'Politiska bekymmer', *Finsk Tidskrift*, Vol. 87 (1919), p. 250; A. Lille, *Framtidsuppgifter* (Frågor för dagen, 16) (Helsingfors, H. Schildt, 1918), p. 24.
7. *Svenska Finlands Folkting, 19–28 maj 1919* (Helsingfors, H. Schildt, 1919), pp. 172–3 (Rabbe Wrede's speech).
8. On the Swedish-speaking minority, see: J. Sundberg, *Svenskhetens dilemma i Finland: Finlandssvenskarnas samling och splittring under 1900-talet* (Bildrag till kännedom av Finlands natur och folk, 133) (Helsingfors, Svenska Litteratursällskapet i Finland, 1985). On the Anglo-Irish, O. MacDonagh, *States of Mind: A Study of Anglo-Irish Conflict, 1780–1980* (London, Alan & Unwin, 1983), and P. Buckland, *The Anglo-Irish and the New Ireland, 1885–1922* (Dublin, Gill and McMillan, 1972).
9. K. Kautsky, *Nationalität und Internationalität* (Die Neue Zeit: Ergänzungshefte, 1) (Stuttgart, 1908), pp. 5ff.

10. T. Brown, *Ireland: A Social and Cultural History, 1922–79* (London, Fontana/ Collins, 1981), p. 79.
11. L. Kerekes, *Von St. Germain bis Genf: Österreich und seine Nachbarn, 1918–1922* (Vienna, Hermann Böhlhaus Nachf., 1979), p. 85.
12. J.H. Whyte, *Church and State in Modern Ireland, 1923–1970* (Dublin, Gill and McMillan, 1971), p. 12.
13. Brown, *Ireland*, op. cit., p. 40.
14. *Valtiopäivät 1921. Pöytäkirjat I*, p. 192.
15. G. Castren, 'Förbudslagen', *Nya Argus*, Vol. 12 (1919), p. 84.
16. D.G. Kirby, *Finland in the Twentieth Century* (London, Hurst, 1979), p. 102; Brown, *Ireland*, op. cit., p. 147.
17. Cited in Brown, *Ireland*, op. cit., pp. 137, 158.
18. F.S.L. Lyons, *Culture and Anarchy in Ireland, 1890–1939* (Oxford, Oxford University Press, 1982), pp. 7ff.
19. E. Evi, 'Suomalainen—europpalainen?', *Tulenkantajat*, Vol. 1 (1928), p. 12. Evi argued that it was the Finnish Odysseus who had smuggled the wooden horse of Europeanism into the Troy of artificial Swedishness.
20. D.G. Kirby, *Finland and Russia 1808–1920: From Autonomy to Independence. A Selection of Documents* (London, Macmillan, 1975), pp. 70–1. The importance of the fully fledged state is also stressed by J. Jussila, 'Finlands steg från provins till stat', *Historisk Tidskrift för Finland*, Vol. 72, No. 3 (1975), pp. 437–56.

8 Authoritarian and national socialist conceptions of nation, state and Europe

Peter M.R. Stirk

The national socialist idea of Europe has often been seen as a distortion of an essentially liberal and peaceful, if not pacifistic, tradition and dream.[1] By comparison with this tradition the national socialist espousal of the idea of Europe during the Second World War appears as cynical propaganda.[2] The reality of national socialism is regarded as the expression of a militaristic hyper-nationalism which is fundamentally incompatible with the trans-national idea of Europe. There is a great deal of truth in this view. National socialists usually exhibited few scruples in consciously purloining and exploiting ideas for which they had no respect whatsoever. The reality of the national socialist New Order in Europe was brought about by conquest and maintained by forms of domination which were so crude that they provoked resistance where there had previously been none.

Nevertheless, this chapter will suggest that to treat the national socialists' ideas of Europe as propaganda in the service of conquest is too simple. It is too simple because it ignores precisely those problems which inevitably led to the reduction of Europe to a slogan in the service of conquest, even when this was dysfunctional in terms of the maintenance of national socialist power in Europe. It is too simple because it treats propaganda as mere propaganda. It fails to recognise Europe as a contested concept and it fails to recognise national socialist ideology and practice as an attempt to 'make Europe', to bring Europe into existence. To talk of national socialist efforts to make Europe is not to condone them. Nor is it to suggest that national socialists had a clear and consistent conception of Europe. It is, indeed, more accurate to talk about national socialist conceptions of Europe.

What, then, did Europe mean to the national socialists? A starting point is offered by critics of the national socialist claim to have been nationalists at all. A.D. Smith, for example, holds that the nationalist doctrine envisages a pluralist universe in which the right of other nations to exist is conceded.[3]

National socialism, on the other hand, was, in his view, a racist doctrine which evidently denied that nationalist assumption. As a racist doctrine it was also inherently transnational. Although Smith's comments are not unproblematic they at least have the virtue of focusing attention on the basic elements of the national socialist view of Europe, namely, races, nations and peoples (*Völker*). Others see the national socialist idea of Europe as a virulent manifestation of a wider stream of thought which predated national socialism. The central concept here is that of *Mitteleuropa*. The idea of *Mitteleuropa* is, of course, thoroughly discussed by adherents to the 'propaganda thesis'. There is, however, a difference between this sort of commentary upon that idea and those who talk about *Mitteleuropa* as an alternative strategy for European unity. A fairly strong formulation of the latter can be found in W.A. McDougall's statement that the First World War '. . . offered two models for further European integration. One was *Mitteleuropa*, the other a painstakingly negotiated co-operation among the beleagured Allies'.[4] To the extent that the national socialist idea of Europe was a manifestation of this tradition there would, however, be nothing distinctively national socialist about it. This observation points to another problem in accounting for the national socialist view of Europe. National socialism is often distinguished from contemporaneous authoritarianism by virtue of the role ascribed to the state in the respective doctrines. National socialism is seen as being a movement-oriented doctrine which disparages the idea of the state and seeks to replace it by the idea of the permanent mobilisation of the people. Authoritarianism is seen as advocating a strong state bolstered by a socially conservative élite. Depoliticisation, not mobilisation, is prescribed for the non-élite. The question is, does the difference concerning the internal role of the state also entail a difference concerning the external relations of the state, and hence a difference between national socialism and authoritarianism in their respective conceptions of *Mitteleuropa*, and of Europe in general?

These preliminary considerations have been intended to identify the ideas of race, nation and people on the one hand and the state on the other hand as ideas which have a prima facie bearing upon the idea of Europe. The following discussion will seek to show that although there is no unified and distinctive idea of a national socialist Europe which was espoused by all national socialists, there are certain key problems concerning the relationship of race, nation, state and people which acquired particular prominence in national socialist ideology and practice and that these problems affected the national socialist view of Europe. Reflection upon the ideas of authoritarians in the interwar period will help to clarify what, if anything, was distinctive of the national socialist view of Europe. It will also be claimed that ultimately the national socialist view of Europe was impoverished because its conceptions of the state were impoverished and hence that when national socialism was confronted with the task of ruling the newly conquered Europe its guiding principle could be no other than sheer domination, the precise nature of which varied according to the fortunes of the competing bureaucracies within the new *Reich*.

The terms nation, race and *Volk* all refer to types of social collectivity which have been held to be natural or appropriate bases for the existence of states. To that extent they all make the state secondary to membership of a prepolitical type of community. There were, however, significant differences between these terms, especially in the eyes of the authoritarians and national socialists. But both the *völkisch* orthodoxy upon which national socialism drew, and the authoritarians experienced difficulty in explaining the relationship between the prepolitical community and the state. The *völkisch* tendency provided the most vigorous assertion of the prepolitical community: 'Both history and personal experience teach us that the economy of a people is not its fate, nor is its social structure its life-nerve. Behind and beyond such transient structures stand eternal forces in which the possibility and the limits of history are prescribed.'[5] Here the prepolitical character of the *Volk* is taken to its logical conclusion: the characteristics of the *Volk* become immune to the vicissitudes of time. In this atemporal realm the ideas of *Volk* and race become indistinguishable. Individuals are ascribed to one unit or another and have no choice in the matter. Conversion, voluntary or forced, is not an option. It is well known that Hitler subscribed to this view and even used it to assuage fears of his military ambitions, claiming that it was futile to try to incorporate alien peoples into one's own.[6] From the viewpoint of the prepolitical community, the state, its form and development are simply swept aside.

Part of the antipathy to any close relationship between nation and state sprang from the association of the idea of the nation-state with France. According to its authoritarian critics the nation-state engendered by the French Revolution was a centralised state, legitimated through the idea of popular sovereignty, which exports such notions by force of arms. The critics rejected the French idea on various grounds. M.H. Boehm, who led the *Institut für Grenz- und Auslandsstudien*, set out from the geographic dispersion of the German people to argue that the closed nation-state was simply inappropriate for the Germans.[7] The German people could fulfil its destiny only in the form of a non-imperialistic *Reich*. The demographic confusion of Central and Eastern Europe had implications for other peoples too. If the geographically dispersed Germans could not turn to the nation-state then neither could the other peoples who were intermixed with Germans and each other. The key question, of course, is what was to take the place of the nation-state. For the moment, however, it must suffice to note that the idea of the nation and nation-state was suspect to many because of the peculiarities which were discerned in Central Europe. Other critics adopted a more polemical opposition to the French idea. *Die Tat*, for instance, saw the nation and the nationalism which was born in the French Revolution as inherently 'extensive' and 'expansive'.[8] That is, it inevitably issued in imperialist conquest in order to divert attention from internal tension and division by means of the exploitation of other nations. German nationalism by contrast was said to be intensive and inner directed, and hence presumably of no danger to its neighbours.

Despite the implication that German nationalism would produce a more strongly consolidated and tightly bound community *Die Tat* also advocated the idea of a federal and multinational *Reich* whose lack of long-established borders and political identity was held to be a virtue. According to one of the *Tatkreis*, E.W. Eschmann, the continuity of the nation-state in the west had promoted egoism and rigidity from which the members of the proposed *Reich* were thankfully free.[9] How this inner-directed nationalism was to be reconciled with a multinational state remained conveniently opaque.

These initial difficulties are compounded when we take a closer look at the idea of the *Volk*. For although the characteristics of the *Volk* are immutable the existence of the *Volk* or race is not guaranteed. Indeed, the prophets of the *Volk* or race were often motivated by the belief that it was radically threatened. Various conclusions could be drawn from this concern. The leading advocates of the Nordic Idea, Hans F.K. Günther and F. Lenz, both opposed war on the grounds that the already weakened Nordic race would suffer disproportionate losses in any war compared with the other racial elements in the *Volk*.[10] Hitler was of course much more concerned with the supposed threat from the Jewish race posed by interbreeding with Aryans and much more confident of finding a solution, namely the physical elimination of that threat. Yet he too discerned other threats to the German *Volk*. The racial value of the *Volk* was dependent not only upon its purity but also upon the possession of adequate *Lebensraum* and the enjoyment of a rising standard of living.[11] Foreign domination could prove disastrous too.[12] If the purity of blood alone was an insufficient guarantee against economic and political depredations it was also true that political and economic strategies could improve the inner qualities of the *Volk*. Hence Ley recalled Hitler's attitude to the establishment of the *Kraft durch Freude* programme: 'Make sure that the German *Volk* has sound nerves. I want a sound *Volk* with strong nerves, because only with a *Volk* which holds its nerve can one conduct truly great politics.'[13]

The primacy of political and economic strategy is clearly revealed in the developments in Czechoslovakia after 1933. Smelser and Jacobsen have described in great detail the conflict between the 'traditionalists', who are closer ideologically to those described as authoritarian here, and Nazis, within the ranks of *Volkstum* activists.[14] Despite numerous and ultimately decisive similarities each had different notions of the *Volk* and the state. The so-called traditionalists, who included Hans Steinacher, the Haushofers and even Konrad Henlein and possibly Hess, shared the national socialist desire to rally the whole *Volk* but also upheld the distinctive and specific virtues of the diverse groups of ethnic Germans living outside the Reich. The national socialists emphasised the Core State (*Kernstaat*) and neglected the diversity which was praised by the traditionalists. The incompatibility of these positions was evident from the outset when Steinacher met Hitler on 15 November 1933. Steinacher recorded, 'Then Hitler made a half-hour speech on the significance of the German core-state. This must be strong. Then everything else can be gotten. But only by this means. I cannot get around this basic attitude . . .'[15] This was much more than a difference over means. It reflected a basic disagreement over the nature of the *Volk*, the state and the relationship between the two. The unfolding of this disagreement was, as is characteristic of national socialist politics, complicated by the competing claims over the authority and scope of the ill-coordinated agencies of the Third Reich. It was also complicated by the fact that the supporters of Henlein and Steinacher within the *Sudetendeutscher Heimatfront/Sudetendeutsche Partei* (SHF/SdP) came predominantly from the *Kameradschaftsbund* which was inspired by the élitist theories of Othmar Spann. The *Kameradschaftsbund* was hated by national socialist radicals because they saw it was an élitist organisation, rightly so, as Catholic and as sympathetic to Mussolini, Dolfuss and Schuschnigg. The *Kameradschaftsbund* envisaged élites, of which they themselves would form the core, presiding over apolitical Germanic communities. The opponents of Henlein and the *Kameradschaftsbund* concurred with Hitler in demanding the politicisation and mobilisation of the whole *Volk* in the service of the *Reich*. There were, to be sure, some differences between the radicals from the *DNSAP* like Karl Viererbl and Hitler. Hitler, who stood on the sidelines in the early history of the dispute over the direction of the SHF/SdP, was not initially prepared to risk inciting international conflict by the employment of the diplomatically unorthodox tactics of the radicals, especially after the débâcle of the failed Nazi coup in Austria in 1934. In one sense, however, Hitler was the true radical and he was the true radical because he placed so much emphasis upon the nature of the *Volk* as a politicised community which was brought into being by the movement and state which he controlled.[16] His approach to the *Volk* beyond the *Reich* was essentially the same as his approach to the *Volk* within the *Reich*. Speaking to the Party on 22 January 1933 he declared: 'If their origins, traditions and imaginations tear men apart then political will must somehow pull them together again.'[17] The notion of the *Volk* as product of the movement and the state seems to reverse the emphasis envisaged by the *völkisch* orthodoxy according to which the immutable characteristics of the *Volk* have explanatory and causal priority *vis-à-vis* economic, social and political forms. Yet Hitler, of course, also espoused the priority of the prepolitical community. In, for instance, his account of the relationship between race and state which emerges in his comments upon Slavs, Jews and Germans, Slavs and Jews are denied the ability to create states. This incapacity is held to signify their inferiority. He avoided the obvious conclusion of his own belief in Jewish control of states, which was necessary to Hitler's conspiracy theory and manic fear for his *Volk*, only by ascribing this control to their parasitic character. It did not signify their inherent superiority over other races. Here, the *völkisch* orthodoxy asserts itself: the prepolitical community creates the state, not vice versa.

The authoritarians suffered from the same dilemma. For, as Sontheimer notes in his summary of the main points of the authoritarian anti-liberal idea of the state, 'To be sure political unity is produced and represented through the sovereign, decision-making power of the state, but at the same time this state is supposed to be the expression of the living will of the *Volk*.'[18] The state had to be represented as decisive and pre-eminent in order to meet the authoritarians' desire for élite rule. By the same token, however, that élitism required a fairly strong and direct form of legitimacy. The state had to be the creator of political unity and its expression. The basic ambiguity is the same for both authoritarians and for national socialists. Henlein, Steinacher and the other 'traditionalists' did differ from the radicals by virtue of their opposition to the supremacy of the 'core state'. Yet they accepted the *völkisch* idea of unifying the nation in the service of the *Reich*, and could not resist Hitler's success in this quarter.

The distinctiveness of Hitler's position is revealed by considering what he meant by race, *Volk* and state. The first point here is that race is not synonymous with *Volk*. The *Volk* is composed of several races one of which is predominant. It is the predominant core race, designated as Aryan or nordic, which is ascribed responsibility for creating states. Indeed, Hitler drew on the theories of a Pan-European Aryan or nordic ruling caste to explain the existence of any state worthy of note throughout Europe. The distinction between *Volk* and race points towards the meaning of state for Hitler. States exist where the racially superior, but numerically few, dominate the majority. The proviso that only specific races, or in fact only one race, the nordic or Aryan, could create states meant that the absence of nordic superiority entailed the impossibility of the existence of states. Evidence to the contrary, for example, the existence of a Russian state, was explained by the claim that the state had been created by nordic elements and was now in the process of terminal decline. Equally common was the assertion that states did not exist, that is that 'chaos' reigned. The imagery of chaos was invoked wherever Slavs were deemed to live without the benefit of nordic rule. The first meaning of state then is simply the rule of the racially superior over the racially inferior.

The second meaning of state arises from the first. The state is an instrument by means of which the racially superior exercise their domination. The various political and economic strategies for improving the quality of the *Volk* fall within this meaning of state. Eradication of Jews and the cultivation of the nordic element form part of these strategies. The view of the state as instrument had another function too. It served as a weapon against the authoritarians' conservatism and veneration of the state as an end in itself. The authoritarians were no less élitist than Hitler but they too readily identified their élite with institutions like the army and bureaucracy and derived the legitimacy of the élite from its service to the state. Hitler disagreed, for in so far as the idea of the state meant more than racial superiority and instrumentality he dismissed it as ephemeral: 'It is no accident that religions are more stable than states. They generally sink their roots deeper into the earth; they would be inconceivable without the broad masses.'[19]

These conflicting ideas about race, people, nation and state have a direct significance for authoritarian and national socialist views of international relations, and vice versa. Hitler's antipathy to the state, for instance, reflected his view of Germany's international position. When Hitler disparaged the international law derived from 'statist thinking'[20] there were two objects of criticism which he had in mind. Firstly, there was the Versailles settlement and secondly the doctrine of the equality of sovereign, territorially defined states. Initially Hitler, like the numerous conservative and national socialist lawyers, was prepared to appeal to doctrines of the equality of states in order to argue for a revision of Versailles and especially German rearmament. After the introduction of military conscription he proclaimed, 'The restoration of German national authority in matters of armament is a reparation of the violated sovereignty of a great power.'[21] One of the earliest attempts to produce a comprehensive national socialist doctrine of international law, Rauchhaupt's *Völkerrecht* came to much the same conclusion. Yet Rauchhaupt for all his denunciation of Versailles and even his defence of the Nuremburg Laws remained within the traditional framework of international law: 'Both the subject and the object of international relations are the states which are internationally recognised.'[22] In other words states are members of a community of states. Membership of the community is achieved through mutual recognition. Possession of arms and armies is, from this perspective, one of the signs by means of which states recognise each other as states.

For various reasons, however, the integrity of the sovereign state was increasingly being called into question during the interwar period. From the viewpoint of the prophets of the *Volk* denigration of the state was welcome. The idea of the territorially defined state was, claimed Hans Keller, ungermanic.[23] It was derived from the Italian Renaissance and Roman law, the idea of an absolute monarchy developed by France and the nineteenth-century French idea of the nation-state. Keller's objection to the territorially defined state was that individuals were defined in terms of citizenship of such states and hence of course numerous 'Germans' were defined as Poles, Czechs and so on. Existing attempts to cover such problems by securing rights of appeal by individuals belonging to national minorities were, however, firmly rejected on the grounds that such guarantees presaged the emergence of a 'universal' state which was composed of individuals. Against this Keller upheld peoples (*Völker*) as the only natural entities which could and ought to possess rights. In the place of individuals whose rights were recognised by international law or citizens of states he put the idea of the *Volksgenosse*. It was not territoriality that defined membership of the community but 'personality', i.e. membership of the *Volk*. The problem which arose from this was how were the resulting peoples to relate to each other and were there any binding rules for their intercourse? There were two responses. One was that peoples were distinct and self-contained entities with no obligations to each other. Rights existed purely within peoples and international relations were legally anarchic. This approach implicitly drew on the traditional view which derived right from the will of the state and denied that this will could be bound in any way. There was of course a significant difference in so far as states were replaced by peoples. National socialists who wished to maintain that this legal anarchy posed no threat to peace usually had recourse to some sort of natural harmony amongst peoples as a substitute for adherence to the recognition of legal restraint. This, at least, seems to be the implication of Werner Best's idea that though international relations had nothing to do with right they could be *'regelhaft'* in the sense that all natural entities exhibited some sort of regularity of behaviour.[24]

Best's approach is consistent with Hitler's view of international relations as the expression of interests. Legal arrangements, i.e. treaties, were viewed as purely matters of convenience which were to be broken as soon as the constellation of interests which induced them changed. Multilateral treaties were therefore to be avoided since the repercusions of violating them could be more problematic than those resulting from the violation of bilateral treaties. Though Hitler held that this was what all statesmen did anyway, he also operated on another assumption, namely that the conviction of others that international law ought to be binding could be turned against them to Germany's advantage. National socialist lawyers openly blurted out the truth that so long as Germany remained militarily weak it had no interest in rejecting international law. To the contrary it had an interest in an international law which bound the stronger powers as much as possible.[25] Like Best, however, Hitler believed in some sort of natural harmony, at least between certain states. His recurrent assumptions of English indifference to German ambitions in the east were based on the supposed diversity of interests of the two states. Such considerations have led Lutzhöft to claim that Hitler's alliance policy ignored racial similarity in favour of national interests. From the viewpoint of the convinced theorist of the nordic community an alliance with Italy (15 per cent nordic) in opposition to France (25 per cent nordic) was as senseless as war with the United States (30 per cent nordic).[26] This goes too far for the racial theories were, as was suggested above, of sufficient flexibility to account for all sorts of unanticipated events. Nevertheless the general point is valid: Hitler did believe that some states could coexist at least by virtue of a division of interests which corresponded to their natural or organic orientation. This view of the external behaviour of states corresponds to the instrumentalist view of the states discussed earlier. International law and treaties are mere instruments serving the interests of the various *Völker*. Coexistence is possible only where these interests are mutually indifferent.

The alternative to instrumentalism, which was promulgated by Helmut Nicolai, involved again setting out from the derivation of law from the will of the *Volk* and from racially distinctive perceptions of right.[27] International law then had to be based upon the similarity of such perceptions which meant that international law existed in extent and substance only so far as racial similarity existed. If, however, peoples not states are the true subjects of international relations and if some of these share conceptions of right and law to a significant extent the line between alliances between different peoples and a community which incorporates one people currently divided by territorial boundaries becomes blurred. The idea of a Nordic Community reflects this sort of logic. The *völkisch* alternative then points towards racially defined systems of states or trans-state communities. It left the problem of how to relate peoples whose 'racial' similarity was insufficient to establish a system of states or community. The answer goes back to the impoverishment of the national socialist conception of what a state is in the first place. It was suggested above that when Hitler invoked the image of order against chaos and assigned the Aryan race a state-creating will which he denied to others, what was involved was simply the idea of the domination of the racially superior over the racially inferior. Once the integrity and sovereignty of states is dispensed with this becomes the model for what others would call international relations. In a less extreme form the inequality of races or peoples and their respective states was expressed in terms of a division of labour or tasks. This division of tasks was presented under the slogan of 'organic division' and 'natural diversity' which was contrasted with 'equality' (*Gleichheit*). The derivation of such terminology from ideas about domestic social order was explicit. Commenting upon a speech by Hitler, Helmut Dietze proclaimed, 'Here, he [Hitler] carries over the idea of community from the individual life of the people to the common life of peoples.'[28] What exactly was entailed by 'organic division' in international relations was not, however, immediately evident. In part at least it pointed towards the conception of Germany's leading political role in central Europe which pervaded the political spectrum and was rampant in conservative and authoritarian circles. It also drew on equally widespread economic arguments which advocated increased trading links between an industrialised Germany and the 'agrarian' states of Southern and Eastern Europe. Attempts by these 'agrarian' states to promote domestic industries were dismissed as 'unnatural'.[29] Their markets were said to be too small and general conditions too difficult to enable them to compete with Western European industry.[30] In the long run, however, the slogan of 'organic structure' made more sense if the 'organism' as a whole could be identified, and defined by some common purpose. The organism was in fact usually Europe or the marginally more restricted one of Central Europe.

Both authoritarians and national socialists had shown scant respect or liking for the idea of a system of equal sovereign nation-states. In the case of the national socialists this arose from the instrumentalisation or impoverishment of the state, though the same conclusion could be reached by those who set out from the primacy of each state's interest in its own existence: 'Their own preservation is seen as an unconditional duty by all states, *even by those which are not worthy of existence.*'[31] In both cases the domestic and international dimensions of the state were closely linked, as, indeed, they were for the authoritarians. The authoritarians were, as has often been pointed out, motivated by the desire to salvage both the power (*potestas*) and the authority (*auctoritas*) of the state. But every step they took towards this goal threatened to draw the mass of the population into politics. Thus the circle around the *Hochschule für nationale Politik* split in the early 1920s over the alternatives of either pursuing politics within an élitist club which would itself seek influence over leading personalities or seeking to realise van den Bruck's idea of national solidarity.[32] This ambiguity was induced by a crisis of power in view of the demand for greater participation in society. As Michael Geyer has argued, this was one side of the dual crisis confronting Weimar. The other was the crisis of sovereignty which arose from the international competition for power.[33] One answer to the dilemma lay in the construction of a 'federalistic central European confederation whose economy is strictly and centrally organised, but which leaves the member states a greater spiritual and cultural autonomy than today'.[34] Much the same result could be derived from a concern with the authority of the state rather than simply with the power of the state. A.E. Gunther derived the state's loss of authority from secularisation and sought a substitute in a *'metaphysischen Reichsauftrag'*. In both cases there was an attempt to solve the problems of domestic power and authority on the one hand, and the international challenge from other states on the other, by a single stroke.

All these visions entailed a 'new order' in Europe. The character of that order varied with the associated conceptions of race, nation, people and state. Before commenting upon national socialist and authoritarian conceptions it is worth recalling that Europe has shown considerable geographical flexibility. As his critics never tired of pointing out, Coudenhove-Kalergi's map of Pan-Europe exhibits some surprising features. Great Britain is excluded but French possessions in Africa are included. Russia was excluded but the possibility was left open that it might be included at some point in the future. The extent of Europe varied with the type of argument, cultural, economic, racial and so on, which was used to define it. Some arguments were not at all susceptible to a geographic definition. Those who viewed Europe as a spiritual expression could display a resistance to any type of 'mechanical' fixation of Europe. The varieties of Europe are worth recalling because some of the images to be discussed below might appear to be discrepant to that of Europe. Cartographically *Pan-Europa*, *Mitteleuropa*, the *Nordic Gemeinschaft*, and *Zwischeneuropa* are radically different. Some of them were indeed recognised as being to various extents images of parts of a wider notion of Europe. There is, however, no more inherent absurdity in talking about these images as images of Europe than there is in treating the postwar EEC as an expression of European Unity. It is probably futile to worry over which, if any, of these images is truer to Europe. It is certainly misleading for Europe is much more a form which has to be made than it is a natural, that is, prepolitical, entity.

One form in which European unity was conceived was that of racial similarity. Here it should be noted that the students of nationalism who deny that national socialist racism was truly nationalist are right. The very ambitions of the racial theories inevitably issued in tension with the orthodox nationalism for which the contours of the nation were effectively drawn in part by the efforts of states to stabilise their boundaries. National socialists did not normally acknowledge this, preferring to believe that state formation marked the fulfilment of the national destiny. The tension between racial and nationalist doctrines was evident when Günther felt obliged to defend himself against the accusation by 'patriotic men' that his beloved nordic community would submerge the feeling of being German, English or American in a wider enthusiasm for being nordic.[35]

Günther was one of the main prophets of the 'nordic idea' who gathered around the Nordic Society in Lübeck. According to Lutzhöft's detailed study they were not markedly anti-semitic and exercised little influence in the high politics of the Third Reich. Their ideas are, however, of interest for several reasons. The nordic idea was, in the first place, evidently normative in the sense that the sound nordic man was to be held up as an example and criterion of selection amongst Germans and 'nordically defined' peoples. In other words the nordic community was admitted to be a mixture of artifice and nature. The nordic idea also had relatively clear implications for foreign policy, namely alliances, possibly culminating in some sort of federation, between Germany and the Scandinavian countries. Its very clarity, relative clarity that is, was of course its downfall. Initial disappointments could be overcome by the flexibility of the racial doctrine. Appearances could be saved. When the Scandinavians refused to play their allotted role Rosenberg explained that, 'Scandinavia has had it too easy, it has become satisfied and lazy. The Vikings have emigrated, the bourgeois remain. Only a severe misfortune will make the *old* blood rebellious again.'[36] The nordic idea suffered, however, the same limitations as the ideas of the *völkisch* legal theorists who sought to derive a model of international community from an underlying common perception of right. Even if the inherent absurdity of these notions are ignored they were still highly restrictive and were difficult to adapt to the more wide-ranging ambitions of national socialist Germany. These ambitions could be accounted for but only at the expense of expedients like equating nordic with white. Rosenberg was particularly fond of this strategy because it meant he could portray France as the enemy of Europe as a whole. France, he said, was planning to mobilise armies of black men from its colonies who were to be pitched against Germany and/or Italy.[37]

More flexibility was offered by those who set out from the idea of a trans-European nordic ruling caste. Their doctrine points to an international ruling caste which is characterised as much by the division between it and the subordinate strata in individual states as it is by anything else. It could of course be employed to point towards a nordic international. The link between these two elements emerges in the writings of Otto Bangert who envisaged a revival of the *Abendland* by nordic blood and saw fascist Italy as a step in this direction on the grounds that Italian fascism was led by nordic elements from Italy. He feared, however, that these nordic elements would be overwhelmed in the long run if the much stronger nordic forces in Germany did not come to their aid.[38] The idea of an international nordic ruling caste whose common origins prescribed a united front against the diverse, racially inferior subordinate strata was incompatible with the idea of a nordic community spanning Germany and Scandinavia let alone the idea of the primacy of the German *Volk*. It was also weakened by the lack of any institutional structure at least until Himmler sought to develop the *Waffen SS* as the core of the new international caste.[39]

The idea of the *Reich* as an alternative to the system of sovereign states, especially in Eastern and South-eastern Europe, was widespread in the interwar years. It was propounded by the *Tatkreis*, a group of publicists centred around the journal *Die Tat*, who even conceded that the *Reich* should be federal in structure. There is, however, no doubt that their commitment to federalism was weak. Like most authoritarian prophets of the *Reich* they showed more concern with the idea of the *Reich* as a symbol of spiritual renewal and the restoration of the power and authority of the state. The counterposition of a federal *Reich* to the ideology of the nation-state in Eastern Europe (*Zwischeneuropa*) served more to deny the states in that region their sovereignty than to relativise German claims to leadership. This does not mean that all advocates of the *Reich* supported the claims of Bismarck's heirs. A strong Austro-Catholic strand of thought longed for the revival of the Danubian monarchy or for the realisation of a Greater Germany under Austrian rather than German leadership. Indeed such ideas were not alien to the national socialist Seyss-Inquart, but received short shrift from Hitler.[40] The Austro-Catholic idea of the *Reich* as symbol and embodiment of a new Europe rested heavily upon filling out the idea of the *Reich* with Catholic corporatist doctrines. According to Ernst Karl Winter, the rebirth of Austria would spark off the rebirth of Europe, and Austria would be reborn by virtue of the restoration of a Catholic way of life and Catholic corporatism.[41] Ultimately the idea of the *Reich* functioned only as a critique of the existing nation-state. Its ideologists had little to put in its place and too readily succumbed to the division of labour suggested by Martin Spahn on the tenth anniversary of the *Politische Kolleg*. The educators and publicists had the duty of inflaming the desire to coordinate *Reich* and *Raum*, *Reich* and *Volk*. The actual coordination remained the task of the statesman.[42]

Carl Schmitt, a highly influential legal and political theorist, appeared to offer a more sophisticated and concrete alternative to the vacuity of authoritarian and national socialist conceptions. Closer examination, however, reveals that Schmitt's theory did little more than to justify the emergent new order. In *Völkerrechtliche Grossraumordnung* he sought to provide a new framework for international relations which was to supersede the model of equal and sovereign states. The doctrine of the equality of sovereign states had had, he conceded, a certain validity up to the twentieth century; but it now served merely as a cover for the hegemony of France and England. In reality there was a 'rank order' amongst states. More importantly, Schmitt claimed to discern new political entities which he called *Grossräume*. A *Grossraum* was a union of states bound together by a specific type of principle which Schmitt mistakenly believed was exemplified by the American Monroe Doctrine. The core of this principle was '. . . the connection of a politically awakened people, a political idea and the exclusion of foreign intervention from the *Grossraum* which is dominated by this idea'.[43] One nation, and one alone, was to provide this political idea for the union as a whole. These leading states were designated *Reiche*. In the place of the doctrine of equal and sovereign states Schmitt offered a model which contained three types of political bodies: *Grossräume*, Reiche and nations. Within this framework there were to be four types of relationship: firstly, relationships between *Grossräume*, which appear to be mainly economic; secondly, those between the leading *Reiche*; thirdly, the international relationships within *Grossräume*; fourthly, the international relationships between nations of different *Grossräume*. The latter are the only ones which are specifically restricted in that 'intervention' by one nation in the affairs of those of another *Grossraum* is prohibited.

Although Schmitt did not specify in any detail what the international (*zwischen-völkische*) relationships within a *Grossraum* were to be, it is not too difficult to discern their general character. He subscribed to the view that the existence of a state required an unspecified degree of 'internal, predictable (*berechenbarer*) organisation and internal discipline'.[44] Such qualities were essential to the existence of any sort of international community too. Not all peoples, however, had measured up to these requirements. Furthermore, 'A people which is incapable of becoming a state in this purely organisational sense can in no way be a legal subject in international law.'[45] The Abyssinians, for example, had failed to pass the test. Abyssinia was not, in fact, a state at all. Schmitt simply enshrined military power by denying the victims of such power any legal status in international law.

Further clarification of relationships within *Grossräume* can be gained by reflection on Schmitt's view of the nature of federations as expounded in 1928. According to Murray Forsyth,[46] Schmitt says that a *Bund* (union of states) as opposed to a confederation or federal state exists where the traditional dilemma of the sovereignty of the union or the members is left open. Other acknowledged problems are the renunciation of the *ius belli* by member-states, despite the fact that they have entered the union for reasons of self-presentation, and the interference of the *Bund* in the affairs of the member-states, despite the desire of each to maintain its political independence. Schmitt's solution to these dilemmas was the 'homogeneity' or 'substantive similarity' of the member states. This homogeneity was to exclude the decisive conflicts which involved conflicting claims to sovereignty. It was to dissolve the conflict between the renunciation of the *ius belli* and the goal of self-preservation. It was also to remove the objectionable character of the interference of the *Bund* in the affairs of member-states since 'interference' was objectionable because it was 'foreign' and the interference of a *Bund* in the affairs of member-states within a homogenous society was not foreign.

The relevance of these views expressed in 1928 is evident from a long footnote in *Völkerrechtliche Grossraumordnung* where Schmitt extols the virtues of the 'higher' categories of *Bund, Reich* and *Grossraum*.[47] The internal relationships within the *Grossraum* are thereby associated with those within a *Bund*, which Schmitt had discussed in 1928. There is indeed a strong similarity in that both *Bund* and *Grossraum* are alternatives to the sovereignty of states. The difference is that in 1928 Schmitt wrote of the 'homogeneity' of all members of the *Bund*. In *Völkerrechtliche Grossraumordnung* he wrote of a 'political idea' imparted by one member of the *Grossraum*, namely the *Reich*. Whereas in 1928 a vague 'homogeneity' was to justify the loss of sovereign rights by all members of the *Bund*, the loss of sovereign rights by *some* members of the *Grossraum* was now justified by the imposition of a 'political idea' by one member, the *Reich*. In terms of Schmitt's theory the 'homogeneity' within the *Bund* or the leading 'political idea' within a *Grossraum* plays an essential role in facilitating the unity of the supra-national political entity. But Schmitt himself remains vague about both 'homogeneity' and, more importantly, about the 'political idea'. Since *Völkerrechtliche Grossraumordnung* was republished throughout the Second World War it is, however, difficult to see how the 'political idea' for Europe could be anything other than national socialism.

Within the era of *Grossräume* envisaged by Schmitt small states had at best a subordinate role. Leading national socialists went further, speculating about the revision of territorial boundaries. When they did so the fate of small states was clear. They were to be abolished, incorporated into the *Reich*, or reduced to dependency upon the *Reich*. The contempt for small states was more usually reflected by the complete neglect of them in the broader discussions about German foreign policy and the future of Europe. The only states which mattered, apart from Germany itself, were England, France, Italy, Russia and America. In the long run Russia was to be pushed back or dismembered in the interests of the expansion of German *Lebensraum*. In the short run Russia could be drawn into the calculation of interests which Hitler and Rosenberg used to regulate German foreign policy. A striking feature of these calculations is the extent to which the resulting constellation of interests was often marked by the mutual indifference of interests. To be sure the pragmatic decision to conceal long-term goals was prominent in the public expression of these calculations, but there is another factor rooted in the national socialist view of history. Here the need for *Lebensraum* is seen as the motor of behaviour. To the national socialist the fact that this driving force was natural also meant that it was justifiable. Thus

Rosenberg proudly contrasted *völkisch* imperialism with militaristic imperialism. French imperialism was '. . . a purely militaristic imperialism which doesn't spring from internal *völkischen* necessity, that is out of the necessity to obtain living-space but rather, incorporates new areas out of the lust for plunder and adventure'.[48] A different formulation was later offered by Werner Best. As has been noted, Best denied that there was any such thing as international law. Yet other states had nothing to fear from Germany for the *völkisch* theory of law did not ascribe one state any rights over another. Right was merely the expression of the will of the *Volk* and that will can only be oriented towards the maintenance of the *Volk* and the unfolding of *its* possibilities.[49] Both Rosenberg and Best then sought to justify an expansionist programme and yet to claim that other states need not feel threatened by this. In one sense this is clearly ludicrous. The expansion had to be at someone's expense. The underlying assumption is that some states simply did not count. The only ones which did count were the major powers listed above. Each of these was allocated a specific area in which it could act out the natural law 'which no single nation, so far as it wants to maintain the ability to be a nation, can deny'.[50] Conflict between these states can be avoided only so far as their respective spheres of interest do not come into conflict. Mutual indifference is the only guarantee of peace. From this perspective there are two images of Europe. The first conceives of Europe as a community of four states, Germany, England, France and Italy, each of which is to follow its natural interests and consequently would have no ambitions *vis-à-vis* any of the others. Smaller states have no role or right in this picture. Or rather their only role is one of subordination to one of the main powers. This is what was meant by Dietze when he denied that the European community could be 'a sum composed of equal parts', as proposed by the advocates of Pan-Europe, but could only be 'structured whole' whose ultimate meaning was to be found in a correctly understood Four Power Pact.[51] Coexisting with this image of Europe was another which placed more emphasis upon the actual division of interest envisaged in the first. All of the powers save Germany were ascribed interests which lay wholly (England and France) or substantially (Italy) overseas. Within a planetary division of interests Germany appears as the only power with an exclusively European interest. It is a small step from this, especially under the later conditions of military success, to identifying Germany with Europe as a whole.

National socialists clearly felt that the community of mutual indifference was insufficient for they often advocated a stronger form of community in which the relevant states and peoples were bound by a common interest. That common interest was either the politico-cultural community of Europe or the European *Grossraumwirtschaft*. In both cases unity was defined in opposition to either or both of the emergent superpowers, America and Russia. England also entered the picture as an Anglo-Saxon or western power (France was also included in the latter) or, from the economic perspective as an independent *Grossraum*. The most prominent adversary, Bolshevist Russia, was denounced in a vitriolic circle of cultural and racial abuse.

The common focus was the idea that Russia and Bolshevism signified chaos, lack of order, anarchy. The reasons varied. Rosenberg, for instance, offered different versions of a racial theory to account for this distinctive lack of order. Sometimes disorder was traced back to racial intermixture, which was consistent with the explanation of disorder within Germany. At other times, however, disorder appeared to be an inherent characteristic of an asiatic race: 'Bolshevism means the revolt of the mongol against the nordic form of culture. It is the desire for the steppe, it is the hatred of the nomad for a rooted personality, it means the attempt to wipe out Europe completely.'[52] The antipathy to Bolshevist chaos was not, however, undisputed even within the ranks of the national socialists. There was a broad stream of thought which stretched over the line between authoritarians and national socialists which saw the threat, and source of unity, in western decadence and ossification rather than Bolshevist chaos. Goebbels, as Rosenberg was later to recall, had espoused these views. So too did the *Tatkreis* and Hans Schwarz of the *Politische Kolleg*. The anti-western idea of Europe envisaged a revolt against the western domination exemplified by the Versailles Treaty in which the youthful nations of the east would liberate themselves from the shackles of the west.

Beyond such general images, however, the anti-western tendency displayed considerable variety. The identity of a distinct Europe sometimes evaporated amidst an apocalyptic conflict between west and east.[53] A more stable and clearly defined image of Europe was presented by those, like the *Tatkreis*, who drew upon the *Mitteleuropa* tradition and saw Russia as an ally but also as a distinct entity.

Given Hitler's own anti-Bolshevist attitudes and, more importantly, the fact that he discerned the expansion of German *Lebensraum* in the east, it was the anti-Bolshevist alternative which became official policy. Within this framework of European unity two alternative conceptions of the internal organisation of Europe were available. The first saw a solution in the 'fascistisation' of all European states. Here the Bolshevist menace appeared as an international phenomenon which sapped states from within. The consequence that the menace had to be removed at the national level, state by state, left the problem of how the ensuing fascist states were to organise their relationships with each other. Italian initiatives for a fascist international had not been particularly promising, partly at least because of the national socialist emphasis on race. More prominent was the other solution which did not rely upon ideologically based cooperation, namely the idea of an 'organic structure'. What was meant by 'organic structure' often remained stubbornly opaque. Despite the prominence which it played, as a slogan, within Keller's *Das Recht der Völker* it was never defined. The *'organische Weltbild'* consisted solely of denunciations of the equality of states, of putting the state before the *Volk* and so on. The economist Werner Daitz appeared to go a little further in assigning specific states specific tasks. England he said had the duty, 'to shield Europe against the overseas continents with its Empire . . .', Italy the duty, 'to hold off the pressure of Africa . . .', and Germany, 'to protect Europe from central Asia after the disappearance of Bolshevism by means of its east European Ottawa, by means of an east European working community of peoples which must stretch to the Urals'.[54] The striking feature of this division of tasks is that it sounds suspiciously like the advocacy of what was described above as the politics of mutual indifference. Only one country, Germany, has a task which actually concerns the internal organisation of Europe and even then only part of Europe is mentioned. This limitation was not always observed even in the prewar years. In 1936 Daitz was writing of a new European order which would stretch from Flanders to Reval.[55] Nevertheless the focus on Central and Eastern Europe is revealing for it points to the basis of an idea of organised structure which does actually entail some symbiotic relationship within Europe. That relationship was economic. Daitz's version of the new economic order was marked by the idea of isolation from the vicissitudes of world trade and the threat posed by the emerging economic blocs of the Americas, the British Empire, China, Japan and Russia. Economies within the new order were to be largely self-sufficient but such trade as there was was to be controlled by Germany and Germans. It is no surprise therefore that Daitz's writings are littered with references to the, suitably embellished, role of the Hanse towns in medieval Europe. He even suggested, in 1934, a division of labour with France whereby the French were to become the financiers of a continental *Grossraumwirtschaft* but control of transit trade was to be left to Germany. A similar emphasis upon trade was evident in Matthes Ziegler's 'Um die Gestaltung Europas' (1939) according to which economic unity was to be based upon a system of river-borne trade linking the North Sea and the Baltic with the Black Sea.[56] A somewhat different sort of 'organic structure' was advocated by those who took more cognisance of Germany's industrial economy. Again Eastern Europe was the focus of unity but with German industrial goods being exchanged for eastern agricultural products and raw materials. In both cases the states of Eastern and South-eastern Europe were to be subordinate to Germany but the political shape of this subordination remained opaque or confused though the general intent was clear enough and occasionally explicitly so. Although the states of Eastern Europe were promised the restoration of their sovereignty which was threatened by the vicissitudes of the world market and dependency upon foreign, usually French, loans, the cure was even more of a threat to their sovereignty. Whether economic unity was to be based upon the monopolisation of trade or a European wide division of labour between industrial and agrarian states, the management of economic affairs was to be centralised, in German hands.

That it was to be centralised followed from the assumption that the economic crisis which broke out in 1929 was not a temporary, if severe, disruption of world trade but rather signalled the emergence of a new economic world order characterised by state-controlled, large-sphere economies. In the words of Zadow, the new era would witness 'a stronger implementation of the political and economic claims of states against other states'.[57] At the least this would entail centralised control of trade tariffs, currency flows and price levels. In fact it entailed considerably more. The argument about the necessity of large-sphere economies was far from being a purely economic one. The advocates were often motivated by considerations of sovereignty and memories of the war economy of 1914–18. Maintenance of sovereignty was seen as incompatible with extensive involvement in world trade, especially under conditions of a free market. Disinvolvement from the world market could not, however, be achieved within the confines of the boundaries of the Versailles Treaty. Expansion of the sovereign economy of Germany was therefore incompatible with the economic sovereignty of neighbouring states.

Of these notions of a *Grossraumwirtschaft* the one closest to Hitler's view was the one which focused on the symbiosis of industrial Germany on the one hand and the agrarian states and suppliers of raw materials on the other. As L. Herbst has argued, Hitler held that the agrarian states were necessary not only as suppliers but also as markets for German industrial goods. Both industrial production, of consumer goods, and the supply of foodstuffs were necessary in order to maintain and raise the living standards of the Aryan race which in turn strengthened the racial value of that race. How strongly he held to this association of living standards and racial value is evident from his rejection of international trade on the grounds that it tended to equalise living standards and hence could threaten the performance of the white race. Applied within Europe this model points to the perpetual agrarianisation and suppression of living standards for inferior races. It may not, however, have meant malnutrition and low living standards for all non-Germans, at least not in the long run. Even by his own distorted standards he recognised the military and industrial power of America and Russia. Pitted against these, especially the former, the German *Volk* may have seemed too small for he speculated that '. . . in the far future it may be possible to think of a new association of nations, consisting of individual states with a high national value, which could then stand up to the threatening overwhelming of the world by the American Union.'[58] The implied European unity was, however, promptly curtailed for he added, 'Pan-Europe cannot be summoned to the solution of this problem, but only a Europe with free and independent national states whose areas of interest are divergent and precisely limited.'[59] Hitler could not reconcile his recognition of the need for European unity in the envisaged conflict with the economic and military giants with his conception of a *Volksgemeinschaft*. In the words of Werner Daitz, '*Volksgemeinschaft* means an armed community facing outwards and, facing inwards, an harmonious community.'[60] Such communities could coexist only by virtue of mutual indifference generated by an appropriate division of spheres of interest. Mutual indifference and division of interest are, however, evidently contrary to the unity proclaimed earlier. There was of course one other sort of relationship between peoples. The racially superior could dominate the racially inferior. If, however, the racially superior were equated purely with Germans the problem of whether there are sufficient Germans reappears. Hence Hitler's rejection of emigration as a solution to the supposed problem of overpopulation. There were other solutions too. Nordic elements could be discerned in Holland, Flanders, Switzerland, Norway, Sweden, Denmark in addition to those Germans scattered throughout Eastern Europe. It was not, however, until the war that the idea of a European wide racial élite gained any significant manifestation and even then it remained far more a future dream than a reality.

The characteristics of the national socialist idea of Europe were inherently contradictory, as were those of the *Volk* and the state. The *Volk* was supposed to be a cohesive and creative community, yet it was also regarded as the product of political and economic strategies. The state appeared as mere instrument and yet as the manifestation of the inner value of a people. Europe appeared as an economic and cultural community yet its internal structure could be envisaged only in terms of mutually indifferent states or in terms of the dream of a racial élite. Into the political vacuum created by this confusion and particularly by the poverty of the national socialist concept of the state stepped the various paladins each with his own multinational apparatus.

Conservative images of Europe offered little resistance to this outcome. Despite the conservative emphasis upon the state *vis-à-vis* the supremacy of the *Volk* and the political mobilisation of the masses, the conservative state frequently exhibited no more self-restraint than the national socialist *Volk*. Out of perceived economic necessity or the supposed need for a sense of mission transcending class divisions conservatives dismissed the claims to sovereignty of many states, especially in Eastern Europe. It is true that some conservatives, and not only conservatives, were ready to make genuine concessions to foreign peoples, partially to dissolve the concentration of power in their own lands within some larger unit. In other words they took federalism seriously. National socialists did not. Nor did many conservatives, for much the same reason. The conservative state like the national socialist *Volksgemeinschaft* meant the 'restoration', in fact the creation, of an intensely high degree of social integration and social control. The institutions through which this was to be achieved provided the point of dispute between national socialists and conservatives. Between such intensely integrated communities relationships had to be kept to a minimum. The only alternative was the expansion of one such community and its incorporation of the others. Conservatives could, at least apparently, avoid this option by virtue of their concern for the state. The traditional discourse about the state included doctrines of federalism which could be polemically pitted against the egoistic nation-state in the name of a greater *Reich*. Both the *Tatkreis* and Carl Schmitt availed themselves of this discourse, as did Othmar Spann and M.H. Boehm. The internal unity which they desired for domestic reasons crept over, however, into their transnational conceptions. Giselher Wirsing called for the application of Smend's notion of *Staatsintegration* to *Raumintegration*[61]. Schmitt defined the leading political idea as part of any genuine *Grossraum* principle. The dilemma for conservatives with a transnational orientation was the same as that for national socialists. The decisive question was integration and autarky within one's own boundaries or expansion. Expansion was in fact prescribed by the demand for the revision of Versailles, the welcome dissolution of the world market economy, and the postulation of a German mission in Europe. The incorporation of other communities was, however, no easy matter. Ideas about how it was to be achieved were limited. The defence of European culture against Bolshevist anarchy and western decadence, of a European *Grossraum* against emerging competitors may have been the most appealing but left open the question of what sort of order was to exist in Europe. National socialist *Völkerrechtlehre* offered what by the account of its own adherents was a limited solution, and one which tended to counterpose the claims of national socialism to Italian 'universalism'. In fact the disparagement of the unified state in favour of *Volk* and movement already indicated the solution, as did the periodic revelation of the *Volk* as product rather than as cause and agent. Into the place of the unified state stepped various public and semi-public organisations each of which sought to create order, to rebuild the state, in its own image. In the wake of the German army these agencies would each seek to create order in Europe as they had sought to create it in the *Reich*, competing with each other to extend their respective spheres of domination.

The ultimate vacuity of the national socialist images of Europe should not be taken as a sanction for dismissing them as pure propaganda against which we can set some true European heritage. Even prior to the war efforts were made to institutionalise and disseminate diverse conceptions of Europe. The *Nordic Gesellschaft* did seek to create a Nordic Community. Individuals like Werner Daitz pursued their schemes, in his case the establishment of a *Grossraumswirtschaft*. Hitler and Rosenberg propounded, and believed in, a division of interests between the great powers of Europe which was consonant with the overarching, if not necessarily pre-eminent, goals of the defence of the Aryan or 'white' race. These conceptions may be obnoxious or deluded, or usually both, but their role in shaping the idea and reality of Europe was no less significant for that.

Notes

1.   W. Lipgens, *A History of European Integration, 1945–1947 (Oxford, Clarendon Press, 1982), Vol. I, pp. 18–35.*
2.   R.E. Herzstein, *When Nazi Dreams Come True* (London, Abacus, 1982).
3.   A.D. Smith, *Nationalism in the Twentieth Century* (London, Robertson, 1979), pp. 43–85.
4.   W.A. McDougall, 'Political economy versus national sovereignty: French structures for German economic integration after Versailles', *Journal of Modern History*, Vol. 51 (1979), p. 7.
5.   Adolf Spamer, 'Wesen und Aufgabe der Volkskunde', in Adolf Spamer (ed.), *Die Deutsche Volkskunde*, Vol. 1 (Leipzig, Bibliographisches Institut, 1934), p. 1.
6.   G. Weinberg has pointed out that the impossibility of political incorporation left open another strategy, depopulation and genocide, *The Foreign Policy of Hitler's Germany: Diplomatic Revolution in Europe, 1933–1936* (Chicago, University of Chicago Press, 1970), p. 64.
7.   Paul Sweet, 'Recent German literature on Mitteleuropa', *Journal of Central European Affairs*, Vol. 3 (1943), p. 4.
8.   Klaus Fritzsche, *Politische Romantik und Gegenrevolution* (Frankfurt-on-Main, Suhrkamp, 1976), p. 208.
9.   Hans Hecker, *Die Tat und ihr Osteuropa Bild, 1909–1938* (Cologne, Wissenschaft und Politik, 1974), pp. 142–4.
10.   Hans-Jurgen Lutzhöft, *Der Nordische Gedanke in Deutschland, 1920–1949* (Stuttgart, Klett, 1971), pp. 255–6 and 261. Hitler used the same argument, albeit less honestly, in an interview in 1933. See Max Domarus, *Hitler: Reden und Proklamationen, 1932–1945* (Munich, Süddeutscher Verlag, 1965), Vol. I, p. 333.
11.   Ludolf Herbst, *Der Totale Krieg und die Ordnung der Wirtschaft* (Stuttgart, DVA, 1982), pp. 84–92.
12.   As Rosenberg recorded. See Wolfgang Michalka (ed) *Das Dritte Reich* (Munich, DTV, 1985), Vol. 2, p. 117.
13.   Domarus, *Hitler: Reden und Proklamationen*, op. cit., Vol. I, pp. 334–5.
14.   Ronald M. Smelser, *The Sudeten Problem 1933–1938* (Folkestone, Dawson, 1975) Hans-Adolf Jacobsen, *Nationalsozialistische Aussenpolitik 1933–1938* (Frankfurt-on-Main, Metzner, 1968).

15. Quoted by Smelser, *Sudeten Problem*, op. cit., p. 18.
16. National socialist legal theorists went further, identifying the Führer as the source and creator of the community. See Jurgen Meinck, *Weimarer Staatslehre* (Frankfurt, Campus, 1978), pp. 63–66.
17. Domarus, *Hitler: Reden und Proklamationen*, op. cit., Vol. I, p. 181.
18. Kurt Sontheimer, *Antidemokratisches Denken in der Weimarer Republik* (Munich, Nymphenburger, 1962).
19. Domarus, *Hitler: Reden und Proklamationen*, op. cit., Vol. I, p. 268.
20. Domarus, *Hitler: Reden und Proklamationen*, op. cit., Vol. I, p. 271.
21. Norman H. Baynes, *The Speeches of Adolf Hitler* (London, RIIA, 1942), p. 1212.
22. Fr. W. von Rauchhaupt, *Völkerrecht* (Munich and Leipzig, Voglrieder, 1936), p. 33.
23. Hans K.E.L. Keller, *Das Recht der Volker* (Berlin, Vahlen, 1938), pp. 105–110.
24. Werner Best, 'Rechtsbegriff und "Völkerrecht"', *Deutsches Recht* Vol. 9 (1939), p. 1347.
25. Edouard Bristler, *Die Völkerrechtlehre des Nationalsozialismus* (Zurich, Europa, 1938), pp. 67–8.
26. Lutzhöft, *Nordische Gedanke*, op. cit., pp. 262ff.
27. See Bristler, *Völkerrechtlehre*, pp. 68–71.
28. Hans Helmut Dietze, 'Europa als Einheit', *Zeitschrift für Völkerrecht* (1936), p. 299.
29. By Hans Posse. See Eckart Teichert, *Autarkie und Grossraumwirtschaft in Deutschland 1930–1939* (Munich, Steiner, 1984), p. 111.
30. Erwin Wiskemann, *Mitteleuropa* (Berlin, 1933) as quoted in Reinhard Opitz (ed.), *Europastrategien des deutschen Kapitels, 1900–1945* (Cologne, Rugenstein, 1977), p. 167.
31. H. Krauss, 'Interesse und Zwischenstaatliche Ordnung', *Niemeyers Zeitschrift für Internationales Recht* (1934), p. 44.
32. Joachim Petzold, *Konservative Theoretiker des deutschen Faschismus*, (Berlin, VEB, 1978), p. 128.
33. Michael Geyer, 'Nation, Klasse, und Macht', *Archiv für Sozialgeschichte*, Vol. 26 (1986), p. 31.
34. Quoted by Fritzsche, *Politische Romantik*, op. cit., p. 213.
35. Lutzhöft, *Nordische Gedanke*, op. cit., p. 258.
36. Quoted by Lutzhöft, ibid., p. 339.
37. See, for example, A. Rosenberg, *Der Zukunftsweg einer deutschen Aussenpolitik* (Munich, Eher, 1927), p. 52.
38. Klaus-Peter Hoepke, *Die deutsche Rechte und der italienische Fascishmus* (Dusseldorf, Droste, 1968), pp. 135–6.
39. Bernd Wegner, *Hitlers Politische Soldaten* (Paderborn, Schöningh, 1982).
40. Peter R. Black, *Ernst Kaltenbrunner: Ideological Soldier of the Third Reich* (Princeton, Princeton University Press, 1984), p. 113.
41. Quoted by Klaus Breuning, *Die Vision des Reiches* (Munich, Hueber, 1969), p. 29.
42. ibid., pp. 101–2.
43. Carl Schmitt, *Völkerrechtliche Grossraumordnung* (Berlin, Deutscher Rechtsverlag, 1941), p. 20.

44. ibid., p. 43.
45. ibid., p. 45.
46. Murray Forsyth, *Unions of States* (New York, Holmes and Meier, 1981), pp. 146–55.
47. Schmitt, *Völkerrechtliche Grossraumordnung*, op. cit., pp. 39–40.
48. Rosenberg, *Zukunftsweg*, op. cit., p. 14.
49. Best, 'Rechtsbegriff und Völkerrecht', op. cit., p. 1347.
50. Rosenberg, *Zukunftsweg*, op. cit., p. 14.
51. Hans Helmut Dietze, 'Die Problematik der europäischen Rechtseinheit', *Geist der Zeit*, Vol. 16, (1938) p. 314.
52. Alfred Rosenberg, *Der Mythus des 20 Jahrhunderts* (Munich, Eher, 1934), p. 113.
53. The term Europe was thus associated with the 'west' by Ernst Niekisch. See O.E. Schüddenkopf, *Linke Leute von Rechts* (Stuttgart, Kohlhammer, 1960), pp. 357, 360.
54. Werner Daitz, *Der Weg zur Volkswirtschaft, Grossraumwirtschaft und Grossraumpolitik* (Dresden, Meinhold, 1945), p. 16.
55. ibid., p. 119.
56. Matthes Ziegler, 'Um die Gestaltung Europas', *Nationalsozialistische Monatshefte* (April 1939), pp. 291–5.
57. Quoted by Teichert, *Autarkie und Grossraumwirtschaft*, op. cit., p. 149.
58. Telford Taylor (ed.), *Hitler's Secret Book* (New York, Grove, 1961), p. 209.
59. ibid., p. 209.
60. Daitz, *Der Weg zur Volkswirtschaft*, op. cit., p. 114.
61. Giselher Wirsing, *Zwischeneuropa und die deutsche zukunft* (Jena, Diederich, 1932), p. 9. On the ideas of Rudolph Smend see Meinck, *Weimarer Staatslehre*, op. cit., pp. 56–8.

9 Ideas for a New Order in France, Britain and the Low Countries in the 1930s

M.L. Smith

In an assessment of the forces behind patterns of Western European integration the history of the 1930s has a dismal place. These 'nine troubled years', themselves part of a deeper 'twenty years crisis' that touched and distorted every area of life have not easily led to more positive conclusions. Indeed, the inexorable drift towards a war that, for many, came almost as a relief has provided the exemplar of the worst effects of disunity.[1] Where there have been attempts made at positive assessments these have been directed to the didactic purpose of learning from the consequences of division. In particular, the history of the 1930s has provided a series of warnings as to the relation between economic crisis and political and social disorder. Fascism—especially its most virulent form, Nazism—is agreed to have fed on the dislocations of the Depression, attracting support for a nationalist and autarkic vision that could ultimately only be sustained by recourse to war and conquest as the direct result of the despair and anger engendered by underproduction and long-term unemployment. Above all else it was the phenomenon of unemployment that, in the words of a *Times* leader that was looking towards the means of assuring the conditions of postwar stability, had been 'the most insidious and most corroding malady of our generation.'[2] Unemployment stood out acknowledged as the mainspring of the claims to the success of fascism; its persistence through the 1930s was a demonstration of the failure of the democracies to address the problem of making fundamental defensive changes to the system of capitalism that might have provided an effective and credible counter-cyclical policy.

Those who in 1945 sought to rebuild a Europe that would never again fall prey to such destructive forces as those that Nazism expressed had of necessity to distance themselves from the decade in which fascism had been allowed to portray itself as holding a viable solution to economic disorder. For many the process of looking to the future had started in the Resistance.

149

For resistance in itself represented a fundamental refusal to accept that the Nazi version of a New European Order was valid. And in so far as that version had its origins in a critique of the liberal democracies against which those societies themselves had found little defence, its rejection by the Resistance tended inevitably to be accompanied by a parallel refusal to perceive a positive value in pure restoration. Whether it was the agreement in France that the Third Republic was dead, the push for *doorbraak* (breakthrough) of the over-compartmentalised political and social life in the Low Countries, or the shift to a New Deal for Britain, the Western Europe of 1945 appeared decisively to turn its back on much of the past.

Of course, a *tabula rasa* was neither a realistic assumption in view of the developing threat of the superpowers, nor what the plans and projects that actually emerged from the European Resistance envisaged. In any case, at least after June 1941, the Resistance had had to become a meeting ground of all those people of goodwill who, regardless of past political affiliation, were drawn into a coalition motivated by the pluralist and humane values that Nazism affronted. Naturally, such a coalition presented its own dilemmas. On the one hand, there stood the radical desire to have done with the paralysis in the face of economic crisis, compromises and shameful subservience to force that had characterised the politics of the 1930s. Against this, the desire to rebuild by sweeping away the worst features—if no more— of a system that had proved itself divisive and dangerous to peace was tempered by the knowledge that others had argued just this before the war. For the legitimacy of the liberal parliamentary states had been extensively challenged, and not only by fascists. Throughout Europe the 1930s had been, in the words of a recent observation, 'a seething cauldron of ideas' infused by a critical and often dismissive impatience with the status quo and, most of all, questioning the automatic assumption that the form of liberal democracy that had consolidated itself in Europe after 1919 was necessarily for the best.[3]

Fascism during its formative years in the 1920s and the Nazis in their drive to power had also tried, with some partial success, to occupy this ground. Yet, as many in 1945 knew from their own intellectual histories, an identity of target did not *ipso facto* make all those who had expressed misgivings and a desire for radical change in this sphere fascists, or even fellow-travellers of fascist ideology.[4] In fact the pervasive dissatisfaction with the working of the parliamentary system was also motivated (as one pioneering contemporary study, *Intellectual Ferment in France*, noted) by a negative appraisal of its capacity to deal with the dangers that were inherent in both the economic crisis *and* the rise of Hitler.[5] Intellectual, young, arrogant and certainly often enjoying the notoriety of their attack on sacred respectabilities, the 'nonconformists' of the 1930s, as they have been aptly named, laid a bed of ideas which inhabited a world critical and independent of fascism although related and reactive to it.[6] Fascism they took as the great challenge as much as the great reality of the time. Against it they proposed not an electoral coalition but the creation of a counter new order: a 'constructive revolution'[7] premised (in a typically paradoxical formulation) on being 'neither Communism nor capitalism', 'neither Right nor Left', 'neither liberalism nor fascism.'[8]

The wider significance of these currents of thought will be discussed at length below. The point to be made first is that for radical reconstructionists at the end of the war not only was some of the ground of fundamental renewal to a considerable degree pre-empted, but it was also occupied by discredited representatives of a discredited decade. It could be, and was, argued that all that the ferment of the 1930s had achieved was to assure the penetration and ultimate success of fascism. Even more damningly, the non-conformist, non-Marxist challenge to liberal democracy had not come to an end in 1939. For, in so far as fascism was the dominant form in which the challenge became reality, inevitably as its success increased by conquest and an apparently long-term hegemony over Europe, it drew others into its orbit throughout the war years themselves. In 1945 it was sadly evident that the progress of many of those who had been in the forefront of the most exciting critiques in the 1930s had been not towards the Resistance but to the Collaboration.

The rejection of those who had made the choice of collaboration with fascism was neither difficult nor controversial in 1945. More problematic was to avoid doing so in a way that appeared to defend the political record of the 1930s. Yet some form of continuity was needed if the process of forging, or at least maintaining, a consensus adequate to meet the demands of reconstruction was to be achieved. The very uncertainty of the trajectories of those who, from an initial position critical of the inadequacies of capitalist and fascist solutions to the crisis alike, had ended in the Collaboration made it essential to redefine a normative politics that would link the two worlds either side of the war. Of course some linkage was provided by the continuity of purpose in the opposition to fascism that had found a common expression from Germany to the battlefields of the Spanish Republic and the final liberation of continental Europe. This progressive history had early coalesced in some parts of Europe into the structured defensive purpose that informed the Popular Front — the idea around which the majority of the European Left had sought to reassert its dwindling authority and effectiveness. But here again there were problems. Neither its economic policies based on theories of underconsumption, nor the practice of collective security as methods of stopping fascism had met with startling success. At a more fundamental level, too, that was of particular relevance to the postwar period, the uneasy and temporary truce between social democrats and communists had left not so much the basis for future cooperation as a legacy of bitterness and distrust that the common effort in the latter part of the war had done little to erase.

Nonetheless, the need to define a normative tradition was urgent. For the first progressive postwar governments had to face two major realities which shaped their reconstructionist thinking. First, the effective break-up of the Resistance coalition in a foretaste of the conflicts that were to harden into the Cold War meant that communist participation was rapidly dispensed with and the parameters of a new majority coalition accordingly modified. Second, and in part as a consequence, there was a pressing need for a stable and positive political settlement that would allow the process of building a better society to start. These two constraints channelled politics away from the path of initiating fundamental changes and towards consolidation and renewal; and it was in this respect that the idea of creating a different Popular Front could be made to provide an attractive normative direction.

Naturally, it had been accepted by all parties in the 1930s that the continuing economic crisis played increasingly into the demagogic strengths of fascism. Remedies remained, however, vastly different. At the very time that the Nazis were achieving their electoral breakthrough, orthodox opinion in most European countries still held to the pursuit of a policy of deflation, sound money and a balanced budget, believing this to be the surest way of restoring business confidence and, thereby, answering the challenge of fascism by denying it its fertile recruiting ground of dissatisfaction and impoverishment. It was in reaction to such policies that the Left—broadly defined—began to propose an alternative which, in some countries became, briefly, the policy of new governments. Although more committed to the idea that fascism was in large measure the response of capitalism in crisis, they nevertheless saw themselves restrained by their electoral mandates and the defence of a parliamentary majority to pursue programmes that would essentially fight the effects of the Depression by what, subsequently, became known as Keynesian means. The ravages of an unrestrained capitalism were to be moderated by the assurance of a more just and humane operation of the economy. In both responses there was a reluctance to touch on deeper reforms, in the first case because there was no disposition to look further than regulatory fiscal mechanisms, and, in the second, because the emphasis was placed on the effect of a redistribution of wealth rather than on the problem of its production.[9] The remedies that underpinned the idea of a positive coalition against the spread of fascism expressed, therefore, the assumption that limited counter-cyclical policies were both tactically necessary and of greater utility in this battle than more fundamental prescriptions. Most important was the desire to sustain a consensus round an ameliorative vision committed to bringing about conditions of greater social justice.

It was precisely on this point that the junction between pre- and postwar could be made. The use of a parliamentary majority together with the incorporation of the power of the trade unions became seen as the means to avoid rocking an already fragile situation: to control capitalism and, ultimately, revitalise it. The process was encouraged by the fact that the war itself had created throughout Western Europe what has been called 'the social democratic consensus', i.e. the desire for widespread and immediate social reform with, in particular, demands for change in the areas of education, housing, health care, social security and employment—in short, an agreement that centred on the wish for a redistributive welfarism.[10] Such a consensus now provided exactly the social and political base that had been lacking in the 1930s, and whose absence had fatally undermined the defence against fascism. On this new base the way was open to complete unfinished business and it took much the same shape across Western Europe: a commitment to the idea of the mixed economy; an active and interventionist state willing to extend the boundaries of public ownership; the encouragement of a free and vigorous trade union movement; the use of the instrument of planning and forecasting; and, lastly, the achievement of social peace by means of tripartite summit organisations. All of this structure of neo-corporatism, by which recovery and growth were sustained in the first two or more decades of the peace, could be said to be following the lines first laid down in the 1930s and refined during the test of the war.[11]

The assertion of a normative line of descent from the 1930s to the postwar period created, however, its victims and cut off from proper evaluation a large part of the history of ideas that had typified the prewar period. In particular, the requirements of the postwar settlement made it difficult to assess the full weight of the European-wide response to fascism that had actually occurred. The limitations of the channels of postwar reconstructionist thinking to those that rested on defining the continuity of a social democratic tradition played down the fact that there had existed another relationship. This was between fascism and those who, although outside any embryonic Popular Front coalition and explicitly anti-Marxist, had still regarded themselves as its opponents. It is to the delineation of the contours of this other, hidden, dialogue that it is again time to turn.

In contrast to the remedies to the economic crisis, sketched above, there emerged in the early and mid-1930s an increasingly distinct position which, distanced from the mainstream of socialist parties and, most especially, from the positions taken by the Comintern, believed that structural reforms were the absolutely necessary condition for successfully tackling the crisis. To this way of thinking economic depression and fascism were related expressions of a deeper crisis in western societies and of their inability, as presently constituted, to mount effective counter-measures. The origins of those people who made such an analysis were extremely diverse. Cultural pessimists rubbed shoulders with anti-materialists who focused on the enslavement of the individual in developed capitalism, and anti-liberals who deplored the waning of communal bonds in the modern liberal state. However, within and at the heart of this diversity where the crank and the marginal were well represented was a solid and respectable core. This had three common points of reference: first, a clear anti-capitalism in so far as capitalism was no longer regarded as a creative force behind social or economic organisation; second, a firm anti-statism; last, and most determinant, an anti-Marxism expressed as often as not in terms of anti-communism or anti-collectivism.[12]

The period of the early 1930s proved to be a watershed in creating a cohesiveness among these convictions which, though powerfully held hitherto, had lacked coordinated force. It should be remembered that it was not only the new fascist states and movements that drew the attention of those who sought remedies for the European crisis. The Soviet state in its influence over the European labour movement since 1919 through the Third International had always held out a clear alternative to the fumbling attempts after Versailles to re-establish a bourgeois Europe. Now the Soviet drive to the collectivisation of agriculture and the accompanying Five-Year Plan offered the largest contrast and challenge yet to market capitalism and the ineffectual policies of the liberal democracies after the crash of 1929. By 1933 the Soviets, on the basis of a renewed and powerful state, could at last substantiate their claim to have a better and, as it appeared, successful form of economic and social organisation. Such a claim, spurious as it now seems, served only to deepen the division within European socialism that had been forced by the isolation of the Russian Revolution from the mainstream of western thought. For the resurgence of Soviet Russia hit at the very weakest spot in the armour of western social democracy: its inability after four years of mounting unemployment to provide its supporters with convincing remedies of its own. But, at the same time, if Soviet success was hard to gainsay, the ethos of the Plan with its forced mass movement of populations and its model of new Stakhanovite labour confirmed a view that if this was the price for the replacement of capitalism it was not worth paying. The emerging Stalinist dictatorship and progress by means of the intensification of the class struggle—a Third Revolution—with all its attendant miseries, drove many to conclude that socialism, at least in its dominant Marxist–Leninist form, had reached its logical dead-end.

In fact such sentiments found a powerful support and cohesive force in the revisionist analysis that had been made even before the economic downswing by the Belgian socialist and future leader of the Belgian Socialist Party, Hendrik de Man. In his book *Zur Psychologie des Sozialismus (On the Psychology of Socialism)* published in 1926 and, revealingly perhaps, translated into French under the title *Au-delà du Marxisme (Beyond Marxism)*, de Man had argued the need to recognise the determinist idea of the class struggle as the impediment it was and, instead, to proceed to a voluntarist stance that put 'man himself, as a spiritual individuality at the centre of a new doctrine'.[13] This revision he continued a year later in *Der Kampf um die Arbeitsfreude* (*The Fight for Joy in Work*) and in articles and lectures that proposed a socialism which would depend on and recognise a new state of will transcending the collective egoism of a given class.[14] To those people who, as the Depression worsened, feared the increasing confidence of a Soviet system ruthlessly developing its own state power under the cover of furthering the historic interests of one class, yet who also understood the urgent necessity of tackling the crisis, de Man became through his writings an increasingly central figure and one whose influence extended beyond Socialist Party circles.[15]

The common thread of anti-Marxism, applied especially to Soviet Russia, although deep, did not in itself offer a sufficient impetus to create a comprehensive programme of action. The starting point for this was provided by an analysis of the relation between fascism and communism and, in particular, of fascism's debt to a resurgent Soviet state. If there was a new spirit that emerged in Europe in the years 1933–4 that was anti-Marxist it rested equally on the conviction that the crisis in western society was both the cause of, and was deepened by, the appeal of the mass movements which claimed to be able to master it and were prepared to back that claim by the use of state power and the marshalling of the energies of the nation. In part this view took the form of recognising that fascism fed on the fear of Red revolution. More subtly, there was a fear which affected a wide social spectrum that the means to hand for western states to combat the economic crisis would themselves create the conditions of collectivism. Fascism, in that case, would attract people as much because of the anti-crisis prescriptions that its own presence encouraged as because of the direct threat of Communism in the shape of the organised working-class movement.

An important component of this analysis was an acknowledgement of fascism's own transformational energy toward society. It was not enough to regard the growth of these movements simply as the defensive posture of a desperate capitalism. Rather, so the analysis went, they too sought to widen and utilise for their own radical ends the contradictions that the crisis had brought into being. In particular, this could be seen in the link that fascism forged between those parts of the working class and of the middle class most affected by the Depression in a type of anti-capitalist coalition. This unpalatable perspective was clearly put by de Man to the special Congress of the Belgian Socialist Party held at Christmas 1933, and whose considerable wider significance will be addressed at length below. In de Man's conception the real division that fascism exploited was between the unemployed — including those who felt threatened with the loss of their livelihood — from whatever class or social grouping they came and those in work. From within the working class itself, argued de Man, there had formed a new 'fifth' social *stand* composed of those 'who have no hope ever of finding work again'. It was they who, in Germany, had moved away from a Social Democratic Party which they regarded as concerned with protecting the interests of those still in work, and who had drifted subsequently, sometimes by way of Communism, into the trap of fascist nationalism.[16] There they joined others more obviously attracted as a consequence of their own sense of powerlessness by the fascist promise to crush the restrictive and alien power of socialism. Fascism, therefore, so far from merely countering the crisis of the old regime was engaged at root in building a new coalition across classes—a coalition itself encouraged by the fact of unemployment and social dislocation and bound together by the twin attractions of nationalist and totalitarian prescriptions.

It seemed clear to those who thought along similar lines to de Man that fascism's creative exploitation of the deficiencies of liberal capitalism together with the unattractiveness of the Communist alternative required the response of a quite different defensive strategy from that hitherto supposed. The idea that fascism in itself formed and was sustained by a new energy that the traditional political parties and allegiances—especially within old-fashioned social democracy—repressed led to the conclusion that the challenge had to consist of more than either a recourse to palliative measures or to a purely negative and defensive critique. Anti-fascism together with anti-communism and anti-liberalism may have faithfully represented the starting position for a correct analysis of the crisis but they were hardly rallying cries for positive and ever more urgent action.[17] The attraction which fascism continued to exert could only be counterbalanced by the formation of an equally powerful rallying round a broadly based coalition with its own shaping theme. But if such a *rassemblement* were to transcend, as it would have to, the limited aims of protecting the position and allegiance of the working class and move towards the equal association within it of other groups in society, there were of course dangers: first, that its ideological and intellectual cohesion would be lost, in some awful parody of fascism, in pure action or pure relativism; second, that the 'accentuation of the positive' that would be needed to form the basis of a new spirit of defence was also at the heart of both fascist and Soviet strategies of mass mobilisation. The *élan* necessary to create and maintain the effort to neutralise fascism was, then, likely to lead straight to the type of solution proffered by its supposed opponent.

These preoccupations naturally troubled those socialists who saw their historic ideal of a movement bleeding to death in Germany but who realised to their despair that their own parties could find little by way of compensatory strategy to offer other Western European societies. To them the path taken by socialism in Italy and Germany, historically justified but practically disastrous, seemed destined to be repeated everywhere. So, too, among revisionist socialist groups or outside the socialist movement among those who were beginning to develop the idea that fascism would only be halted by realising a new social and political consensus there was a growing sense that there was no obvious mobilising theme to aid this construction. 'More than anyone we have a taste for the concrete, a horror of debates that are academic and ineffectual,' concluded the manifesto in 1932 of the group *Révolution Constructive* who wished to prepare a new spirit and a new activism that would fight fascism by attacking the operational structure of capitalism. 'But, in reality, how is one to act if one is not able to think, and how to think without the lightning conductor of ideology?'[18] In much the same way those who were starting to argue in favour of a 'third way' that would combine and draw on the strengths of socialist community and capitalist organisation as a new binding principle found it hard to see how this could be made to penetrate and convince a broad enough cross-section of the population.[19]

To all these tendencies de Man acted as a catalyst, as much by a provocative revisionism as by his practical proposals. With respect to the former he put forward three general ideas as to how a real cooperation across classes could be achieved and, thereby, turn the main weapon of fascism against itself. Firstly, his emphasis on voluntarism itself held pluralist implications. Second, there was what proved subsequently to be a contentious and divisive focus on the nation. De Man's analysis of fascism as a movement which united various strands of anti-capitalism also recognised that it did so by using the potential counter-force of the nation. What was true as a critique of fascism's recruiting power was, in his mind, also true of the most effective defence against it. De Man had long argued that the working class needed to 'learn their mother tongue' before they could 'speak a universal language'.[20] To this notion, as the threat of Nazism in particular grew, was added the idea that even if the deep causes of the Depression and the means of its eventual solution were supra-national, the perception of its effects and, most of all, the terrain on which it would first be checked were rooted at the national level. Those who were squeezed in the direction of fascism by unemployment or fear were victims less of a generalised 'capitalism' than of a failure to control its operation—specifically the monopoly power of finance—in their own society. Farmers, civil servants, middle managers, employees and rentiers were, in this respect, no better off and no less threatened than the industrial working class.[21] In this case the nation did, and could, elsewhere provide the resources of a community of action against the crisis. But for this to be realised socialists would need to change their concept of the state. Lastly, then, and most critical in tapping the root of an anti-Marxist coalition, de Man's third contribution was a view of the state as quite different from an instrument of class domination. Rather, it was a 'sociological structure with a separate existence of its own', an 'alien power' to be identified neither with the rule of the proletariat as a class (as supposedly in Russia or, in aspiration in German socialism) nor with that of the capitalist class (as in Marxist sociology), but able and prepared to intervene in the extended area of moral and political relationships.[22]

These three interrelated revisions established the path for the first practical anti-crisis strategy for which de Man was to lobby tirelessly.[23] Once the capture of state power in the name of the proletariat was regarded as unnecessary—and in some senses counter-productive—the way was open for the incorporation of those other groups threatened by the Depression and as equally hostile to capitalism as alienated from the idea of Soviet collectivism, and for them to unite in a common effort. What de Man's theories offered was an alliance between historic social democracy with its experience of solidarity and its commitment to social justice, but shorn of the authoritarian consequences of its class analysis, with the energy and creativity—as already demonstrated by the use to which the Nazis had turned the raw force of discontent—of a majority in the nation. More than a consensus, there would come into being a true social majority. By 1933, therefore, what was lacking to start the offensive against the success of fascism was not a potential will, nor the theme of a counter new order, rather a mechanism to bring it to reality.

Once more de Man provided the way forward in the shape of a 'Plan'. If de Man has here received lengthy attention as the major figure defining and facilitating a new spirit in the early 1930s, it is for the reason that the idea of mobilising the fight against depression and its consequences by means of a Plan was, for a time, at the very centre of the European stage. Commissioned at the end of 1931 to return from Frankfurt to Belgium and write an anti-crisis strategy for the Belgian Socialist Party, de Man produced a synthesis of his revisionist thinking which he placed before the Party in 1933 as the *Plan van de Arbeid* (Labour Plan).[24] This document, in favour of which the special Congress convened at Christmas 1933 voted nearly unanimously, consisted of a mere eight pages with seven indicative headings that set out the general principles that informed the Plan and the areas of immediate action, such as the nationalisation of credit and the establishment of an Economic Council, which the Plan would realise.[25] The full exegesis of these indications in detailed chapters took until 1935 and will not be discussed here.[26] It is in the difference between these two stages that de Man's broader influence lay.

In one respect the Plan that de Man proposed was a purely Belgian affair directed to specific problems of the Belgian economy in depression and motivated by the desire of the Party to take positive measures in a new front with other groups in Belgian society, most notably the Catholics. But the choice of de Man as its progenitor was no accident. At another level the Plan was the statement of its own general philosophy; a philosophy which became known, encouraged by de Man, as *planisme*. Thus, in his long and enthusiastically heard speech to the Congress, de Man, while insisting on sober conviction and assiduous attention to the technical detail of what he was laying before the meeting, also made it plain that these belonged to the second stage of its realisation as a whole. Before the detail there needed to come a 'mobilisation and military action plan'. If the achievement of the Plan would be to free the country from the crisis by such means as would prevent new and recurrent crises from emerging, these demanded the prior coming together of belief and will in defining the mechanisms to achieve their goal. The proposal before the Congress, stated de Man, was not a programme which registered finite and limited intentions. It was 'the exact expression of a definite will', a dynamic entity in as much as from the point of view of its own prescriptions—i.e. of its precise indications of the detail of new legislation—'the Plan is nothing, the action for the Plan is everything'.[27] The end purpose of seeking to halt the conditions which were tending to the triumph of fascism remained the controlling factor of the Plan at two levels: conviction and practical activity. Indeed, de Man's careful statement of the necessary interdependence of the two stages of the Plan, in his opinion, made his proposals quite different from simply developing Bernstein's Revisionist position that the movement was everything. Nonetheless, *planisme*, or 'anti-crisis socialism' as he was himself to define it almost exactly a year later, in the *élan* that it required to come into being did lean heavily on voluntarism and belief.[28] The Plan was, as its final version demonstrated, a coherent series of economic and social strategies to combat the conjunctural crisis; much more it was, and was so conceived, a crusade.[29]

De Man certainly hoped to launch a new form of action. Even so it is striking that from his initiative there followed across Europe what can only be termed an explosion of 'plan-mania' that paid tribute in varying degrees to the content of the Belgian proposals but was largely faithful to the spirit. Within the next year Dutch socialists established a Study Commission to prepare their own *Plan van de Arbeid* which borrowed heavily and publicly from de Man and eventually became the major electoral strategy of a party anxious to form a coalition across the classes, and pillars, of Dutch society. In France there emerged no fewer than ten Plans representing almost the whole political spectrum and of whose number, one, in the form of the Plan of 9 July 1934, was itself a coalition of politically diverse forces. Similarly in Britain, an existing movement of the centre-right, Political and Economic Planning (PEP), founded originally in 1931 to explore the possibility of a national plan to combat the economic crisis, turned in 1934 to the advocacy—in terms extraordinarily close to de Man's—of a Plan that would seize the initiative from fascism and communism and create a harmony of forces in the nation moving 'organically' towards a dynamic equilibrium.[30] To this must be added a British Plan from the Left; a Polish Plan, and Plans, to one degree or another, put into practice in Switzerland and Czechoslovakia completed the bandwagon.[31]

It would be wrong to attribute the plan phenomenon entirely to de Man or to an imitation of his recommendations to the Belgian Congress. There is no doubt that he had been extensively read, particularly among the young. But in many countries there had been considerble discussion of planning before 1933. In both Holland and France the Left, and renegades from it, had, since the beginning of the decade, engaged in a substantial critique of socialist economics and had especially explored corporatist directions. These questionings had also involved Catholic circles. The year 1934 saw the issue, as the end product of a large debate, of the Papal Encyclical *Quadragesimo Anno* which also pointed in a corporatist direction as necessary to combat the crisis. It had been the desire to form a political alliance with the Catholic Party that had, after all, first motivated the Belgian socialists to encourage de Man's Plan. It would be equally wrong to overstate the extent of the breakthrough of the phenomenon into government policy and the thinking in official circles. With few exceptions the pressure to introduce and act upon a Plan was resisted and kept within left and progressive strata. Even in Belgium, de Man's eventual entry into government led, in the opinion of many, to the abandonment of his own Plan.

Yet it is hard to ignore the evidence that for a brief period of about two years the idea of a Plan and of planning was more than simply in vogue. Between 1934 and 1936 it offered an often central reference point to those outside government in the search for a counter-crisis strategy; it also put on the political agenda the conditions for the elimination of unemployment and a return to stable conditions of production and exchange. Moreover, it did so with a great degree of conformity across national boundaries and political systems. While it is true that the Plans that were published inevitably varied in detail, and to some degree in balance—largely in their acknowledgement or otherwise of the extent of corporatist intermediary institutions—their shared characteristics were far greater than the differences between them.[32] All, naturally, posited the attack on unemployment as the first and major objective to which the state, committed to the Plan, would direct its energies. All, too, encouraged some form of mixed economy in which there would be a 'planned' and a 'free' sector; control of banking and credit as fundamental and a regular economic budget facilitated by an inbuilt forecasting mechanism, together with some form of Economic Council or Parliament, completed the common technical ensemble of measures by which the Plans defined themselves.

These precise and often exhaustively worked-out common proposals are, it is important to stress, an indication that plan-mania was in no sense a shallow and emotionally based reaction to a worsening crisis. The Plans were in general detailed and serious. But beyond the conformity of technical agreement, which in any case may have reflected a truism that all Plans must resemble each other, lay a distinctive conformity in the dimension of their *modus operandi*. Firstly, the Plans looked, just as de Man had argued to his Belgian colleagues, towards forming a new constituency which was at one and the same time created by the idea and the essential basis of its effectiveness. The nation was seen as becoming a community involved by, as well as in, the Plan. Second, all the Plans sought to define their operation within a context of political freedom. The direction or nationalisation of key areas of the economy was to be achieved—and this was the very reason why the Plan was thought to be necessary in the first place—without substituting an authoritarian regime for one that, with all its shortcomings, rested on an idea and practice of democracy. It was these two principles taken together that distinguished Plans from anything that had been proposed before. In addition, they distanced the idea of the Plan as it crystallised in the mid-1930s not just from fascist and communist prescriptions for the crisis but, equally, from the rigid failure of the class-based answer of the socialists. Indeed, the very diversity of the provenance of those Plans that appeared subsequent to de Man's exemplifies this point. What was created in this period was a belief in the necessity of a belief that would be tempered by a realistic and technically precise outward form. If, as indicated earlier, de Man offered a new solution to the stalemate in the debate between reformists who had no credible reforms and revolutionaries without a revolution,[33] so too it was his concept of the Plan as an activity that drew on a broad current of passionately felt goodwill that allowed his influence to be received so much more widely than the confines and preoccupations of his original audience.[34]

The Plan phenomenon should, then, be recognised as a singular one in the recent European past. Yet the question as to why the idea of a Plan as a rallying agent should have proved so cogent among intellectuals that it was, even if for a brief period, to be found on a European-wide scale is a legitimate one. One answer must look to an explanation at the level of political events. The political conjunction from the end of 1933 and, most especially, during the whole of 1934 provided what many at the time took as definitive evidence that the fundamental challenge to the European system from fascism and communism had reached the point of decisive breakthrough. In this year Hitler began to consolidate a Nazi regime and revealed his determination to destroy the basis of the postwar settlement by removing Germany from the League. In France the forces opposed to the Third Republic, checked in February in a desire to overthrow what they regarded as a corrupt parliamentary regime, seemed poised to pursue a successful counter-revolution. Léon Degrelle in Belgium, Antoon Mussert in The Netherlands, as well as Oswald Mosley in Britain, headed anti-system movements which began to make considerable inroads into the structure of existing political allegiance. The list is a long one and could be extended. It is not hard, therefore, to argue that Europeans at this time were afraid and that the Plan was, somehow, the expression both of that fear and of a determination to overcome it. Plans were gauges of order, stability and predictability amidst fear, arbitrariness and violence.

This explanation should not be played down, although, as will be the contention below, it underestimates if not misreads the fundamental and undeniable change of political climate in these years. The sense was growing after 1933 that unless some initiative to control the economy was undertaken by the democracies, then others, less concerned with liberty and more authoritarian, would do so instead. In fact in one of the first scholarly analyses of the phenomenon published in October 1934, and still the most comprehensive survey, the author Henri Noyelle was largely sympathetic to the idea that expectations that arose from political uncertainty were what motivated much of the urgency on which the Plans fed. He identified in this context a current that ran through all the Plans of that year which he saw expressed as the desire for a confident and immediately realisable direction of the economy that would balance the claims of authority and freedom. The Plans, he concluded, were firmly located in a response that, in part, made them seem to be 'political programmes inspired by popular impatience in the face of the crisis'.[35] Yet, although acknowledging this desire for order behind the Plans, Noyelle also sensed something darker. His reaction is worth citing in full:

> And if one looks back to the origins of this planning movement, of this fashion, what does one see? *At one and the same time* fascism and antifascism. Plans are everywhere. But behind these Plans which vary more in their doctrines than in the means to carry them out, there is a political preoccupation, certainly legitimate and legitimate in itself, but yet too predominant for the economic base not to suffer: the economic crisis, the moral crisis, the political crisis—whatever order of 'causality' one might wish to assign between them—together signify want, suffering, rebellion, restlessness, disorder, longing for reforms, the will to recovery whatever the cost, demands, threats. Something must be done.[36]

What is recognised by this contemporary account is that Plans went beyond simply reacting to a generally perceived fear of fascism, or limiting themselves to proposing a series of coordinated adjustments to the way the economy functioned by means of particular mechanisms of control. It is true that the language in which the Plans were written, as well as the measures they outlined, had a certain precision. Indeed, it has already been noted that all the Plans had a broad similarity of shape in terms of the mechanisms they envisaged in their operation. But the precision was, as Noyelle's commentary picked up, in large part an illusory or, at best, a dependent condition. As Jacques Branger put it, somewhat cynically perhaps, to a conference on *planisme* held in Paris in early 1935: 'Today *planisme* is a fact. It even preoccupies economists.'[37] De Man had made much the same point to the Belgian Congress when he separated the preparatory action for the Plan, the will for it to work, from its detailed provisions. This line was followed by his first 'disciples' in France in *Révolution Constructive*, who wrote of 'renewing the atmosphere' as the starting point for winning the battle to eliminate the context in which fascism was permitted to thrive.[38] For these activists Plans called on emotions more than technical solutions.[39] The force of the fear that had created the space for planning was the same as that which would make its precise recommendations work. In the end, fascism and those who placed the concept of the Plan against it inhabited, albeit for different purposes and with different motivations, the same terrain of political, ideological and social despair and the same conviction of the need to build a New Order rather than reordering what was already there.

The effect of such an analysis ought to make us wary of regarding the plan phenomenon as essentially a strategy for achieving a disguised stasis, a way of protecting, more or less, the established order. Plans were subversive in that if they were to achieve their purpose they would have to create a climate in which the crisis was seen as structural not cyclical.[40] They could operate only by disturbing the political and social status quo. The commitment to planning, whether or not it followed closely de Man's Belgian model, demanded, as we have seen, the broadest possible mobilisation to operate. This was conceived, however, otherwise than in numerical terms. Thus, the Dutch *Plan van de Arbeid*, which saw itself as closely indebted to de Man, felt it necessary to stress in the introductory statement of its general principles that its realisation would require not just a government convinced of the Plan and prepared to put it into practice but a population actually 'pervaded' by Plan-thinking.[41] Noyelle, again with de Man in mind, concluded his long review with the assertion that the carrying through of a Plan needed 'a mystique, an *élan*, a faith, a credo' if it was to fulfil itself.[42] This sentiment was echoed by Alexandre Marc, of the youthful French movement *Ordre Nouveau*, when he laid down the first condition of any plan as being an 'attitude',[43] and repeated later in the *Bulletin* of the very different, techno-cratically minded group, *X-Crise* for whom, as late as spring 1935, the essence of a Plan was seen as relying on enthusiasm and moral *élan* from across a wide range of individuals of 'goodwill'; the Plan required, indeed, 'almost a heroic attitude'.[44] In Britain, too, which in general has not been included in an assessment of the phenomenon, Harold Macmillan, working his path in 1934 to what he was to call 'The Middle Way', stipulated that the acceptance of the idea of planning that he advocated as essential for reconstruction had to be at once radical and popular, appealing of necessity to a broad section of public opinion.[45] These sentiments were extended in what might be regarded as the first fully worked-out British Plan, *The Next Five Years* which Macmillan, together with over two hundred signatories distinguished in public life, collectively put out in July 1935. Here too, as well as the call for collaboration across the political spectrum and the acceptance of a mixed economy, was set out the primary need for enthusiasm and release of energy in the service of rallying the nation.[46]

There is always a danger in finding—especially fifty years after their first publication—false points of contact and congruity between texts and statements that came from very different political milieux. The problem is compounded if national boundaries are also crossed. Yet from the perspectives cited above it does seem that a distinct spirit that found similar forms of expression can be properly identified across Western Europe. In many parts it became known as *planisme*. It might equally well be called '1934ism'. For to locate it so precisely in time is to recognise the forces of its parentage and its relatively short duration as a focal point of a response to unemployment, fascism and the dangers of war. The current emanated from the Left or, more precisely, was led by the sense of crisis and impotence within a socialist movement faced with the real power of Nazism and unconvinced of the Soviet response. But if that was its starting point, its development broadened to seek the involvement of the middle classes and, most particularly, intellectuals and specialists, to the extent that during the two years in which the Plan was put forward as offering a permanent way out of crisis it is not easy to put it under any other label than progressive.

Is the phenomenon, however, of any more than marginal importance in the history of contemporary Europe? In part, the later recourse to a brief and unsuccessful popular frontism, the failure of the policy of collective security, and in general the collapse of social democracy before 1939, all would suggest that the answer should be no. In addition there is the accusation that *planisme* had a negative influence. This is reflected in the fact that many—though by no means a majority of its advocates—drifted in 1940 and 1941 towards the orbit of a different New Order, but one that also purported to want to mobilise the resources of Europe to create a prosperous society in which sterile class conflict was superseded. In short, de Man and Déat (the two leaders of European socialist thinking in the 1930s, as Vandervelde had identified them) moved to accommodate with fascism because that was always implicit in the nature of their doctrine as it centred round the Plan.[47]

This judgement addresses the heart of the problem as to what *planisme* was or was not. The need to create a mystique of belief, the mobilisation of a coalition to unblock the structural causes of the general crisis could not easily, if at all, given the existence of fascism, be contained within the boundaries of traditional liberties and democratic forms. Dissatisfaction with the working—more accurately, the failure to function adequately—of parliaments was widespread and gave rise in much of Europe to the seductive notion that they represented an 'established disorder' which it was proper to attack.[48] *Planisme*, however, went both less far and more deep. de Man himself, in the 'Theses' which he presented at the Abbey of Pontigny in September 1934 and which form the clearest statement of what he regarded as the essential of his thinking, took great pains to locate his action for the Plan in the legal and constitutional matrices of the democratic state.[49] But he also stipulated that the very processes of the Plan, once it was engaged upon, by creating what he termed the 'economic state' would force a change in the classical doctrine of bourgeois democracy. The present forms of liberal democracy, he suggested, no longer would correspond to the tasks laid down by the Plan. In practice for de Man this came down to the recommendation that the executive would need strengthening and that representative institutions based on individual suffrage would take on more the role of scrutiny.[50] Such ideas of reform were as much the consequence of the corporatist elements—especially the problem of defining the function and powers of an economic council—that lay within all planning solutions, and which exercised a more powerful fascination than is often realised over a cross-section of opinion in the 1930s. For *planistes*, too, in line with de Man's thinking, it was more the corporatist implications of the Plan than an antipathy for parliament as such that encouraged the re-examination of the liberal state. The drift to corporatism should not, then, be taken by itself as indicative of a synchronous drift to fascism. In France corporatism became the universal concomitant of advocacy of a Plan. More surprisingly in Holland, where Catholics already had a long experience of initiating corporatist legislation, the Socialist Party, as it moved to adopt *planisme*, also happily accepted corporatist limitations on the traditional sphere of parliamentary competence.[51] Even more unexpectedly, at any rate in terms of later historiography, the British *rassemblement* gathered in *The Next Five Years* initiative in its turn put forward a corporatist case for the 'refashioning' of the democratic system. If, as the group's manifesto made clear in its introduction, there was no intention of undermining the central place of parliament based on the principle of universal suffrage, it was nonetheless accepted that parliament could not meet the needs that the system of planning would place on it. In thoughts strikingly close to de Man's, the relation that planning imposed between the elected chamber and a kind of economic parliament was resolved only with a substantial loss of day-to-day power by the former.[52]

If 'informed men of moderate opinion',[53] as the British group saw themselves, were at least thinking along similar lines to French syndicalists and revisionist socialists, then the context in which this could happen does need to be noticed. *Planisme* for a time engaged a far wider constituency than has been supposed. Its ambiguity toward the automatic defence of values and forms which fascism was attacking expressed both the nature of its origins and its weakness in the deteriorating Europe of the late 1930s. But its contributions need also to be rediscovered. The analysis of fascism on which it was premised, the role it found for intellectuals as well as for a wider middle class within a mass society, and its emphasis on social cohesion as the base for constructing a more humane society, all had a positive value. More than all these, perhaps, its insistence that the crisis was deeper than many wished to believe, or certainly act upon, and that it must, therefore, be tackled if Europe was not to be submerged by extremism, led it to ask hard questions about social and political organisation. That it did not always give acceptable—or sometimes sensible—answers does not mean that its proposals were always without value, to later generations.

Notes

1. S.J.G. Hoare (1st Viscount Templewood), *Nine Troubled Years* (London, Collins, 1954); E.H. Carr, *The Twenty Years Crisis* (London, Macmillan, 1939).
2. *The Times*, 23 January 1943, cit. in H.W. Arndt, *The Economic Lessons of the Nineteen-Thirties* (2nd edn., London, Cass, 1963), p. 250.
3. F. Bédarida in D. Peschanski (ed.), *Vichy 1940–1944: Quaderni e documenti inediti di Angelo Tasca* (Milano, Feltrinelli, 1986), p. XIII; M. Sadoun, 'Les contraintes de la position', in Peschanski (ed.), *Vichy*, p. 63.
4. The contrary position is taken in relation to France by Z. Sternhell, most especially in Z. Sternhell, *Ni droite, ni gauche: L'idéologie fasciste en France* (Paris, Seuil, 1983), and the same author's 'Emmanuel Mounier et la contestation de la démocratie libérale dans la France des années trente', *Revue Française de Science Politique*, Vol. 6, (1984), pp. 1141–80. But see, in a debate which has great relevance outside the confines of French history, the critique by J. Julliard, 'Sur un fascisme imaginaire', *Annales*, Vol. 4 (1984), pp. 849–61.
5. D.M. Pickles, 'Intellectual Ferment in France', *Politica*, Vol. 2 (1936), p. 58.
6. J.-L. Loubet del Bayle, *Les non-conformistes des années 30. Une tentative de renouvellement de la pensée politique française* (Paris, Seuil, 1969).
7. G. Lefranc, P. Boivin and M. Deixonne, *Révolution constructive* (Paris, Valois, 1932).
8. R. Aron and A. Dandieu, *La Révolution nécessaire* (Paris, Grasset, 1933), p. 269. So far the 'non-conformists' have received the greatest attention in France—

perhaps because there were so many groups there in the 1930s. Less has been written regarding the Low Countries, but see A.A. de Jonge, *Crisis en critiek der democratie: Anti-democratische stromingen en de daarin levende denkbeelden over de staat in Nederland tussen de wereldoorlogen* (Assen, van Gorcum, 1968); P.W. Klein and G.J. Borger (eds), *De jaren dertig: Aspecten van crisis en werkloosheid* (Amsterdam, Meulenhoff, 1979); E. Gerard, *De Katholieke Partij in crisis: Partijpolitiek leven in België (1918–40)* (Leuven, Kritak, 1985).

9.   For a clear statement of this policy, see J.-M. Jeanneney, 'La politique économique de Léon Blum', in P. Renouvin and R. Rémond (eds), *Léon Blum: Chef de gouvernement* (Paris, FNSP, 1969), pp. 207–32.

10. J. Tomlinson, *Employment Policy: The Crucial Years, 1939–1955* (Oxford, Clarendon, 1987), p. 46.

11. P. Addison, *The Road to 1945: British Politics and the Second World War*, (London, Cape, 1975); R.F. Kuisel, *Capitalism and the State in Modern France: Renovation and Economic Management in the Twentieth Century*, (Cambridge, Cambridge University Press, 1981); P.W. Klein, 'Wegen naar economisch herstel 1945–59', *Bijdragen en Mededelingen betreffende de geschiedenis der Nederlanden*, Vol. 96 (1981).

12. J. Touchard, 'L'esprit des années 1930', in G. Michaud (ed.), *Tendances politiques dans la vie française depuis 1789* (Paris, Hachette, 1960), pp. 89–118.

13. H. de Man, *The Psychology of Socialism* (London, Allen and Unwin, 1928), p. 452.

14. See H. de Man, 'La crise due socialisme' in P. Dodge (ed.), *Hendrik de Man, Socialist Critic of Marxism* (Princeton, Princeton University Press, 1979), pp. 158–79.

15. The most extensive discussion of the spread of de Man's ideas in the Europe of the late 1920s and early 1930s is to be found in the Special Number of the *Cahiers Vilfredo Pareto, Revue européenne des sciences sociales*, Vol. XII, No. 31 (1974). Of particular relevance to this study: H. Brugmans, 'Henri de Man et les Pays-Bas', ibid., pp. 142–9; A.G. Slama, 'Henri de Man et les néo-traditionalistes français (1933–1936)', ibid., pp. 169–88; G. Lefranc, 'Les conférences internationales des Plans', ibid., pp. 189–96; and G. Lefranc, 'La diffusion des idées planistes en France', ibid., pp. 152–66.

16. Belgische Werkliedenpartij, Algemene Raad, *XXXXVIIIste Congres: Brussel, 24 en 25 December 1933. Stenographisch Verslag* (Brussel, De Wilde Roos, 1934), pp. 22–3.

17. *Ordre Nouveau*, Vol. 21 (May 1935), p. 1.

18. G. Lefranc, *Révolution constructive*, op. cit., p. 253.

19. M. Bouvier, *L'Etat sans politique: Tradition et modernité* (Paris, Librairie Générale de Droit et de Jurisprudence, 1986), pp. 75–6. See also de Man's statement that 'Socialism must contribute towards the realisation of some of the aims of *capitalism as a method of production*, while continuing to fight *capitalism as a form of social domination*', H. de Man, *Psychology*, op. cit., p. 301 (italics in the original).

20. de Man, *Psychology*, op. cit., pp. 313–9.

21. See the article which he wrote in 1932, 'Het nieuwe Duitse Nationaal-

Socialisme', in H. Balthazar (ed.), *Hendrik de Man. Persoon en ideeën*, Vol. 5, *Een halve eeuw doctrine. Verspreide geschriften* (Antwerp, Standaard, 1976), pp. 253–65.

22. de Man, *Psychology*, op. cit., pp. 197–9.
23. See de Man's restatement of the themes to a seminar held in Paris at the Institut Supérieur Ouvrier on 12 July 1934, G. Lefranc, 'La diffusion des idées planistes', *Cahiers Vilfredo Pareto* (1974), p. 163.
24. The origins of the Belgian Socialist Party's move toward the Plan are covered in E. Hansen, 'Hendrik de Man and the theoretical foundations of economic planning: the Belgian experience, 1933–40', *European Studies Review*, Vol. 2 (1978), pp. 234–57; a detailed description of the content of the full Plan in E. Hansen, 'Depression decade crisis: social democracy and planisme in Belgium and the Netherlands, 1929–39', *Journal of Contemporary History*, Vol. 16 (1981), pp. 293–322.
25. *Congres*, pp. 161–8.
26. H. de Man, *De uitvoering van het Plan van de Arbeid* in P. Frantzen (ed.), *Hendrik de Man: Persoon en ideeën*, Vol. 4, *Planisme* (Antwerp, Standaard, 1975), pp. 73–300.
27. *Congres*, pp. 12–21.
28. H. de Man, *Socialisme en Planisme*, in *Persoon en ideeën*, op. cit., Vol. 4, p. 303.
29. This dynamic relationship was one which united de Man's views with the reformulation occurring at this time within French socialism around the controversial figure of Marcel Déat. At the congress, Vandervelde, the elder statesman of the Belgian Party specifically linked the two men as the 'stoutest heads of the new generation'. Déat himself who enthusiastically embraced *planisme*, always emphasised its psychological aspects, arguing, for instance, that the force of the movement lay in the necessary relation 'between the technical disposition of the Plan and the psychological conditions of its realisation', *Congres*, p. 47; Centre polytechnicien d'études, X-Crise, *Bulletin*, Vols 20–21 (March-April 1935), p. 17.
30. 'Political and economic planning', *Planning*, Vol. 35 (9 October 1934), pp. 6–12.
31. For 'plan-mania': *Cahiers Vilfredo Pareto*; Kuisel, *Capitalism*, op. cit., Ch. 4; J. Jackson, *The Politics of Depression in France* (Cambridge, Cambridge University Press, 1985), Ch. 7; H. Noyelle, 'Plans d'économie dirigée', *Revue d'Economie Politique* (October 1934), pp. 1595–1668.
32. Noyelle, 'Plans', op. cit., provides a very thorough survey of the content of the majority of Plans. To his list ought to be added some of the currents of thought in Britain identified by A. Marwick, 'Middle opinion in the thirties: planning, progress and political "agreement" ', *The English Historical Review*, Vol. CCCXI (1964), pp. 285–98. Marwick seems to be unaware of de Man or developments on the Continent.
33. Brugmans, 'Henri de Man et les Pays-Bas', *Cahiers Vilfredo Pareto*, p. 147.
34. It is this linkage that led some contemporaries as well as more recent critics to see in *planisme* the fatal agent that weakened socialism in the interwar period and left it open to fascist impregnation. See, especially, Sternhell, *Ni droite, ni gauche*, op. cit., pp. 211–31.

35. Noyelle, 'Plans', op. cit., pp. 1595–97, 1668.
36. ibid., p. 1667.
37. J. Branger, 'Le contenu économique des Plans' in X-Crise, *Bulletin*, Vols 20–21 (March-April 1935), p. 7.
38. G. Lefranc, *Révolution constructive*, op. cit., p. 227.
39. A point made by Kuisel, *Capitalism*, op. cit., p. 101.
40. de Man himself always stressed the revolutionary character of *planisme*. See, for instance, de Man, *Socialisme en planisme, Persoon en ideeën*, op. cit., Vol. 4, p. 317.
41. Sociaal-Democratische Arbeiders Partij, *Het Plan van de Arbeid* (Amsterdam, Arbeiderspers, 1935), p. 22.
42. Noyelle, 'Plans', op. cit., p. 1668.
43. A. Marc, 'Un destin? Ton destin', *Ordre Nouveau*, Vol. 11 (May 1934), p. 3.
44. X-Crise, *Bulletin*, Vols. 20–21 (March-April 1935), pp. 12–13.
45. H. Macmillan, *Reconstruction: A Plea for a National Policy* (London, Macmillan, 1934), pp. 6–7.
46. *The Next Five Years: An Essay in Political Agreement* (London, Macmillan, 1935), pp. 1–8. See also the unpubished constitution of the group, in Marwick, 'Middle opinion', op. cit., pp. 294–5.
47. *Congres*, p. 47.
48. Touchard, 'L'esprit', op. cit., pp. 97–9.
49. de Man, *De belangrijkste stellingen van het planisme*, in *Persoon en ideeën*, op. cit., Vol. 4, p. 315.
50. ibid., pp. 313–14.
51. See M.L. Smith, 'Some historical problems of corporatist development in the Netherlands', in A. Cox and N. O'Sullivan (eds), *The Corporate State* (London, Elgar, 1988), pp. 170–97.
52. *The Next Five Years*, op. cit., pp. 7–20.
53. ibid., p. 7.

10 The Crisis of Scandinavia and the Collapse of Interwar Ideals, 1938–1940

Anthony Upton

The situation in the Baltic area after 1918 was abnormal because the two dominant powers, Germany and Russia, were temporarily neutered and the area ceased to be of major concern in the international power struggle. This was ideal for the Scandinavian kingdoms, Denmark, Norway and Sweden, which, having nothing to fear from the great powers and, despite their own minor disputes, could assume there would be no armed conflict in the region. Their former policies of strict neutrality became redundant and were replaced by a cautious adherence to the League of Nations, including the obligations of Article XVI of the Covenant to uphold collective security. This Baltic status quo was wholly satisfactory, and if it were threatened they could call on the League to apply the principles of collective security to maintain it. The situation was disturbed only by the existence after 1918 of a new Baltic power, the independent republic of Finland. Finland had a recent history quite different from that of the three kingdoms, which had a tradition of peaceful constitutional development and avoidance of war. Finland had won independence after 1918 through a prolonged struggle with Russia and a violent civil war. This left her internal politics prone to extremist disruption from the illegal communist movement on one side, and authoritarian, nationalist radicalism on the other, while externally she had a hostile great power neighbour in the Soviet Union. Although Finland and the Soviet Union had made peace in 1920, their subsequent relations, though formally correct, could not conceal the mutual distrust and malevolence that prevailed between them, expressed in repeated, bad-tempered frontier incidents and mutual accusations of espionage and subversion. The existence of independent Finland disturbed an otherwise stable region, though it had the advantage that Finland stood as a buffer zone, keeping the Soviet Union at a distance from the three kingdoms. Sweden's military leaders appreciated this, and through the 1920s established close contacts with their Finnish counterparts and developed joint plans in case the Soviet Union attacked Finland. Then, under the League's collective security system, Sweden would move forces into Finland to repel the aggression. There were no corresponding political agreements, but government leaders in both countries knew of the contacts and did not disown them. A further possibility for resolving Finnish–Russian antagonism and securing against the danger that Finland align herself with the other neighbours of the Soviet Union, led by Poland, or with an anti-Soviet great power, would be to include Finland in a Nordic neutrality bloc with the three kingdoms, thus stabilising both her internal and external politics. Some thoughtful men in the Nordic countries were already thinking about this option in the 1920s.

These trends developed further in the 1930s. The Swedish government set up a Defence Commission in 1931, and the officer members, led by C.G. Ehrensvärd and A. Rappe, worked through it to produce the memorandum of 1935 which recommended that Sweden's armed forces be reorganised so they could act, under the League, to defend Sweden beyond her borders. Three areas were specified, joint action with Finland to repel Russian aggression, joint action with Norway and Finland to secure Lapland from external attack, and joint action with Denmark to defend the Danish islands from Germany. These ideas were incorporated into the official Swedish war plans, finalised in 1937. The political leadership, which had discussed the plans, did not endorse them, but did not repudiate them either. When C.G. Mannerheim became chairman of Finland's Defence Council in 1931 he used all his influence to persuade the country's leaders that Finland could only be defended from Soviet attack with the help of Sweden, and that to secure this Finland should declare publicly her willingness to adopt a Scandinavian orientation and adhere to a Nordic neutrality bloc. By 1934 the Prime Minister, T. Kivimäki, and the Foreign Minister, A. Hackzell, were persuaded and informal approaches were made to the Swedish Foreign Minister, R. Sandler. They focused on a possible joint defence of the Åland islands and a divergence of approach was revealed from the start. The Finns wanted Swedish support in a conflict with the Soviet Union which they saw as inevitable; the Swedes wanted to conciliate the Soviet Union, on the basis that a Finland committed to Scandinavian neutrality would become a good neighbour. The one country thought in terms of preparing for war, the other was seeking to avoid it. But a course had been set for both countries and was signalled in September 1934, when Hackzell was invited to join the regular, half-yearly meeting of Scandinavian Foreign Ministers in Stockholm, tacitly accepting Finland as a member of the Nordic bloc. The subsequent pressure from the Finnish leaders, encouraged by the Swedish military, to win some commitment from Sweden met with disappointment, but in December 1935 Finland acted unilaterally by declaring in parliament the country's formal adoption of a policy based on Nordic neutrality. The declaration was carried unanimously and stated:

> Because Finland's interests demand above all the preservation of the nation's neutrality, it is natural that Finland's orientation shall develop towards Scandinavia . . . It is the most basic task of Finland's foreign policy to bring about joint action between Finland and the Scandinavian countries to secure their common neutrality.

While this was happening the international situation in the Nordic region was beginning to change. The resurgence of Germany as a great power, with the declared aim of revising the postwar settlements and of driving back the menace of communism, revived the possibility of war between Germany and the Soviet Union in the Baltic. Sweden in particular could see two dangers arising from the new situation. The Åland islands, which belonged to Finland, were neutralised under an international Convention of 1921, and in their defenceless condition invited a swift seizure by a belligerent. Further, in Finland there was a powerful germanophile tradition that held that only a strong Germany could protect Finland against Russia. In a Russo-German war, Finland might be involved either willingly or unwillingly as a base for German operations, and the Soviet Union could be tempted to launch a preemptive strike. Then, as the danger of war in the Baltic increased, two supposed safeguards collapsed. The Anglo-German naval agreement of 1935 implied that Britain renounced the possibility of armed intervention in the Baltic, leaving only the Soviet Union to face a dominant Germany. At the same time, the main guarantee of the status quo, collective security under the League, lost all credibility with the failure of sanctions against Italy in 1936. The security system prevailing in the Baltic since 1920 was recognised by the Nordic countries themselves as defunct.

A new system was needed, and it emerged from two convergent thrusts — the drive of the Finnish leaders to use their Nordic orientation to win support against the Russian threat, and the vision of the Swedish Foreign Minister, R. Sandler. He wanted to translate traditional ideas of Nordic solidarity into a system where, instead of four small countries, each trying to avoid involvement in great power conflict, there would be a common Nordic neutrality policy, under which the four would pool their resources to ensure the inviolability of the whole region, if necessary and as a last resource by the joint use of force. These thrusts were convergent but not identical: the Finns wanted to prepare for war that was bound to come, while Sandler believed that advance preparation would deter aggressors and there would be no war. Sandler was trying to inject new meanings into traditional concepts of Nordic unity. These had a real basis in language, historic tradition, the Lutheran religion, almost identical legal systems and very similar politics. They were liberal, parliamentary states which in the 1930s all established progressive coalition governments of social democrats and small farmer parties, which gave them stable, majority government. All Nordic countries were fiercely independent and committed to their separate identities, but all acknowledged that they had a shared range of common interests — Finland always being a partial exception. These common interests were institutionalized at many levels, in foreign policy in the half-yearly meetings of the foreign ministers. It was easy to be cynical about Nordic collaboration. It has been described as 'taking a common position at Geneva on matters not directly of concern to the Nordic countries and producing rhetoric for domestic consumption'. The rhetoric existed; phrases like 'a community of fate', or 'complete solidarity', or 'the Nordic countries stand side by side in defence of their common interests' were widespread in speeches and articles and few challenged what they really meant. Politicians could get carried away, as when Stauning told the Danish parliament in 1933 that 'our land frontier to the south is the frontier of Scandinavia and an attack there would become the business of Scandinavia as a whole'. He was challenged privately by the Swedish leader, P.A. Hansson, who reported:

> I did not suppose Stauning had been alluding to any kind of defence alliance. He said he had not been thinking of anything like that, whereupon I added that if there was a threat to Denmark's integrity, they could always be assured of our sympathy and moral support.

Stauning was no fool — he said himself in 1937, 'a Nordic defence alliance belongs to Utopia'.

Sandler, whose public utterances were rarely models of clarity, had evident difficulty in defining his new concept. One of the more coherent expositions was in a radio address on 4 April 1938:

> We are all deeply conscious of the essential value to everyone of Nordic security within its borders. In face of tension it can only become more obvious that there is only one way for a united Nordic policy. That is, in a conflict of the great powers, to safeguard our own right of self-determination of policy which keeps the Nordic countries out of war.

He dismissed military alliances as 'meaningless, more, perhaps harmful' and continued:

> The true common line of Nordic policy is nothing other than a united endeavour not to be involved in war, so it is no longer a question of a defence alliance . . . but concerns a preparation for neutrality which extends to military preparation as well

. . . Is there a limited field and objective in which it is true that some coordination of all, or most Nordic Countries' defence forces could give additional support to our chances of avoiding war? No other common enemy than the risk of war is in question. Today, I can only say it is worth trying.

He knew that his ideas were novel and might alarm a traditionalist audience and conceded this was a new concept of neutrality, because 'in some critical situations it will be possible to say that a neutrality that has become Nordic is no longer neutrality, because thereby Sweden does not take a neutral stance towards a brother country'.

The practical difficulties were shown in an area where cooperation should have been easy, planning common economic measures for a war situation. The aim was, by stockpiling necessities, to make the neutrals less exposed to economic blackmail by the belligerents. The Swedish Foreign Ministry had drafted a plan in July 1936; by March 1938 it had been 'adopted as a base for continuing work by the delegations of the respective countries' governments'. But when the crisis came, in September 1939, the governments were still wholly unprepared to implement even such tentative agreements as had been reached. Hansson's secretary described the meeting on the subject as degenerating into 'general mumbling and after that was entirely abandoned'. In face of this, the programme set out by Sandler at the conference in Oslo in April 1938, for collaboration in the defence of Åland, Lapland and the Öresund, planned stockpiling of strategic goods, and a common programme for producing war materials, sounds unrealistic. It raises doubts whether he was serious, or was using the concept to make a close bilateral relationship of Sweden and Finland acceptable to public opinion. Certainly the Åland question, which concerned Denmark and Norway only marginally, was the only item in his programme that Sandler pursued with vigour. He seems realistic enough to have recognised the limitations of joint political action. Once, when he was asked why he had not simply promoted an alliance between Sweden and Finland, he said 'naturally because I did not see there was any possibility present for furthering such a proposal', and added, 'I also thought that perhaps it was not necessary'. This is consistent with the view that Sandler saw joint action with Finland to secure the neutrality of Åland as realizable, and something that might open the way to further collaborations, but to make it acceptable it had to be presented in a context of Nordic solidarity.

The Åland problem was complex. For any power waging war in the Baltic the islands were a major strategic interest. They commanded the Gulf of Bothnia and could inhibit sea communication between Sweden and Finland, and control the shipment of Swedish iron ore. Neither Germany nor the Soviet Union would willingly see the other take possession. The military importance to Finland is obvious, that to Sweden less evident but probably greater. If Åland was in friendly hands, there was virtually no need to defend central Sweden, and her forces could be concentrated to defend Skåne from the German threat, and Norrland against the Soviet Union. If central Sweden had to be defended as well the strategic problems became critical. In particular, Stockholm would be very vulnerable to air attack from Åland. There was also a political complication. Although the islands were the sovereign territory of Finland, their inhabitants were wholly Swedish in language and culture and looked to Sweden to protect them. All these problems had been resolved by the ten-power international Convention of 1921, under the auspices of the League, which neutralised the islands permanently, allowing no military installations of any kind. If they came under attack, the Council of the League would take the action necessary to preserve their integrity. This had satisfied everyone except the Soviet Union, which was not a signatory and had protested formally that she did not recognise the Convention, and Finland who begrudged the limitations on her sovereignty. But the effectiveness of the Convention depended on the absence of great power conflict in the Baltic, and the effectiveness of the League of Nations. By 1936 both Sweden and Finland could see that neither condition applied any longer. The immediate danger was of a pre-emptive strike by either Germany or the Soviet Union, which could only be deterred if there were some permanent defences in place. Finland wanted to abolish all restriction on her right to defend Åland; Sweden could not agree, fearing that Finland was thinking only of the Soviet Union and might even welcome a German occupation. Sweden was also sensitive to the prevailing nationalist agitation in Finland against Swedish language rights which seemed a threat to the cultural status of the Ålanders. She pressed for an international agreement to permit Finland and Sweden jointly to organise basic defences. These would make a surprise seizure impractical and should reassure both Germany and the Soviet Union and encourage them to respect the islands' neutrality.

The initial pressure to do something about Åland came from Finland. The Swedish military leaders were enthusiastic, but Sandler remained unconvinced. It was the *Anschluss* in March 1938 that seems to have changed his mind. His ambassador in Helsinki warned that Finnish opinion was excited by the rising power of Germany: 'in all sorts, respect for Germany has increased enormously . . . It is high time that something concrete emerge in the matter of collaboration between Sweden and Finland.' A conference of leading ministers and defence chiefs was held in Stockholm on 17 March 1938, at which the leading military expert, Ehrensvärd, noted that 'many members of the government had a critical attitude to Sandler and especially his Nordic policy. Above all he was seen as excessively friendly to Finland'.

This suggests that Sandler was convinced of the need to make a commitment to Finland, saw Åland as the means of doing it, and was using the Nordic ideal to sell his policy. On 31 March a reluctant Swedish government authorised exploratory conversations with the Finns. The Finnish Foreign Minister, now R. Holsti, was told at the Foreign Ministers' meeting in Oslo, where Sandler stressed that Germany and the Soviet Union must be considered equally, and the talks confined to upholding the neutrality of Åland. Holsti was reluctant to concede that the Soviet Union had a legitimate interest, but Sandler was adamant and after some delay Holsti conceded. The next stage was to inform the Foreign Affairs Committee of the Swedish parliament. Sandler explained that his sole concern was 'increasing the security of Åland as a neutralised zone'. These was no enthusiasm in the committee but a grudging acceptance of the need to keep Finland out of the clutches of Germany. On 6 May the Swedish government gave formal consent for negotiations to begin and, since the technical problems had already been settled by the military experts, an agreed report was ready for the two governments by July. The problems had been political. Finland had proposed a bilateral treaty to supersede the Convention. The Swedes saw this as a trap to draw them into an alliance and insisted instead on amending the Convention by international consent. Sandler was blunt about Sweden's position. 'Sweden's concern that Åland should not come into the hands of a great power is probably not so great that Sweden will let herself be drawn into a general war to prevent such an eventuality.' Since for Finland any agreement was better than none she had to accept the Swedish proposal. This was that the agreement applied only to upholding the neutrality of Åland and hence could only be activated while both countries remained neutral. Then the obligations were not automatic, but could only be put into effect at the request of Finland with the consent of Sweden. There were strict safeguards for the culture of the islanders, any garrison would consist of Swedish-speaking Finnish troops, supported by a local militia and reinforced at need by Swedish troops.

This agreement was the most that could be achieved, and its very limitations won it the endorsement of the Swedish Foreign Affairs Committee in August 1938. It seems that in the Munich crisis in September it was almost put into effect, the two governments agreed to take emergency measures in Åland, but the crisis ended so quickly that the Swedish government did not actually order its armed forces to move into Åland. But Sandler said later:

> Although, naturally, no commitments can be made in respect of the unforeseen in the future, it can be said of the concrete situation last September that, had war broken out in the Baltic, and Finland proposed joint action for the protection of

the neutralised area, the Swedish government, in view of Sweden's interests, would have given a positive answer.

The Finnish historian, M. Jakobson, has remarked that this was the peak point of Swedish–Finnish cooperation. The Swedish government never went so far again and Sandler's career eventually broke because of it.

By this time a new complication had developed. The Soviet Union launched an initiative on Finland in 1938 through a series of confidential approaches to Finnish ministers by B. Jartsev, nominally a second secretary at the Helsinki Legation, but actually the messenger of the Politburo. He said the Soviet Union, in face of rising fascist aggression, could not be satisfied with Finland's Nordic neutrality policy. Finland could not sustain neutrality in face of great power pressures. Unless Finland would accept the support of the Soviet Union in upholding her neutrality it had no credibility. Jartsev told Holsti in October that Finland's Nordic policy was fine in peacetime, but in war only the Soviet Union could ensure Finland's integrity. These approaches confirmed all the worst fears of the Finnish leaders about Russian intentions. Their response was entirely negative; they sheltered behind the concept of Nordic neutrality to refuse even to discuss any kind of commitment to the Soviet Union. The immediate effect was to make the Finnish leaders (for no one else in Finland was told) ever more determined to get some Swedish promise of support. Sandler knew about the Soviet proposals and encouraged the Finns to refuse all concessions. Sandler probably did not take the Soviet Union seriously; he doubted she had the will or the military capacity to be an aggressor, while Munich seemed to confirm the international marginalisation of the Soviet Union. Sandler also knew that there was no possibility that Finland would enter into an arrangement with the Soviet Union, but if she became sufficiently alarmed she might turn to Germany. Further, if any Nordic country entered into any arrangement with a great power, the whole Nordic neutrality concept, aimed at insulating the region from great power conflict, would be dead. He was assisted by a new Finnish Foreign Minister, E. Erkko, who replaced Holsti at the end of 1938. Erkko was more committed to a Nordic policy, for him it was a matter of conviction, not tactics, and he was a more forceful and independent character than Holsti.

On 7 January 1939 Erkko led a Finnish delegation to Stockholm which signed what was technically 'The Report of the Finnish and Swedish delegations on their negotiations on the Åland islands'. This is usually referred to as 'The Stockholm Plan'. The preamble spoke of 'the weakening of the League of Nations' security system, and the political and military difficulties which affected the guarantee system envisaged under the 1921 Convention'. The Plan had three main elements. First the two powers proposed to modify the Convention by changing the limits of the neutral zone. This would exclude the southernmost, uninhabited islands and allow Finland to fortify them and establish garrisons. This would create a trip-wire defence such that Åland could not be seized by a military raid. Sweden had no commitment here, except that to be effective the defence must be linked to defences in Sweden's territorial waters. Secondly, in the remaining neutral zone, the League would authorise Finland to conscript a local militia, and send troops, and both Swedish and Finnish warships could use the surrounding waters. The specific defensive measures must be agreed between Sweden and Finland, so that Sweden held a veto over them. Thirdly there was a declaration by Sweden:

> In the event of an immediate threat of war in the Baltic area, Sweden reserves the right, as the closest guarantor, and in view of her vital interests, at the request of Finland, to assist defensive measures designed to secure the neutrality of the Åland islands.

This emphasised that there was no automatic commitment, and that it was applicable only under threat of war, while both countries were still neutral. If Finland was actually attacked, it would not apply — the purpose was deterrence of a threatened aggression.

The Plan had to be sold to the domestic constituencies first. In Finland this was no problem for obvious reasons, despite some nationalist resentment at Sweden's patronage of the islanders. In Sweden, Hansson, now Prime Minister, declared the government was solidly behind the Plan. 'Mr Sandler does not represent a personal policy in matters of foreign affairs, but that of the government.' According to credible anecdote, however, when an opponent of the Plan approached Hansson he said 'you can stay calm, nothing will come of it, and I shall not be the one to grieve over it'. Parliamentary opposition was almost entirely from conservatives concerned about the rights of the islanders, all other groups supported the government. The opponents challenged Sandler with a hostile interpellation on 22 March, and he turned on his critics: Åland is where it is and the international order is such as it is . . . we want to stimulate the will of neutrality and Nordic collaboration in a neighbour country.' He challenged them to suggest a better way, but the alternatives, to leave the islands undefended, or leave Finland to do it by herself, were both unattractive.

The next step was to get international agreement to amend the Convention. On 16 January 1939 in all signatory powers, the Swedish and Finnish ambassadors presented a joint note asking for consent to amendments to the Convention, and by the end of May they had all agreed. The Soviet Union, which was not a signatory, was also sent a note at Sweden's insistence, expressing the hope that the Soviet Union 'would comply with the proposals now made'. The immediate Russian response was a new approach to Finland. On 5 March, Litvinov suggested that Finland lease, or exchange for territory elsewhere, her islands in the Gulf of Finland for use in the defence of Leningrad. Although Mannerheim favoured concessions, Erkko refused to discuss the proposals, and was encouraged by Sandler, even though it appeared this might be the Soviet price for agreeing to the Plan. He told the Soviet government that 'the Swedish government is entirely at one with the Finnish government over this'. Soviet anger was manifest; Litvinov told the Swedish ambassador 'he could not see what Sweden had to do with the affair'. The displeasure of the Soviet Union was further expressed by a studied refusal to reply to the joint note on the Plan. Then, when the Council of the League met in May 1939 and was asked to approve the changes in the Åland Convention, the Soviet Union insisted that a decision must be postponed—in effect the Soviet Union had vetoed the Plan. Sandler was slow to admit this; he told the press on his return from Geneva:

> The Åland Plan will be a contribution to collaboration between all the Baltic countries and to heightened security in the region. The Council's proceedings, in the Foreign Minister's view, do not give rise to any alteration in the Swedish government's position, so we must now proceed further with the matter.

Any lingering ambiguity was crushed when Molotov, the new Foreign Minister, told the Supreme Soviet 'the Soviet Union does not approve the Swedish and Finnish proposals'. J.K. Paasikivi, the Finnish ambassador, came to Sandler on 30 May, and said that Finland wanted to proceed with implementation, in spite of the Soviet position, but Sandler admitted that for the Swedish government Molotov's statement had created a new situation. The following day the Swedish government dicusssed the matter, and it was Sandler's doomsday. He tried to take a bold line: the Soviet Union would see sense and Sweden should stand firm, his colleagues 'do not know how the Russians should be handled'. None of his colleagues supported him and it was decided that the proposals before parliament to ratify the Plan should be withdrawn on the excuse of lack of parliamentary time. This gave Sandler the chance to make another approach to Moscow, but Molotov's reply to a further note of 11 June was that the Plan was unacceptable. With that it was dead, Hansson withdrew support for it, and E. Wigforss, Sandler's most determined ministerial opponent said 'we should not even mention the question further for the time being'. Soon after this, the Nazi–Soviet Non-Aggression Pact made the Plan redundant from Sweden's point of view, since if Germany and the Soviet Union were cooperating, the threat to Åland disappeared, while Finland could not choose the German option but must adhere to Sweden. Mannerheim had summed up what had happened when he heard that Sweden would yield to Soviet objections: 'The Soviet Union has tested the content of Nordic cooperation and could draw its own conclusions from what has happened.' It is easy to agree with that harsh verdict; Nordic cooperation had looked like a beautiful dream that collapsed at the first touch of reality. Whether Sandler had been a dreamer, or a manipulator who had tried to carry a Swedish–Finnish alliance designed as Nordic collaboration, he emerges as a failure, who should have known better. Yet the sequel showed that there were political forces that could have been rallied for Nordic solidarity by a politician luckier, or more gifted, than Sandler.

When war broke out on 1 September, all the Nordic countries declared neutrality and there seemed some prospect of upholding it until the Soviet Union forced mutual assistance treaties on Estonia, Latvia and Lithuania. The Swedish Commander-in-Chief, General O. Thornell, sent a memorandum to Sandler that the Soviet Union would certainly follow this with pressure on Finland and the Stockholm Plan should be implemented at once. Sandler agreed and took the proposal to the government on 1 October. It would not be necessary to send Swedish troops yet, but Finland should be urged to start constructing defences, on the understanding that there would be 'joint Swedish–Finnish resistance' if the islands were attacked, and that Sweden would 'guarantee' Finland's neutrality. Sandler lobbied his ministerial colleagues intensely: 'it is a question of securing Åland for Scandinavia. The Swedish government has it in its power, in a favourable situation, to declare solidarity with Finland.' He argued: 'it would be of decisive importance for Finland if Sweden now gave a guarantee equivalent to a defence alliance'. But he found no support for his revived Nordic solidarity policy—no minister agreed with him. When the blow actually fell on 5 October, and the Soviet Union requested talks with Finland, Erkko sent at once to ask what support Sweden would give. Initially it seemed as though Nordic solidarity might rise to the challenge for, on 12 October, the ambassadors of Denmark, Norway and Sweden presented a joint note in Moscow, expressing their wish to keep Nordic neutrality inviolate and that the Soviet Union 'would not propose anything which would create obstacles for Finland, in full independence, to continue in that neutral position which she has adopted in close collaboration with the other Nordic countries'. This was followed by an invitation from the King of Sweden for the heads of state and foreign ministers of the four countries to confer on the crisis in Stockholm on 18 October. This was done and there were speeches and in the evening a huge mass demonstration outside the royal palace. The Swedish press was enthused; *Sydsvenska Dagbladet* wrote, 'when the rights of neutrals are threatened or trampled on, Nordic unity is a support of no mean character'. *Svenska Dagbladet* declared: 'the 18th of October will be hallowed in Sweden's, as in Scandinavia's history as the hour when, for the first time, Nordic policies ceased to be the affair of statesmen and institutions, and became the concern of the people.' Even allowing for the input from basic anti-communism and historic Russophobia in Sweden, these manifestations suggested that there was a powerful public opinion which believed, as a matter of Nordic solidarity, that Finland should be supported against unacceptable Soviet demands.

But at governmental level it was very different. Sandler pursued his campaign for a promise of armed assistance to defend Åland. He had told the Foreign Affairs Committee on 12 October:

> If we leave Finland to defend Sweden's interests, we must abandon all hope of a Nordic policy. And incur a general risk, if Sweden at this moment shows weakness, it can have fatal consequences. If Sweden does not share positively in the defence of Åland, the danger threatens not only from Russia, but also from Germany.

Sandler admitted there was risk, but also an opportunity—his opponents could only see the risk. Hansson argued back: 'to send troops now could produce inestimable consequences. It could be interpreted as a demonstration, not just for Finland but against Russia.' He doubted there was real popular support for intervention. 'I do not believe this is to be found in the mass of the people, only in certain circles interested in Finland.' Hansson's view prevailed; the Foreign Affairs Committee and the government agreed that Sweden could offer Finland moral support, and some supply of war materials, but should not send troops or promise to do so. In consequence the heads of state, on 18 October, carefully avoided discussing military support, and when Erkko met Hansson, Sandler and P.E. Sköld, the Defence Minister, on 19 October, Hansson outlined the Swedish position. 'Do not count on Swedish troops for Åland.' He said that in spite of the demonstrations, 'it is clear people want to stay out of war as long as possible, especially it is obvious with a people who have had the fortune to enjoy a century of peace'. Sandler, supported by Thornell, continued to press, and on 22 October, the Swedish government considered intervention again. This time Sandler's opponents, led by Wigforss, determined to end the debate. Wigforss threatened resignation and a public campaign against intervention if the government was 'carried away by an inflamed opinion. We may take a step that leads us on and finally lands us in a war that very few, at the outset, have been ready to join'. Sandler asked if this meant a lack of confidence in himself, and Wigforss replied 'you have understood me correctly'. Hansson just averted a government crisis by urging that intervention was still hypothetical and a decision could be postponed.

Hansson's position was inscrutable for he was reluctant to say that in no circumstances should Sweden give Finland military assistance. V. Tanner, the Finnish social democrat leader, challenged him by personal letter to say he refused military help. Hansson's written reply was firm, but Tanner's emissary, K.A. Fagerholm, reported that in conversation, 'Hansson said he personally would go further, but I have to deal with a people selfish about peace. What public opinion would become, if Finland really gets into a war, is another matter'. Sandler added his belief that the Soviet Union was bluffing, but 'there is still the possibility to start acting, as soon as the Russians really begin a war'. In truth the Swedish leadership was paralysed by indecision. Public opinion was divided; the vociferous lobby calling for action in the name of Nordic solidarity was balanced by Hansson's silent majority who wanted to stay out of war at all cost. Everyone believed the Soviet Union was bluffing; only Sandler thought that 'Sweden too can employ a bit of bluff'. He believed that the threat of Swedish intervention would deter aggression, where his opponents believed it was foolhardy and unnecessary, and might encourage the Finns to dangerous bravado. The result of the ambivalence was tragic — Sweden did not deter the Soviet Union, but she did persuade the Finns that if a shooting war began, Sweden would not leave them unsupported.

On 30 November the Soviet Union did attack Finland and further evasion was impossible. The Finnish government asked Sweden to implement the Stockholm Plan. The Swedish reply was determined on 2 December. In the Foreign Affairs Committee only Sandler urged intervention, while the king submitted a personal opinion that it was now too late. In the evening the government confimed a policy of non-intervention and Sandler resigned. In his resignation statement he argued that even at that late stage a show of force by Sweden would have deterred the aggression. But the choice had been made, and Sandler's conception of Nordic solidarity had been rejected. Instead an emasculated version was implemented in all three Nordic countries. They did not declare neutrality in the Russo-Finnish war, they allowed volunteers to be recruited to fight for Finland, and they facilitated the collection and transit of supplies, including war materials, for Finland. The governments had little choice, for there was a surge of public feeling built round the slogan 'Finland's affair is our affair too'. In Sweden, two popular organisations, *Nationalsamlingen för Finland* and *Finlandshjälpen*, collected money and supplies with the government's blessing. The volunteer movement, run by the *Finlandskommittee* eventually sent 8,500 fighting men to the front, equipped from Swedish government stores. But beyond this there was an activist pressure group led by academics, soldiers and business-men demanding 'effective help', by which they meant the despatch of army units in the guise of 'volunteers'. They organised a series of mass rallies and on 9 December set up an organising committee, *Nordens Frihet*. This demanded true Nordic solidarity expressed through actions. But it was significant that no leading politician accepted their invitation to declare support, and Sandler did not put himself at their head, as he could have done.

These activists had been outmanoeuvred by Hansson, who took advantage of Sandler's resignation to transform his coalition government into a government of national unity, which included the conservatives, the major party most sympathetic to intervention. Hansson had wanted to commit the new government to non-intervention in the Finnish war, but the conservatives insisted on a formula that Sweden's position was not predetermined, but would depend on 'Sweden's vital interests and the course of events'. The new Foreign Minister, C. Gunther, defined the policy as 'to keep the country out of the great power conflict and, as far as possible, to defend the common Nordic interest'. The underlying priorities were revealed by Gunther in a New Year's address which declared, 'however deeply we feel for our bleeding brother nation . . . it is still Sweden's fate which, at this hour, occupies our thoughts'. This contrasted with the statement of the activist leader, S. Curman, who said the conflict would determine 'Scandinavia's fate' and demanded 'unlimited sacrifice to the uttermost, readiness to take up our common responsibility for Nordic liberties'. Throughout the war the activists were able to hold packed public meetings, where the atmosphere was that of religious revivalism, but they had been marginalised politically when Hansson took the conservatives into the government. Also Hansson was lucky. The initial surge of feeling was based on the fear of Russian troops sweeping across Finland and arriving at the Swedish frontier, whereas the Finnish defences held until mid-February 1940, so it seemed that Sweden's assistance had been adequate.

But in mid-February the Finnish front cracked, and the Russians began a slow but unstoppable advance. On the other hand, the Swedish government had acted as mediator, and ascertained that Finland could have peace on terms which preserved her independence and which Sweden thought she should accept. The alternative was to fight on with foreign assistance, which was now being offered by Britain and France. But since this could only be implemented by marching Allied troops through Scandinavia, which must embroil the region in the great power war, the Nordic neutrals were desperate to prevent it. However, the Swedish public could not be told that peace was possible, since the mediation was, of necessity, confidential. The public saw Finland in danger of collapse and their own government refusing the necessary help, and driving Finland to appeal for the Allied assistance which would turn Scandinavia into a battlefield. On 13 February 1940 Tanner came for secret talks with the Swedish government and asked directly for military intervention. Hansson refused firmly; neither Swedish opinion nor Germany would allow intervention. If the Allies sought to send troops across Norway and Sweden, transit would be refused. On 16 February the Stockholm newspaper, *Folkets Dagbladet Politiken*, published an accurate account of the secret conversation, almost certainly leaked by an activist sympathiser. In the evening Hansson issued a press statement confirming that the account was true and Finland's plea for help had been rejected. This produced an effect, commonly seen in politics when something is said openly which everyone has accepted tacitly but does not wish to acknowledge—in this case that Sweden had no intention of going to war to rescue Finland. Hansson's statement looked like a betrayal of Finland and released a flood of guilt-fed emotion. The government's position was badly shaken, and a divisive public debate threatened which would give the activists their chance. Hansson was rescued by the king, alarmed at the disunity and probably aware that there were elements among the activists and in the officer corps who had contemplated overthrowing Hansson by a coup. On 19 February the King issued an official declaration of support for his government. It expressed 'admiration for Finland's heroic struggle' and Sweden's resolve to give her all possible assistance, but armed intervention was not possible: 'I am convinced that if Sweden now intervened in the Finnish war, we would be in the greatest danger of being drawn not only into war with Russia, but also into the war between the great powers.'

The magic of monarchy was not dead, even in twentieth-century Sweden; the attack on Hansson collapsed. Curman remarked bitterly: 'The King's statement was the death blow for Finland, perhaps for Scandinavia . . . the King's endorsement of the Prime Minister's statement has rendered it impossible for the opposition to exercise its influence in any successful way.' The activist paper, *Stockholm's Tidningen*, wrote, 'to continue action just now is to speak to deaf ears, the blue-eyed Swedish people will just say, the king has spoken—so Per Albin was right'. Activism and Nordic solidarity were dead; on 22 February *Nordens Frihet* met and decided to support the government.

This cleared the way for the Swedish government to concentrate on pressuring Finland to make peace on Soviet terms, and not to call on the assistance offered by the Allies. In this process, the idea of Nordic solidarity made a brief final appearance. Tanner returned to Stockholm on 22 February to ask what Sweden could to to help Finland if she did make peace, and suggested that Sweden and Norway join Finland in a defensive alliance to guarantee the new settlement. Hansson's answer was typical of the man: 'I was prepared to discuss the question of a defence alliance, but I had not yet thought through the idea and so could not commit myself.' When it was put to the Foreign Affairs Committee, they agreed that in a Nordic framework it could be considered. The Finnish leaders were authorised to mention the possibility when justifying the decision to make peace to their own people. From the first consideration of the idea, a new difficulty emerged. O. Unden had asked in the Foreign Affairs Committee how Sweden could give a guarantee to Finland if she could not control Finland's foreign policy. 'Danger was inseparable from a defensive alliance if we cannot control Finland's foreign policy. But we could . . . propose some sort of union.' The matter was further discussed when the social democrats' *Nordiska Samarbets-kommittée* met in Stockholm on 30 March. Tanner asked, 'were the Nordic states prepared to defend the Nordic region together?' Not one of the leaders present felt able to say no. They had to agree in principle, but Hansson put the point, 'for a defence alliance to be workable, the collaboration must be so extensive that we must be prepared for total union . . . a union of states'. The Norwegian, J. Nygaardsvold, agreed that a political union was probably a precondition. The truth was out: to translate Nordic collaboration from an ideal to a political reality political union was necessary. Four sovereign, democratic states with — except for Finland — long traditions of neutrality and non-militarism, could not commit their peoples to take up arms on behalf of one of their number in circumstances that could not be predicted nor controlled. Only a full Nordic union could pursue a Nordic armed neutrality policy. At which point the German invasion of Denmark and Norway put an end to the debate.

It is probable that the ablest leaders, like Hansson, had always known this truth, and in consequence had defined collaboration in terms of exchanging information and considering options. Advanced commitment to political or military action was dismissed as utopian. Yet they were reluctant to say this in public, always prefacing their rejection of advance commitments with the gloss that, even so, in any specific situation, joint action could be considered. Hansson was a very unemotional politician, but he knew the Nordic ideal could fire the imagination of his compatriots and he could not afford to ignore it. Sandler was a different kind of politician. Perhaps he fell victim to his own vision of a strong, united Nordic neutrality that even the great powers would be compelled to respect. Or he may have been a pragmatic Swedish nationalist who, once the League security system broke down, saw that it was a Swedish interest to uphold an independent, neutral Finland and this required the offer of an alliance. But because alliance was outside the bounds of acceptability to Swedish politicians and their electorate, Sandler pursued his aim behind the screen of Nordic solidarity ideals, and in the end could not see that the ideals were not strong enough to carry the weight he was putting on them. Whatever the case, Sandler's failure is a reminder that although, in a democratic political system, political leaders ignore the forces of idealism at their peril, the real world of competitive sovereign states is dominated by the brutal imperatives of power politics, and these will assert themselves in the end over the highest of ideals.

Bibiliographical note

Any further study of the matters dealt with in this chapter requires a working knowledge of Finnish and Swedish. Some relevant material in the English language is to be found in:

Jakobson, M., *The Diplomacy of the Winter War* (Cambridge, Mass., Harvard University Press, 1961).

Mannerheim, C.G.E., *The Memoirs of Marshal Mannerheim* (London, Cassell, 1953).

Tanner, V., *The Winter War* (Stamford, Stamford University Press, 1957).

Upton, A.F., *Finland 1939–1940* (London, Davies-Poynter, 1974).

There exists a wide range of primary sources in public and private archives in Sweden and Finland, but this chapter was based entirely on published materials, documents, memoirs and scholarly monographs. The following is a select list of the more significant works that were consulted:

Carlgren, W.M., *Svensk utrikespolitik 1939–1945* (Stockholm, Almänna förlaget, 1973), a recent general study of Swedish foreign policy in the Second World War.

——*Varken-eller: reflexioner kring Sveriges Ålandspolitik 1938–1939* (Uddevalla, Militärhistoriska förlaget, 1977). A full and detailed study of Sweden's Åland policy.

Hägglöf, G., *Möte med Europa 1926–1940* (Stockholm, Norstedt, 1971), the memoirs of a senior official of the Swedish Foreign Ministry.

Jakobson, M., *Paaskikivi Tukholmassa: J.K. Paasikiven toiminta Suomen lähettiläänä Tukholmassa 1936–1939* (Helsinki, Otava, 1978), a study of the role of J.K. Paasikivi as Finish ambassador in Stockholm.

Johansson, A., *Finlands sak: Svensk politik och opinion under vinterkriget* (Stockholm, Almänna förlaget, 1973), a study of Swedish public opinion during the Winter War.

Johansson, A., *Per-Albin och kriget: samlingsregeringen och utrikespolitiken under andravärldskriget* (Stockholm, Tidens förlaget, 1984), a study of the Swedish prime-minister and his foreign policy in the Second World War.

Korhonen, K., *Turvallisuuden pettäessä. Suomi neuvostodiplomatiassa Tartosta talvisotaan, II, 1933–1939* (Helsinki, Tammi, 1971), a recent general study of Russo-Finnish relations.

Lönnroth, E., *Den svenska utrikespolitikens historia, V, 1919–1939* (Stockholm, Norstedt, 1959), a volume in the official history of Swedish foreign policy.

Sandler, R., *Strömväxlingar och lärdomar: Utrikespolitiska anföranden, 1937–1939* (Stockholm, Tidens förlaget, 1939), a memoir written immediately after his resignation, and the only full explanation offered by this naturally secretive key figure.

Selen, K., *Genevasta Tukholmaan: Suomen turvallisuuspolitiikan painopisteen siirty-minen Kansainliitosta pohjoismaiseen yhteistyöhön, 1931–1936* (Helsinki, Suomen historiallinen seura, 1974), a study of Finland's change to a policy of Scandinavian neutrality.

Selen, K., *C.G.E. Mannerheim ja hanen puolustusneuvostonsa, 1931–1939* (Helsinki, Otava, 1980), a study of Mannerheim's role in Finnish policy-making in the 1930s.

Suomi, J., *Talvisodan tausta. Neuvostoliitto Suomen ulkopolitiikassa, 1937–1939* (Helsinki, Otava, 1974), a study of Russo-Finnish relations which supplements Korhonen's account.

Tingsten, H., *Svensk utrikesdebatt mellan världskrigen* (Lund, Gleerup, 1964), a study of public discussion in Sweden on foreign policy between the wars.

Turtola, M., *Tornionjoelta Rajajoelle* (Porvoo, Werner Söderström, 1984), a study of the relations of the Finnish and Swedish military leaderships between the wars.

Wahlbäck, K., *Finlandfrågan i svensk politik, 1937–1940* (Stockholm, Norstedt, 1964) a study of Sweden's Åland policy.

Wigforss, E., *Minnen I-III* (Stockholm, Tidens förlaget, 1951–4), the memoirs of a leading Swedish social democrat politician and minister of finance.

11 French Personalist and Federalist Movements in the Interwar Period

John Loughlin

In the study of recent history, 1945 is often accepted as a convenient starting point for what is known as the 'postwar period'. The tendency to begin afresh in 1945 may be due to an understandable desire to forget the events of the 1920s and 1930s and to look ahead to what was hoped would be a better future. While it is true that the postwar period does present a certain coherence and distinctiveness which separates it from earlier periods, the disadvantage of this periodization is that it tends to ignore the continuity with earlier periods: the war itself, and the events which led to the war in the 1920s and 1930s, crucially determined the shape of historical development after 1945.

The tendency to begin in 1945 is reinforced in France by the fact that the schema of French history is portrayed as a succession of 'regimes'. The Vichy regime collapsed in 1945 and was soon replaced by the Fourth Republic. But the early years of the Fourth Republic were dominated by the collapse of the Third, the Defeat, Occupation and Liberation. This continuity with earlier periods is evident in the role France played in the early steps toward European integration. The openness to this integration process on the part of key groups of Frenchmen and a wider public may seem surprising in view of the hostilities between France and Germany which had just ended. In fact, the seeds for this openness had already been sown, at first, among a restricted group of young intellectuals in the early 1930s and, secondly, among the Resistance groups and camp prisoners during the war itself.

The young intellectuals of the 1930s had been revolted by what they regarded as the 'obscene' nature of the French liberal democratic regime and they proposed instead radically different alternatives: some were attracted by the political traditions of the French right such as monarchism or royalism; others by the communist, fascist and Nazi revolutions, finally, a few attempted to rehabilitate the federalist idea, previously associated mainly with the French right and to a lesser extent with Proudhonism, by re-expressing it in terms of contemporary philosophy, a synthesis they termed 'personalism'. While the Third Republic was in place, the proposals advanced by these young intellectuals had little audience. However, in the period immediately following the war, when the old regimes and élites seemed to be discredited, they were presented with an opportunity which they seized without hesitation. The purpose of this chapter is to trace this continuity, to place the movements in the context of the history of French political traditions and to see their relevance for the process of European integration after 1945.

A recurring theme in the history of French political debate is the tension between those who support the centralizing nation-state and those seeking a recognition of the existence of subnational units such as communes, regions and culturally distinct groups.[1] This tension dates from the 1789 Revolution when the Jacobins and Napoleon are generally regarded as having reinforced the centralizing tendencies of the old monarchy, while the Girondins are sometimes credited with being favourable to a more federalist system.[2]. Until recently, the French left has been associated with Jacobinism and distrust of peripheral movements, while the clerical and royalist right attacked the centralized state.

This attack on the state on the part of this right was associated with a distrust of the principles of liberal democracy, that is, the notions that sovereignty came from the people, that their will could be represented in a parliamentary assembly, and that all citizens were equal. The conservative critique claimed that liberalism destroyed the natural living communities such as communes and provinces, with their natural hierarchy of leaders and followers. Such ideas, drawn from a medieval corporatist tradition, were supported by the intransigent opposition of the Roman Catholic Church to liberalism, especially personified by Pius IX and his condemnatory *Syllabus of Errors*.

However, the rejection of the centralized, representative state was not confined to the right. On the extreme left, the anarchist tradition represented by Proudhon (1809–65) shared some of the positions of the clerical right although he interpreted them in a different manner. Of particular importance were Proudhon's advocacy of a federal France composed of 'twelve independent governing units each with legislative and executive authorities elected by the people.[3] This was based on the necessity of an 'administrative decentralization, consituting a resurrection of the life of the commune and the province'.[4] Furthermore, Proudhon linked what he termed 'confederation' with the recognition of the rights of linguistic or racial groups: 'Each group or type of people, each race, each language should be master of its own territory.[5] However, perhaps the most important contribution of Proudhon to French political tradition was his advocacy of federalism in the socio-economic sphere: his influence was most strong in the early French labour movement, whose *syndicats* (trade unions) adopted a federal-type organisation and showed a Proudhonian reluctance to get involved in the parliamentary politics of the Third Republic. However, Proudhon's *political* federalism was largely ignored until it was rediscovered by the young intellectuals of the 1930s. This is understandable since the Right, who might have been sympathetic to this aspect of his thought, would have been repelled by his promotion of 'Revolution', his 'Anarchism', his love of the 'people', and outraged by what seemed to be his blasphemous atheism, 'God is Evil'.[6]

The ideological division between a clerical right opposed to the Republican nation-state and in favour of a decentralized federalism and a Jacobin left took a new twist, however, with the accession to the papacy of Leo XIII at the end of the nineteenth century. Leo tried to reverse the previous position of the Church towards modern developments and encouraged French Catholics to accept the Republic. His most famous encyclical *Rerum Novarum*, sometimes called the 'Workers' Charter', pleaded for the rights of workers and castigated some of the worst aspects of modern industrialism. At the same time, he supported the rights of private property and condemned socialism and communism.

Although, as may be seen from the Dreyfus Affair, the majority of French Catholics took the Pope's advice only with extreme reluctance and maintained reactionary political positions, a small but important minority enthusiastically accepted them. In the early years of this century, groups such as Le Sillon, animated by March Sangnier, attempted to develop a 'social Catholicism', based on Leo's encyclicals, while philosophers such as Jacques Maritain and Etienne Gilson, also under Leo's influence, led the Catholic philosophic revival, known as neo-Thomism. Maritain, in particular, attempted to apply the principles of Thomist philosophy to modern political and social conditions and was an immense influence on this generation of young Catholic intellectuals. Finally, Leo's advocacy of recognising the rights of workers found concrete expression with the founding of a Catholic trade-union movement, the *Confédération française de travail chrétien* (CFTC).

The French federalist movements of the 1930s should be seen as drawing on these various traditions. However, these movements sprang up as a result of a more specific set of circumstances which it will be useful to sketch briefly before looking at the movements themselves.

What is now referred to retrospectively as the 'interwar period' was, in fact, the 'postwar period'. The massacre of millions of men during the First World War, in which France had suffered particularly cruelly, overshadowed everything. First, it put an end to the facile optimism in 'progress' that had characterized the prewar period. This led to two different kinds of reaction: either an effervescent and superficial desire to 'have a good time' (the 'swinging twenties') on the part of the majority; or a sense of philosophical anguish and disgust on the part of a small, mainly young, intellectual minority—it was this which spawned the political and philosophical movements of concern to us here. Secondly, the postwar settlement, embodied in the Treaty of Versailles, was unacceptable to some sections of this minority favourable towards a more generous treatment of Germany. They considered that, far from leading to a new peace, the Treaty seemed to contain the seeds of further conflict and contributed to the growth of fascism and Nazism, Finally, the political élites and parties in France seemed to have changed little in the eyes of this radical youth, and presented a picture of, at best, incompetence and, at worst, corruption.

The first sign that the postwar order was beginning to crumble was the Wall Street 'Crash' in 1929. At first, this affected France less than other industrialised nations, thus creating the illusion among French political élites that their country could survive the crisis.[7] When the economic crisis did reach metropolitan France about 1932, the prestige of the latter was therefore all the more severely compromised. Governments of both the left and the right seemed incapable of meeting the challenge. Political scandals further undermined the regime.[8] Furthermore, while the moderate left upheld the institutions of parliamentary democracy, the right, including some government ministers, seemed to encourage attacks on the latter.[9]

Extra-parliamentary groups on the right and the left intensified these attacks. On the left, the communist party, during what was its most sectarian period, prepared for insurrection, and refused to work with any other left-wing parties and especially not with the socialists of the *Section française de l'Internationale ouvrière* (SFO). On the Right and extreme right, maurassian and overtly fascist leagues formed militias and prepared for street warfare. While the communists were tracked down and imprisoned by the police, the extreme right were given much more lenient treatment, thus leading to suspicions of collusion between those who were supposed to be upholding the institutions of the state and those who were attacking them. This could only intensify the rejection of the regime by the young intellectuals already disgusted with the behaviour of the élites. Demonstrations and street-fighting became common occurrences, while the parliamentarians seemed, in the eyes of their critics, to be incapable of doing no more than impotently debating in the National Assembly. In other words, the economic crisis was giving way to a political crisis.

Finally, on the international level, the Versailles settlement itself was breaking down, thus seemingly confirming the suspicions of the young intellectuals. France could not agree with the United States, and Britain on the questions of reparations. Fascism had triumphed in Italy, while national socialism made rapid progress and finally triumphed in Germany. The economic crisis intensified the difficulties in international relations, especially as inflation had eroded the payment of reparations on the part of Germany. The latter began to rearm and, under Hitler, adopted a more belligerent stance. Finally, the League of Nations, itself based on the acceptance of the legitimacy of the nation-state, was impotent and incapable of resolving these problems and even of lessening the tension. The national political leaders seemed blind to the signs of impending international conflict.

The traditional political classes of the right and left thus seemed to many young intellectuals incapable of providing an answer to the crises in which France found itself. For this reason, they began to form their own extra-parliamentary groups. Some of these groups may be described as extreme left or extreme right, in the sense that they expressed in an extreme form the doctrines held by their more moderate elders. The French communist party and various Trotskyist and anarchist groups belong to the first category, while *Action française* and the extreme right and fascist leagues belong to the second. What distinguishes further some of these groups is that they looked outside of France for their inspiration: either to the Russian Revolution or to Mussolini's Italy and the nascent Hitlerite movement in Germany.

It is within this immediate political and intellectual ferment that the emergence of the French personalist and federalist groups may be placed. Indeed, many of their adherents had begun their political activities in the above-mentioned groups and shared some of their *prises de position*.[10] It is useful at this point to distinguish between two principal tendencies. Although both claimed to be both federalist and personalist, at least in the early 1930s, they each emphasized either personalism or federalism. The first tendency, emphasizing personalism, was the group centred on the review *Esprit*, whose principal leader was Emmanuel Mounier. The second, emphasizing federalism, was *Ordre Nouveau*, founded by Arnaud Dandieu and Robert Aron. At first, there was some overlapping in the membership of these groups, a notable example being that of Alexandre Marc whose concern was always to unite movements sympathetic to federalism. However, despite these differences of emphasis it is convenient to treat the two tendencies as constituting one personalist/federalist movement, at least in the early 1930s. What united them was their common rejection of the capitalist, liberal democratic nation-state as well as of communist regimes and their advocacy of a decentralised federal political system.

The personalist/federalist movement, in common with the other movements of young people in the 1930s, interpreted the crises that France was experiencing as being, in reality, *one* fundamental crisis: *a crisis of civilization*.

This crisis was total: 'It is the entire system, right down to its most vital parts, that is affected and eaten away by a cancer.'[11] Dandieu and Aron, in a book which had a wide impact, *La Révolution nécessaire*, expressed it thus: 'The present crisis is not simply a single social, national or economic crisis: it is a crisis of consciousness, and therefore universal.'[12]

The existing political system, however, was incapable of providing an adequate response because it was itself one of the principal causes of the crisis. The personalists/federalists, again in common with other movements, described the liberal democratic and capitalist system as 'le désorde établi' (established disorder), a phrase much used by Emmanuel Mounier. The 'nation-state', capitalism and communism were interpreted as new idols on the altars of which are sacrificed the individual. As Denis de Rougemont expressed it: 'You already are well aware of these gods: they are the State, nation, race, money and public opinion.'[13]

In effect, this was a new and contemporary formulation of the old conservative critique of the liberal democratic state. The latter was characterized by a centralization which crushes the individual, who is dehumanized because he has been uprooted ('déraciné'), torn away from 'his natural environment of living and thinking, to be submitted to an economic system which denies him'.[14] Daniel-Rops linked the phenomenon of the increase of the powers of the state with the arrival of a period of decadence: 'Every epoch marked by decadence is characterized by the same unhealthy increase of State power.'[15]

The federalist/personalist movement rejected other manifestations of the 'désordre établi' associated with the 'nation-state', and in particular the economic system associated with it which they described as 'liberal capitalism'. It was not simply the techniques of capitalism which were rejected, but also its underlying spirit of greed and individualism. Furthermore, since it led to the creation of social classes and class struggle, it was detrimental to the building of true community. Marxism, interpreted as a system of thought and political organisation which intensified the worst aspects of liberal capitalism, was seen therefore as a still more monstrous version of capitalism. Both capitalism and communism were responsible for what the personalists, and particularly Alexandre Marc, referred to as the 'condition prolétarienne' (proletarian state), which destroyed the dignity of the individual by submitting him to brutal working processes. Instead, a system of 'corporatism' was advocated although it was claimed this was different from the fascist version, despite a certain amount of sympathy and mutual contacts between some personalists and federalist and members of the Nazi and fascist movements in Germany and Italy. In effect, this was the beginning of the attempt to find a 'middle way' between capitalism and socialism that characterised much Catholic social thinking at this period and which later influenced both Christian democracy and social democracy after the Second World War.

The next step was to condemn the political institutions of 'liberal capitalism', the parliamentary system and the system of parties that went with it. The latter were seen as instruments of centralisation. Alexandre Marc expressed it thus: 'the party exists only because of the State, it is the projection of 'statism' in the 'public' life of society. By necessity, therefore, it is abstract, oppressive, and centralising.'[16] The notion of representative democracy was attacked as being based on a form of deception—the notion that the 'people' were represented by periodically elected politicians. Although these critiques may be related to the anarchist critique of the state, the federalists disagreed with the latter by accepting that some kind of state was a necessary evil.

For the personalists/federalists the abomination of abominations was the Jacobin attempt to identify the state with the nation. This allowed the state to substitute itself for society and leads to a *levelling* of the latter. Daniel-Rops summed up this argument thus:

> Today, everything in the State tends toward this abstract uniformity. A centraliza-
> tion which for a long time seemed to be necessary, and whose unhealthiness one is
> only beginning to suspect, leads to a denial of fundamental differences which,
> through regional traditions and customs, and ethnic revivals, are rooted deeply in
> men's hearts.[17]

Finally, this nation-state, oppressive within, was imperialist without, For this reason, it was the real cause of international conflict as different imperialist states, acting as laws unto themselves, inevitably clashed. This, in effect, was the root cause of the failure of the League of Nations and the Wilsonian principles on which it was based. Only when nation-states ceased to claim absolute sovereignty for themselves could the basis for a peaceful international order be laid.

It might be remarked that the above critique of the liberal nation-state is no more than a regurgitation of traditional clerical conservatism with a dose of Proundhonian anarchism thrown in. Indeed, such a remark is probably justified. However, the federalists of the 1930s may also be seen as renovating this critique and updating it by giving it a more contemporary and deeper philosophical basis. Mounier, whose name is most associated with personalism, was clearly influenced by Catholic philosophers such as Bergson, Jacques Maritain and Gabriel Marcel, while the *Ordre Nouveau* group was influenced by some of the German existentialist philosophers such as Karl Jaspers, under whom Alexandre Marc had studied before arriving in France. It seems that Proudhon was an inspiration only at a later stage and was not read by the early founders with the exception perhaps of Dandieu.

This philosophical reflection allowed the federalists to develop an alternative to the 'désordre établi' which took the form of the advocacy of new concrete political institutions, at both the internal and international levels. However, in this matter there was a difference between the two main groups *Esprit* and *Ordre Nouveau*. *Esprit*, under the influence of Mounier, tended to restrict themselves to the elaboration of general principles, while *Ordre Nouveau*, on the contrary, laid emphasis on translating principles into concrete structures and action.

What unified the groups at the beginning was their belief that at the centre of all political, social and economic structures, the human person should be paramount.[18] But this 'person' was different from the abstract individual of liberal democracy and from the Marxist individual whose uniqueness was sacrificed to the interest of class. For the personalists, the 'person' was both a spiritual being and rooted in the rich diversity of concrete experience. Liberalism and Marxism attacked both of these aspects of the person, either by levelling him out in an abstract equality and destroying the natural framework in which he should live, or by reducing him to being a member of an economic class. It was this concept of the person, understood as the spiritual individual rooted in a rich, concrete reality, which formed the basis of the political philosophy of French federalism. It led them to advocate that, rather than a gigantesque and highly centralised state, the political structures of society should take the form of a decentralisation which would respect the rights of natural communities: the family, the commune, the region. In other words, the individual could find his fulfilment only as a member of a natural community: 'contrary to the abstract individual, the person is deeply rooted in an earthly and incarnated reality.'[19]

Such communities possessed a distinct identity of their own which should be respected. As communities they also possessed rights which they must be allowed to exercise. It is clear that such a notion is directly contrary to the notion of 'sovereignty' contained in the traditional Jacobin idea of the 'one and indivisible Republic'.[20] If such communities possess the right to run their own affairs, then sovereignty is many and divided.

What, then, should be the relationship between the state, accepted as a necessary evil, and such entities? The federalists solved this problem by appealing to the principle of subsidiarity, a principle found in Catholic social teaching, which states that each level of society should take decisions appropriate to that level. In other words, opposing the centralized decision-making system of the nation-state is the more personalist and humanistic system of federalism. Such a development was freely acknowledged to be revolutionary: '[a] revolution [based] on an understanding of the world where unity and diversity are in equilibrium. [This revolution] links universalistic personalism to a decentralizing federalism.'[21]

For *Ordre Nouveau*, federalism was not simply a form of political organisation as was the case in the United States or Switzerland, but a new humanism. It had three essential characteristics:

1. it started from small human groups;
2. these groups would federate, not in an arbitrary or hierarchical way, but in relation to their activities and concrete existence;
3. institutions of the state would be simply instruments of coordination.

This plan would apply to functional economic groups such as farmers or workers as well as natural communities such as the commune.

Beginning with this analysis of the existing nation-state, a theory of international relations could be developed. The federalists criticised the League of Nations and proposals for international unity on the grounds that they continued to be based on the continuing salience of the nation-state. The French federalists believed that it was impossible to federate such states: only states that were already federations could federate. However, this did not deter them, even in the 1930s, from promoting the idea of European unity and from making contacts in other countries such as Germany, Britain, Italy and Belgium. The personal contacts of Alexandre Marc, especially in Germany, proved an important source of contacts, while Denis de Rougemont was a Swiss who brought with him a direct knowledge of Swiss federalism.

The French personalists and federalists in the 1930s may be seen as prophets crying in the wilderness. It is unlikely that the key political or administrative élites in France at that time either knew about, or paid much attention to, their ideas. The journals which they produced had a limited circulation, although the considerable output of books and pamphlets reached a wider audience. Furthermore, the federalists refused on principle to form a political party. They therefore did not engage in recruiting campaigns designed to attract the masses. On the contrary, they believed in a certain élitism and their number remained restricted to a small group of intellectuals, largely drawn from the middle classes.

This already small group also showed a tendency to split almost from the very beginning: a meeting between Dandieu, founder of *Ordre Nouveau*, and Mounier (*Esprit*), which had been arranged by Marc showed an incompatibility at the personal level between the two principal leaders, which did little to facilitate collaboration at the level of organisations. More seriously, towards the end of the 1930s, Mounier criticised what he perceived (probably unfairly) to be the fascist tendencies of *Ordre Nouveau* and its dogmatism, while the adherents of *Ordre Nouveau* looked with askance at the continually leftward orientation of Mounier. Eventually, Mounier became 'a man of the left' and reluctant to describe himself as either a personalist or federalist, while the group identified with *Ordre Nouveau* emphasised their federalism and continued to assert that they were 'ni droite, ni gauche' (neither left-wing nor right-wing). Eventually in 1938, as the international crisis grew worse and a new war loomed larger, the organised groups began to disintegrate. However, they left behind them a largely coherent political philosophy and a group of politically conscious young men. When war did break out, these were simply confirmed in their conviction that the old regime of nation-states was politically and morally bankrupt.

After the French defeat, the occupation of part of France and the installation of the Marshall Pétain's regime, some federalists from the *Ordre Nouveau* tendency rallied to the new regime and a few even occupied important positions. This minority thought that Pétain's 'National Revolution' was the 'revolution' which they had struggled for. Indeed, aspects of the Vichy regime seemed to correspond to some of the federalists' proposals: for example, its decentralisation and corporatism. However, most of the federalists and personalists joined the Resistance. Mounier went to prison, while Alexandre Marc took refuge in Switzerland. It seems that it was at this period that these two important thinkers began to read Proudhon more deeply than hitherto and his ideas began to exercise a stronger influence, particularly on Marc.

The idea of a united Europe gained wide acceptance in the Resistance, given the collapse of the old political system of nation-states and the traditional conservative élites associated with it. In 1943, Henri Frenay, founder of the Resistance movement *Combat*, took to task the narrow nationalism he thought he discerned in De Gaulle's entourage in London: 'What we are fighting is an attempt to unite Europe by violence by a totalitarian regime. On the contrary, we are now fighting the very people with whom, after the Liberation, we will have to work together to build a free and democratic Europe.'[22] The theme of European unity as a major goal for postwar Europe appeared frequently in the non-communist clandestine press.[23] This was all the more remarkable given Hitler's annexation of the idea and the fact that Germany was the principal enemy. However, it must be admitted that this 'Europeanism' remained rather vague and was more often inspired by the international pacifism of Briand than by revolutionary federalism.

Nevertheless, more specific federalist options began to be put forward. In 1941, the *Movimento Federalista Europeo* (MFE) was founded in Italy by Altiero Spinelli and Ernesto Rossi. In 1943, the MFE held a meeting in Milan. In June 1944, a French section of the MFE was founded in Lyon. This group diffused a *Projet de déclaration en faveur d'une union fédérale entre les peuples européens*.[24] Meanwhile, Marc continued his activities in Switzerland. With Joseph Voyant, a future *Mouvement Républicaine Populaire*

(MRP) Senator, he drew up a politico-social 'charter', which showed a strong federalist slant and was meant to contribute to the philosophy of what would become the christian democratic MRP. However, already, in these two men, Spinelli and Marc, can be found the great division of postwar federalism: the hamiltonian federalism of the former and the 'fédéralisme intégral' of the latter, i.e. a distinction between federalism understood principally as a political arrangement and federalism as an all-embracing humanistic philosophy.

The commitment and sacrifice of the federalists in the Resistance gave them an audience and prestige which they did not possess before the war. Furthermore, their critique of the old nationalisms based on what they regarded as the discredited nation-state was now shared by a much wider public. The fact of the war itself and the spectacle of Europe in ruins gave an impulse to the European movement to which the federalists contributed and which, in turn, raised their public profile. The events following the war, and the first steps toward European integration, are well known and fall outside the scope of this work.[25]

This chapter has attempted to trace the continuity of ideas and personnel of the French federalist and personalist movement from the 1930s to the period immediately after the war. The argument is that although this movement was confined to a limited group of intellectuals and did not reach a wider mass audience, the seeds were sown which would later sprout as the burgeoning European communities. It could be said that the federalists and personalists adopted certain themes of the traditional French right and renovated them by synthesising them with contemporary philosophical currents. This synthesis was to a large extent the work of the minority of French Catholics who were attempting to update their Church's social and political teaching.

In the early years of the Fourth Republic, at least after the isolation of the Gaullists and communists, the presence of these groups ensured a sympathy on the part of politicians such as Robert Schumann and administrators such as Jean Monnet and J.-F. Gravier to both European integration and regionalism. Although the personalist movement under Mounier's leadership moved significantly to the left and even towards French communism, the record of the French federalists during this period in promoting the European idea is impressive, as Greilsammer has shown in his study of the postwar movements. Furthermore, as this author has tried to illustrate, the French federalists played an important role in the development of consciousness concerning the regional question and in the resurgence of linguistic and cultural minorities.

Finally, the intellectual legacy of the 'angry young men' of the 1930s might even be discerned in many of the themes of 'May '68', although research remains to be carried out in the area. It could also be argued that in the new socialist party of Mitterrand, formed in 1972, important tendencies were influenced by personalist and federalist themes. This may help to explain why the traditionally Jacobin French socialists adopted regionalist policies in the 1960s and 1970s which eventually led to the decentralization reforms of 1982. In the end, however, the federalists could not transform France into a federal state nor Europe into a federal system. What they did do was to assist the opening of minds necessary for the tentative first steps to be taken as well as to return political legitimacy to ideas such as decentralization and regionalism.

Notes

1. See J.E.S. Hayward, *Governing France: The One and Indivisible Republic* (London, Weidenfeld and Nicolson, 1983), 2nd ed, Ch.1.
2. B. Voyenne, *Histoire de l'idée fédéraliste* (Nice, Presses d'Europe, 1973), Vol.1, *Les Sources*.
3. See Proudhon, 'Le principe fédératif', in *Oeuvres choisies*, (Textes présentés par Jean Bancal, Paris, Gallimard, 1967), p. 182.
4. ibid., p. 166.
5. ibid., p.202.
6. But for a nuanced interpretation of Proudhon's approach to Christianity, see H. de Lubac, *The Un-Marxian Socialist: A Study of Proudhon* (London, Sheed and Ward, 1948).
7. See H. Dubief, *Le Déclin de la IIIe République, 1929–1939* (Paris, Editions de Seuil, 1976).
8. ibid., pp. 74–5.
9. ibid., pp. 15–16.
10. See B. Voyenne, *Histoire de l'idée fédéraliste*, op. cit., Vol 3, *Les Lignées proudhoniennes*, Ch. VI, 'Personnalisme et Fédéralisme'; for a more detailed study, see E. Lipiansky and B. Rettenbach, *Ordre et démocratie, deux sociétés de pensée: de l'Order Nouveau au Club Jean-Moulin* (Paris, PUF, 1967).
11. Quoted in ibid.
12. Quoted in ibid.
13. Quoted in ibid., p. 24.
14. Quoted in ibid.
15. ibid.
16. ibid., p. 35.
17. Quoted in ibid., p. 37.
18. See E. Mounier, *Le personnalisme* (Paris, *Que sais-je?*, PUF, 1947); Jean-Marie Domenach *Emmanuel Mounier* (Paris, Editions du Seuil, 1972).
19. Quoted in Lipiansky and Rettenbach, *Ordre et Démocratie*, op.cit., p. 45.

20. See Hayward, *Governing France*, op.cit.
21. Lipiansky and Rettenbach, *Ordre et Démocratie*, op.cit., p. 49.
22. Quoted in Voyenne, *Histoire de l'idée fédéraliste*, op.cit.
23. ibid., p. 198.
24. ibid., p. 201.
25. On developments after 1945, see A. Greilsammer, *Les Mouvements fédéralistes en France de 1945 à 1974* (Nice, Presses d'Europe, 1975); for the relations between federalists and regionalists, see J. Loughlin, 'Federalist and regionalist movements in France', in M. Burgess (ed.), *Federalism and Federation in Western Europe* (London, Croom Helm, 1986), pp. 76–98.

12 Federalism in Britain and Italy: Radicals and the English Liberal Tradition

John Pinder

In 1918, two long articles appeared in the *Corriere della Sera* in the form of letters signed by 'Junius'.[1] They argued that the dogma of sovereignty was the cause of war and must therefore be destroyed. Instead of the alliance or confederation that was likely to be established as the League of Nations, a federal state was required, with its own army, taxation and administration, exercising its powers in direct relation with the citizens, as in the United States of America. Junius contrasted the Pan-Germanist literature, with its stress on protectionism and the supremacy of the state, with the Anglo-Saxon liberal tradition. He was a remarkable precursor of the British federalists who were before long to base their proposals on a similar critique of the League.

Junius was in fact Luigi Einaudi, the eminent liberal economist from Piedmont who was to become the first President of the Italian Republic after the Second World War. When Einaudi wrote the first of the two articles, Attilio Cabiati, another liberal economist who was one of his close friends,[2] was already working with Giovanni Agnelli, the founder of Fiat, on a book that was also published in 1918, under the title *Federazione Europea o Lega delle Nazioni?*[3] In it, they expounded the same idea as Einaudi with greater precision and depth. Whereas Einaudi was less than crystal clear about the extent of the union, they unequivocally proposed a European federation. Its institutions were to include a federal congress, government, and court to ensure the rule of law — on which they laid much emphasis. The federal powers were to comprise foreign policy, armed forces, finance and trade, with the other powers reserved to the member states.

Agnelli and Cabiati foreshadowed much in the British federalist literature of the next two decades. This is less surprising than it may seem, for the book was inspired by the political culture on which the British were nurtured as a matter of course. It shows impressive knowledge of the literature on politics and economics in the English liberal tradition. In its list of twenty-five 'principal works consulted', no less than twenty-one are British. When the authors refer to other schools of thought it is usually to criticise them for glorifying the state and thus sustaining a system that leads to war.[4] They took Bismarck, Treitschke and Von Bulow to task for this, and they were likewise critical of the French concept of national unity, leading to the supremacy of the collective will, in contrast with the English concept of liberty which brings 'benefits to all alike'.[5]

The two authors follow John Locke in contrasting the liberal principle which establishes the citizen's rights with the legitimist principle which defends the sovereign's rights. They cite Acton's proposition that the best guarantee of liberty is a multinational state. When they emphasise that a league of nations is not enough because independent states are prone to go to war with each other, they cite Sidgwick's conclusion that a federal government to enforce the rule of law in Europe is required. On the horrors of modern war, and hence the unviability of absolute sovereignty, they refer to an article by H.G. Wells, and they cite Robertson at length to establish the economic advantages to be derived from the division of labour within a federation.[6]

Agnelli and Cabiati found in the history of the nineteenth century the grounds for an Italian liberal and federalist tradition. In contrast with German unification, attained by a war of aggression with the aim of Prussian supremacy, Italian unity had resulted from a war of liberation; for the Carbonari, the aim of throwing off Austrian rule had been not just Italian unity, but political reform.[7] Had the two authors been less absorbed in the English liberal literature, they could have shown how Carlo Cattaneo had then given a precise exposition of the idea of federalism and of its institutional form, enhancing liberty by the limitation of power at each level of government. He had applied the idea of federalism both to the relationship among the peoples that compose a nation and, beyond the nation, to an international federation, explaining that the two forms of unity are not in conflict because both follow from a single principle: liberty. He sought in this way to reconcile the demands of liberty and unity both within Italy and in Europe as a whole, pointing to Switzerland and the United States as models for the United States of Europe.[8]

Mazzini, too, frequently referred to the ideal of European unity, but he never explored it in any depth. The uniting of Italy was, for him, the all-encompassing priority.[9] Mazzinians of this century have followed him in favouring the idea of European unity, but some have remained attached to the nation-state and thus have found it hard to come to terms with the concept of a federal Europe. A case in point was the brilliant young Torinese Piero Gobetti, who saw the nations as 'fraternal, but sovereign and armed', and whose review of the book of Agnelli and Cabiati criticised it on the grounds that the people would 'never renounce their history . . . (nor) seek Nirvana in an artificial unity.'[10]

Gramsci also attacked Agnelli and Cabiati, but on grounds that had little to do with the contents of the book, which he appeared to have misread.[11] There was, however, no chance of communist approval for federalist proposals since Lenin had pronounced that the class war and the victory of the proletariat through revolution must come first. The communists' devotion to the collective will and, as they became more Stalinist, to the power of the state also made their ideology incompatible with the liberal principle of limited government on which the federalists' proposals were based.

Liberals such as Einaudi at that time saw the marxists as the principal enemies of the liberal order, and his review of Agnelli and Cabiati 'undervalued the nationalist opposition' to any such plans for safeguarding peace.[12] Soon, however, Mussolini was to show himself a deadly enemy of both liberal and federalist principles. He did not believe in the 'utility of permanent peace' and proclaimed the nobility of war. Giovanni Gentile, the leading academic theoretician of fascism, 'endowed it with his neo-Hegelian and ethereal brand of "actual idealism" '.[13] Even when the reality of war was proving less noble than they had hoped, and some of the fascists were attracted to the idea of European unity, their absolutist view of the state made it hard for them to absorb federalist ideas.[14]

The immediate problem after Mussolini marched on Rome in October 1922 was not, however, the incompatibility of principle between fascism and federalism, but the suppression of freedom by a violent authoritarian regime. The fascists persecuted those who strove for a democratic Italy and murdered the leaders of those political tendencies that were to produce most of the committed federalists. The pioneering works of Agnelli, Cabiati and Einaudi disappeared from view and the development of federalist thought was driven into exile and the underground. Meanwhile, the focus must shift to Britain, where federalists remained free to develop their ideas.

Philip Kerr, later Lord Lothian, was private secretary to Lloyd George as Prime Minister during the First World War and afterwards at the Peace Conference. This caused him to reflect deeply about the problem of peace and war, and a spell at the Institute of Politics in Williamstown soon after enabled him to articulate a federalist analysis, based on the premiss that absolute sovereignty leads to war and concluding that the safeguarding of peace requires the establishment of international, and ultimately world, federation.[15] He developed these ideas in a number of publications during the following ten years, culminating in 1935 with *Pacifism is not Enough (nor Patriotism Either)*, which many Italian federalists still regard as one of the fundamental federalist texts.[16]

Lothian's interest in federalism dated from 1905, when he joined other young contemporaries from Oxford to work in Milner's 'Kindergarten', seeking to reconcile the Afrikaners in a relatively liberal South African union after the Boer War.[17] One of those contemporaries was Lionel Curtis, who was to generate and share with him a lifelong federalist commitment. The proximate cause of this was their need to think about a constitution uniting the existing four South African colonies, which led them to a close study of *The Federalist* and of the foundation of the United States.[18] After their plan for a federal constitution had been set aside in favour of a unitary state, they returned to London and founded *The Round Table* quarterly, which from 1910 on propagated the federal idea, with particular reference to the Commonwealth.

Curtis, a passionate advocate of Commonwealth federation, published a book on the subject in 1917, which was extensively quoted by Agnelli and Cabiati to underline his advocacy of responsible government and the rule of law. His idea was that the mission of the Commonwealth was to increase the number of citizens fit for responsible government and to extend control of the supreme functions of government to all of them.[19] Later, in the mid-1930s, he was to write his magnum opus, *Civitas Dei*, in which he envisaged that the process of establishing a world federation would start with the states most experienced in self-government—which, he implied, pointed to the need for Anglo-American leadership.[20]

Lothian was quicker than Curtis to see that the other Commonwealth countries would not federate with Britain and to put his mind, following Versailles, to the idea of wider international federation. In *Pacificism is not Enough*, his critique of the League of Nations and concept of federation were similar to those of Einaudi, Agnelli and Cabiati. Unlike them, he aimed his argument, as his title implied, at the pacifist tendency which had become so widespread in Britain by the mid-1930s. Typical of the naive idealism then prevalent was the suggestion of Gilbert Murray, for many years President of the League of Nations Union, that the governments should secure world peace by acting unanimously to carry out the advice of a council of the world's wisest men.[21] Lothian argued powerfully that law, to be effective, had to be enforceable, and that, since world federation was as yet unattainable, a nucleus of democracies should federate in order to apply this principle.

Although Lothian had resigned from his post as a Liberal minister in the national government over an economic issue when imperial preference was enshrined in the Ottawa Agreement in 1932, he was far from being an economist, and it fell to another distinguished liberal to expound the basic economic arguments for federation. This was Lionel (later Lord) Robbins, who had been given his chair at the London School of Economics in 1929 when he had just turned thirty. He set out his ideas in two books, again still regarded in Italy as classic federalist texts, based on lectures that Professor Rappard had invited him to give at the Institut de Hautes Etudes Internationales in Geneva.[22]

The first book, *Economic Planning and International Order*, published in 1937, linked the case for the division of labour with the need for the framework of an enforceable legal order. Such a political structure existed within the nation-states, but not between them. The failure to understand this had been the great deficiency of nineteenth-century liberalism: the international system it envisaged had been 'not liberal, but anarchist'.[23] He went on to stand the marxist argument for 'socialism first' on its head, arguing to the contrary that socialist central planning was more likely to cause wars than capitalism, because it raised all conflicts of economic interest to the level of national policy.

That book made the economic case for federation in general, but did not indicate who should federate or when. By the summer of 1939, Robbins was quite clear about both the urgency and the membership of the federation he advocated. In *The Economic Causes of War*, whose final section, completed in the first days after the Second World War began, was entitled 'The United States of Europe', he urged that 'unless we destroy the sovereign state, the sovereign state will destroy us', and he concluded that, since world federation would not be feasible for a long time to come and since, 'in our generation at least', the United States would not be ready to federate with other peoples, it was necessary to create a European federation, to be established after the overthrow of nazism and to include a democratic postwar Germany.[24]

With their three books, Lothian and Robbins brought to fruition what Einaudi, Agnelli and Cabiati had started: they provided a strong liberal structure for federalist thought. Although both Lothian and Robbins were Liberals with a capital 'L', their ideas were usable by liberals with a small 'l'. They both wrote pamphlets for the Federal Union movement which was established in 1939, and their works have been much studied, cited and reprinted by federalists in Italy to this day.[25]

The influence of Curtis's books has been less lasting, perhaps because of his concentration on the Empire which was about to pass away. He did, however, persuade the young Winston Churchill to take up the cause of a federal United Kingdom in 1912, which was taken up in turn by Lloyd George and Austen Chamberlain and placed high on the political agenda in 1918, as a means of dealing with the Irish problem.[26] This exposure to the federal idea, which Churchill had seen not just as a way of solving an internal problem but as a step towards a wider Commonwealth federation, may have influenced him when he wrote in 1930 of 'federal links' in an article entitled 'The United States of Europe', and when he took up the same theme in his famous speech in Zurich in September 1946, which launched the postwar movement for European unity.[27] But although Conservatives were to play their part in Federal Union, one of its early leaders being Richard Law, a Conservative MP who was the son of a former Prime Minister, their part in developing the ideas and literature between the wars was a minor one. The credit for the most important works belongs to liberals, with significant contributions from socialists.

British socialists, other than marxists, were predominantly favourable to the federal idea during this period. H.N. Brailsford, Kingsley Martin, Bertrand Russell, Leonard Woolf and H.G. Wells were all advocates of federation who influenced the founders of Federal Union. R.H. Tawney placed national sovereignty along with capitalism as one of the two great evils of the age. G.D.H. Cole was broadly in favour. Among those who were to be Labour's leaders after the war, Bevin called for a United States of Europe and Attlee wrote that 'Europe must federate or perish'.[28]

The federal idea was evidently part of the contemporary political culture for reformist socialists in Britain. But most of the evidence is in the form of fairly short references in works for which this was not the principal theme. Among socialists, the exception was Laski, who devoted a considerable part of his writing to the subject from 1917 onwards. In his *Studies in the Problem of Sovereignty*, published in that year, he expressed his opposition to the monistic view of the state, and his preference for 'a country where sovereignty is distributed'. In his *A Grammar of Politics*, first published in 1925, he included a chapter on 'Authority as Federal', in which he wrote that 'since society is federal, authority must be federal also'. This principle was to apply beyond as well as within the nation-state. He contrasted the 'historical accident of separate states' with the 'scientific fact of world interdependence', and declared that the 'absolute and independent sovereign state' was 'incompatible with the interests of humanity'.[29]

In the mid-1920s, then, Laski had seemed set to precede Lothian and Robbins in the development of federalist ideas. But instead he was to espouse the marxist belief that 'the class-structure of society' must be 'destroyed' first. It was capitalism, not the nation-state, that was 'rooted in a system which makes power the criterion of right and war the ultimate expression of power'. Given the capitalist class relations, it was 'impossible to realise the ideal of an effective international community'. Liberal ideology must be abandoned as the expression of this doomed economic system, and the marxian theory of the state 'holds the field'.[30] Like the Italian marxists, he postponed constructive thought about the international order until capitalism should be overthrown; and British socialists lost their most brilliant federalist pioneer. It was socialists such as Brailsford, Mackay and Wootton, shorter on academic lustre but longer on political judgement, who were to make the subsequent contributions to federalist thinking, working on the assumption that the worst enemy of socialism was war, and the root cause of war was not capitalism but the sovereign nation-state.[31]

By 1938, then, a rich literature on federalism was available to anybody who could read English. Since the First World War there had been the books of Lothian and Curtis, Laski's earlier works and the first of the two books by Lionel Robbins, as well as frequent references in other works. This was on top of the earlier literature, some of which had been cited by Einaudi, Agnelli and Cabiati: the writings on federalism by Acton, J.S. Mill and Sidgwick; *The Federalist* of Hamilton, Jay and Madison; Bryce's monumental *The American Commonwealth*; Dicey's chapter on 'Parliamentary Sovereignty and Federalism' in his classic *Introduction to the Law of the Constitution*; and works by Freeman, Seeley and others on particular federations or on the idea of the United States of Europe.[32] Thus there was no lack of knowledge and thought about federalism. What had been absent until then was the impulse to apply it to a political project in Europe or the wider world.

It was after Munich that three young men, Charles Kimber, Patrick Ransome and Derek Rawnsley, decided to found a federalist movement in Britain, which they called Federal Union. They soon had the active support of Lothian and Curtis, of Wickham Steed, a former Editor of *The Times*, and of Barbara Wootton, then lecturing at London University and subsequently Leader of the Labour Party in the House of Lords. Then came leading academics such as Beveridge, Robbins, Jennings and Joad, and rising politicians such as Richard Law, MP, and R.W.G. Mackay. A stream of pamphlets and books followed, many by distinguished authors. The publication in March 1939 of Clarence Streit's *Union Now* had given a strong boost to the idea of a federation of the democracies, including the United States. But with the onset of war in Europe alongside continued American isolation, Federal Union came to focus on the idea of a European federation launched by Britain and France, to be joined by a democratic postwar Germany after nazism had been overthrown. There was powerful editorial support from *The Times*, *The Guardian* and the *New Statesman*. Membership grew rapidly to ten thousand. The Archbishop of York said that 'The whole scheme of Federal Union has made a staggeringly effective appeal to the British mind'.[33]

The enthusiasm was cut short by the fall of France. The climate of opinion in which the British government did not hesitate to offer an indissoluble union to France can be seen as its culmination. But the French government rejected the offer in favour of capitulation and Britain turned towards the United States. The federalist literature and Federal Union's early success were to be the victims of collective amnesia in Britain. It was in the unpromising ground of Mussolini's prison camps that the British federalist ideas were to take root and start their strongest growth.

While British federalists developed and propagated their ideas with such striking success in the fertile context of the liberal tradition, the political forces that were to carry forward these ideas with yet more success in postwar Italy were meanwhile squeezed between two deadly opponents of liberal thought: the fascists, who idolised the authoritarian nation-state, and marxists, who rejected discussion of its reform, at least for the duration of the class war. Fear of a communist victory, moreover, was one of the motives that led many among the establishment to support or at least tolerate the fascists, thus further narrowing the scope for developing democratic federalism. Pius XI was among those who expressed his sympathy for the regime, and he doubtless reflected a view widely held among the clergy when he expressed his horror, not only of the socialists, but also of the liberal school, whom he described as 'men to whom all laws and regulations . . . were like fetishes.'[34] Fortunately for the future of Italian democracy, however, there were also politically active Catholics who were much more favourable to liberal principles; they included Don Sturzo, a Sicilian aristocrat and priest who founded the Catholic *Partito Popolare Italiano* in 1919, and his lieutenant Alcide De Gasperi, a lawyer from Trento who was, as Prime Minister after the Second World War, to play a decisive part in the foundation of the European Community.

Don Sturzo was opposed to fascism and he led the Congress of the *PPI* in 1923 to condemn the fascist regime.[35] A few months later, Mussolini's squadristi killed Don Minzoni, a politically active priest. Don Sturzo went into exile soon after, living in London until 1940, then in New York until 1946 when he returned to Italy.

In Don Sturzo's first speech in exile, in March 1925, he affirmed the duty to oppose the notion that the nation-state is the only God. But this did not lead him directly to federalism. His commitment was, rather, like that of his social reformist friends (who included Sidney Webb), to internationalism in general and the League of Nations in particular. He argued in 1929 for union as against national sovereignty, but he saw no clear distinction between a federation such as the United States and an international association such as the Commonwealth.[36] By April 1940, however, he had joined the federal unionists in seeing Britain and France as the 'nucleus of a future federation', which must, he insisted, be based on ethical and political principles that excluded dictatorships of right and left.[37] Don Sturzo was certainly in close touch with leading members of Federal Union: he had worked with Wickham Steed in the late 1930s to promote the British Committee for Civil and Religious Peace in Spain.[38]

Italian Catholics were, as Spinelli observed, less attached than mazzinian liberals to the nation-state.[39] If sympathetic, as Don Sturzo was, to liberal constitutional principles, and exposed, as he evidently was in London, to the federalist analysis of the international system, they were apt to espouse the federalist cause. After his postwar return to Italy, Don Sturzo was to support the *Movimento Federalista Europeo* (MFE) and to insist that 'we federalists want solid federations such as the USA or Switzerland, not loose international associations, and must hurry to make them a reality'.[40]

The political scene to which Don Sturzo returned was dominated by De Gasperi. De Gasperi had succeeded Don Sturzo as Secretary General of the PPI, and then underwent a short spell in prison, followed, from 1929 onwards, by a form of exile in the Vatican before becoming Prime Minister in 1945. When the Christian Democratic Party was founded in 1943, as the successor to the PPI, its policy programme, for which De Gasperi had the chief responsibility, called merely for a 'more effective international system', with disarmament, monetary stability and less protection.[41] The federalist influence, already significant among Christian Democrats in North Italy,[42] was, however, soon to be reinforced by the foundation of the MFE, with, as we shall see, its roots in British federalist thought, and, surely encouraged by the example of his former mentor, Don Sturzo, De Gasperi readily made the transition to the federalist policy which gave strong support to the establishment of the European Coal and Steel Community and was to be, with Spinelli's initiative, seminal in the drafting of the Treaty for a European Political Community, which so nearly gave birth to a European federation.[43]

For over half a century after the Russian revolution, the contribution of Italian socialists to federalist thought and action was undermined by the maximalist dogma that war among nation-states was merely an aspect of the class war: 'social transformation' must be completed before thought could be given to a reform of inter-state relations. The maximalist hard core was the Communist Party, founded in 1921. But its negative influence was extended by those socialists, led by Pietro Nenni, whose priority was unity with the Communist Party, and who therefore refused to countenance federalist ideas until the late 1950s.

The maximalists were, however, opposed by the revisionists, who included the socialist leader, Filippo Turati. Turati had, as a young man, been influenced by the federalist strand of *risorgimento* thought. In 1880 he had supported the idea of a United States of Europe on the pattern of the United States of America, and a decade later he was to praise Cattaneo for his faith in that idea.[44] Although he was to enter a marxist phase in the 1890s, he was always open to other currents of opinion, for example inviting Einaudi and Cabiati to contribute to his review, *Critica sociale*, during that period. This openness led him, after the First World War when so many were becoming stranded on the rock of maximalist dogma, to recognise the need to revise 'our outdated ideology' in the light of experience, and an important element in his revision was the recognition that capitalism was not the sole cause of war.[45]

Not long after the leading revisionist, Giacomo Matteotti, was murdered for attacking fascist violence and electoral fraud, Turati escaped to exile in Paris, helped on his way by Carlo Rosselli and Ferruccio Parri, two social liberals who were to play a significant part in Italian federalism.[46] He was soon to return to his early advocacy of federation: a United States of Europe as the supreme aspiration for the democracies, with, like the United States, enough power to keep the peace among the member states, and beyond that a federation of the USA and the USE. At the Fourth Congress of the Socialist International at Vienna in 1931, he went on to explain how the experience of 1914–18 had taught him how much war damages the socialists, who must therefore regard federation as a precondition of socialism, not, as the maximalists insisted, the other way round.[47] He thus anticipated the position taken in Britain by federalist socialists such as Mackay and Wootton, and against Laski's increasingly marxist analysis. But in the following year Turati was to die, and Nenni led the majority of socialists into collaboration with the Communist Party.

A minority of revisionists nevertheless continued to contribute to the Italian federalist tradition. Claudio Treves, who was close to Turati and had, like him, emigrated to Paris in 1926, was one whose influence was to be extended into the postwar period when his protégé, Giuseppe Saragat, founded the pro-European Social Democrat Party. Claudio's two sons, Paolo and Pietro, went to London, advocated European federation, and worked with Federal Union before returning to Italy after the war.[48]

Federalists were also to be found among socialists who had worked with the social liberals who, as we shall see, played a key part in launching the Italian federalist movement. Thus Andrea Caffi, who had been active in the social liberals' leading organization, *Giustizia e Libertà* (GL), in Paris in the mid-1930s, and had moved over to the socialists and to Toulouse where the Italian Socialist Party had its head office, was by 1940 propagating his federalist ideas from there, linking, like the proudhonian Alexandre Marc, the ideas of European federation and local autonomy.[49] When the socialists' office was moved, after the fall of France, to Ignazio Silone's *Centro Estero Socialista* in Zurich, Silone incorporated these ideas into the socialist policy programme. Having been a clandestine communist leader in Italy and expelled from the Communist Party not long after emigrating to Switzerland in 1930, Silone had little time for Nenni's socialist–communist line. He continued to advocate federalism, using the motto *Liberare e Federare* for the weekly paper of the *Centro*; he was to give strong support to the Italian federalist movement and, from the vantage point of the Italian Senate, to the European Union of Federalists, of which he was elected President in 1948.[50] But his ideas then carried little weight with the Italian Socialist Party.

The most important socialist in the founding of the Italian federalist movement, Eugenio Colorni, had also been involved in *Giustizia e Libertà*. After the GL organisation inside Italy was broken by the fascist police in 1935, he too moved over to the socialists, soon becoming one of the leaders of the *Centro Interno Socialista*. Like Turati, he believed that traditional positions must be reviewed and ideologies measured against reality. Like Turati and other revisionists, he was therefore open to federalist ideas. Unlike them, however, he was sent a few months after his arrest in 1938 to confinement in the island of Ventotene, where he was to become a close friend of the founders of the federalist movement. He significantly influenced their thinking and became convinced, in turn, that federation was the primary political goal after the overthrow of fascism. In his preface to their founding document, the Ventotene Manifesto, he affirmed, like Turati, Mackay and Wootton, that federation was the precondition for socialism. After escaping from confinement in 1943, he took part in founding the federalist movement and led a group of young reformist socialists in Rome. He was killed by fascist police in May 1944, just before Rome was liberated.[51]

The reformists in the Italian Socialist Party were to remain eclipsed for some years after the war by those who gave priority to links with the Communist Party and the class war ideology. But the seeds which had been sown by Turati, Treves, Silone, Colorni and others were eventually to bear fruit, when Nenni led the socialists in the late 1950s into a pro-European and eventually a federalist stance. Meanwhile, it was the social liberals who were to make the running for Italian federalism.

From Mussolini's installation in power in 1922 until the fall of fascism in 1943, Einaudi published nothing more on federalism. Indeed, pressure from the fascist police was to cause him to close down the review, *La riforma sociale*, which he had edited from 1908 onwards. But although his liberty of expression was constrained he kept his integrity, and this enabled him to influence young people, including two who were to play crucial parts in the development of Italian federalism: Ernesto Rossi, and Carlo Rosselli, the founder of *Giustizia e Libertà*, which was to bring together so many of the founding fathers of the Italian federalist movement, and who described Einaudi as one of the elite of the previous generation who had 'not forfeited the trust of young people'.[52]

Implicit in Rosselli's respect for Einaudi was condemnation of so many of the liberals of Einaudi's generation who had condoned fascism as a lesser evil than communism. This, together with a feeling that the old liberals did not deal with the workers' problems, drove many of the younger generation towards new groups described as social liberals or liberal socialists. They shared a commitment to a liberal constitution and the liberties that go with it. They were against the dogma of a class war that must be fought and won as a precondition of liberty, but they also opposed the dogma that social justice will follow automatically from *laisser faire*.[53] They valued both justice and liberty—hence the name *Giustizia e Libertà*. The commitment to the principle of a liberal constitution combined with a determination to find the solutions to contemporary problems made them the most fertile of grounds for the growth of federalist ideas.

Giovanni Amendola, a forerunner of the social liberals, founded a National Union of Liberal and Democratic Forces in 1924, whose adherents included both Nello Rosselli and Silvio Trentin, later to be social liberals and federalists.[54] But the fascists saw reformist liberals, like reformist socialists, as dangerous enemies, and they set their thugs to beat up Amendola, as they had done with Matteotti, thus causing his death in 1926. This they followed by assassinating Nello Rosselli with his brother Carlo in 1937 in France, where Carlo had been the principal founder of *Giustizia e Libertà* in 1929.

The Rossellis had strong English and liberal connections. They had British forebears and Carlo was to marry an English wife. He had by 1925 become an assistant to Einaudi at the Bocconi University in Milan. He was, like Cabiati, both active there and teaching at the *Istituto Superiore di Commercio* in Genova. He was also beginning to demonstrate his talent for bold exploits which was to help make GL the most important democratic anti-fascist organisation.[55] He founded, with Nello, the review *Non mollare*, which was to cause a sensation (and to be precipitately shut down) by exposing the fascists' responsibility for Matteotti's murder; one of his collaborators on the review was Rossi, also close to Einaudi and later co-founder of the Italian federalist movement. After helping Turati to escape to France, Rosselli was himself sentenced to confinement, and made in 1929 a spectacular escape to Paris from the island of Lipari, where he had meanwhile written a seminal book entitled *Socialismo liberale*, advocating a liberal constitution, a mixed economy, social justice and international peace.

Once in Paris, Carlo did not delay in founding GL, with the help of Nello, Rossi and Gaetano Salvemini, by then a grand old man for whom Carlo Rosselli and Rossi were 'favourite disciples'.[56] Their journal, *Quaderni di Giustizia e Libertà*, edited by Carlo Rosselli and Caffi, contained from its first issue in 1932 a commitment to European federation, to which theme it returned at intervals. Although the federalist analysis did not compare in depth with that soon to be produced by the federal unionists in Britain, there was a specific advocacy of a European federal constitution and a European government disposing of force at the service of European law, and it appears that the proposal for a constituent assembly, later to be powerfully promoted by Spinelli, was put forward for the first time in the *Quaderni*.[57]

In addition to the Rossellis, Rossi and Caffi, GL was a focus for many of the precursors and founders of the Italian federalist movement. Trentin, who wrote for the *Quaderni*, was one; he founded in Toulouse the resistance group *Libérer et Fédérer* (of which Alexandre Marc was a member and which published a journal under the same name—from which Silone derived the motto for his publication in Zurich). Another was Parri, who was to become the leader of GL's armed resistance during the war and Italy's first postwar prime minister. Colorni participated, as we have seen, in GL before joining the socialists, and met Carlo Rosselli during a visit to Paris in 1937.[58] Among the many other founders of the federalist movement who were active in GL or in its successor, the *Partito d'Azione*, were Aldo Garosci, Ada Gobetti, Manlio Rossi Doria, Gustavo Malan, Mario Rollier, Leo Valiani and Franco Venturi.

Meanwhile another social liberal group was founded by Guido Calogero, Professor of Philosophy at the *Scuola Normale Superiore* at Pisa, whose first manifesto, drawn up in the late 1930s and distributed clandestinely in 1940, called for disarmament, European federation, juridical bodies and means of enforcing international law. The policy as a whole was close to that of GL, and during the period 1942–3 the two groups and some others merged to form the *Partito d'Azione*, whose members, in addition to providing, in Parri, the first postwar prime minister, produced much of the best in federalist thought and action.[59] Most important of all were Rossi and Spinelli, who were to meet each other, along with Colorni, in confinement on Ventotene in 1939.[60]

Altiero Spinelli had reacted to fascism by becoming a leading young communist militant, was given a ten-year prison sentence in 1927, and remained in confinement until the liberation in 1943. From 1929 onwards, however, he began to have doubts about the marxist faith for which he had gone to jail. As he was later to recall his motives, they included the need for 'absolute liberty' of thought and for the right to subject everything to critical appraisal. As he read his way through the literature of philosophy, historiography and economics, his marxism was undermined by his preference for Kant against Hegel and for great liberals such as Benedetto Croce and Alfred Marshall. By 1937 he was expelled from the Communist Party. But his intellectual odyssey was not directed towards an academic destination. Thought, in his view, had to lead to action; 'Spinelli,' a fellow refugee from communism was to say, 'has the stuff of a founder of movements', and the movement he was to found was the answer that he was seeking to the problem of the collapse of Europe that was gathering pace as fascism dragged the Continent into war.[61]

The intellectual content of that answer was profoundly influenced by Rossi and by the thinking of British federalists. Rossi had, on returning to Italy after helping to found GL in Paris, been sentenced in 1930 to twenty years' imprisonment. He was one of the leading lights of GL,[62] seen as a 'legendary hero', who, after his arrival on Ventotene, became for Spinelli 'un maestro della mente'.[63] He appears to have exerted a fundamental liberal influence on the thinking of Spinelli, still in the process of developing his ideas after his escape from communist dogma, and through Spinelli on the Italian federalist movement.

All Rossi's 'chosen affinities' were, according to Spinelli, with the eighteenth-century enlightment, especially that of Britain and France, of which he 'loved the limpid expression, the precise reasoning, the cult of rationality'. His 'cultural formation' was that of 'a rationalist, economist, liberal, brought to see in England the inspiration in the final instance of all the European movement towards the open market economy, towards liberty, parliamentary democracy, social reform'. The latter point was a surprise to Spinelli, who was not among those ex-marxists who flee to the opposite pole of *laisser faire* liberalism and who had expected Rossi to be a conservative in economic and social matters. Instead Spinelli found him to be working on 'innovative ideas' regarding the insertion of some collectivist elements into the market economy, and this in turn convinced Spinelli of the need for the framework of a market, not centrally planned, economy.[64]

While the ideas of mixed economy and welfare state distinguished GL from the old liberals, Rossi's commitment to the liberal constitution and the market economy was at one with that of his old master, Einaudi. Rossi had always been in close touch with Einaudi—he is among the ten individuals most cited in Einaudi's biography. He kept up a correspondence with Einaudi from prison, and it is not surprising that he and Spinelli, in their search for solutions to the problems of war, inter-state relations and the League of Nations, should have found Einaudi's 'Junius' letters of 1918 in a volume of his collected works.[65] Rossi wrote and asked Einaudi for more on the subject, and Einaudi sent him some works by British federalist authors. These certainly included the two books by Robbins, mentioned earlier, which are the most cited sources in the two essays that Spinelli composed following the *Ventotene Manifesto* which Spinelli and Rossi wrote together after they had digested this literature, and a book by von Hayek, then teaching like Robbins at the London School of Economics and active in the Federal Union Research Institute, was cited twice. Spinelli, indeed, translated Robbins's *Economic Causes of War* for publication by Einaudi's publishing house.[66] Federal Union had also by then published pamphlets by Beveridge, Brailsford and Lothian, which may have reached Ventotene via Einaudi; and Spinelli was to extend his reading of British and American federalist works during his stay in Switzerland in 1943–4, adding Layton, Wootton, Streit, Hamilton, Jay and Madison to the list.[67] He was to recall in striking terms the effect that the English federalist writings had on him in Ventotene:

> their analysis of the political and economic perversion that nationalism leads to, and their reasoned presentation of the federal alternative, have remained to this day impressed on my memory as a revelation. Since I was trying to obtain clarity

and precision in thinking, my attention was not drawn by the foggy and contorted ideological federalism of a Proudhon or a Mazzini, but by the clean, precise thinking of these English federalists, in whose writings I found a fairly good method for analysing the chaotic state of affairs into which Europe was plunging and for drawing up alternatives.[68]

When Spinelli and Rossi wrote the Ventotene Manifesto in 1941, its roots in British federalist thought and in the English liberal tradition from Locke onwards were very evident.[69] The first sentence affirmed 'that man is not a mere instrument to be used by others but that every man must be an autonomous centre of life'. The Manifesto then observes that the absolute sovereignty of the nation-state leads to servitude rather than liberty for the citizens. The division of Europe into separate nation-states is diagnosed as the fundamental problem and European federation, with institutions and powers similar to those foreseen by Einaudi and by Federal Union, as the solution. While both authors took responsibility for the whole text, the hand of Rossi is to be seen in the section on 'Postwar tasks. The reform of society', with its advocacy of the mixed economy and welfare state. It was Spinelli's former immersion in the Communist Party, on the other hand, that was reflected in the drawing of a sharp line between reactionaries and progressives —not, to be sure, between two sides in a class war but between those for whom the conquest of national power is the essential aim of politics and those who see the creation of a federal state as the essential task—and in the establishment of a dedicated group to accomplish the federalists' task.[70] Spinelli was later to admit that the section on the 'dedicated group' was expressed in terms that were 'too crudely leninist'.[71] But the sharp distinction between those who were for a European federation and those who were not was to determine his political action for the rest of his life.

The Manifesto was distributed in duplicated form on the Italian mainland from 1941 onwards and was printed for clandestine publication by Colorni, together with Colorni's introduction and the other two essays by Spinelli, in January 1944. It is seen as the foundation text for the Italian federalist movement (*Movimento Federalista Europeo*) that was launched in August 1943, and a principal source for the European Union of Federalists, established four years later. Spinelli was to continue promoting its basic idea up to and beyond the adoption in February 1984 by the European Parliament, thanks mainly to his initiative and effort, of its Draft Treaty for a European Union, developing the Community institutions into a federal legislature, executive and court, and extending its powers to cover money and tax as well as trade, though only tentatively to security; and the Italian federalists continue with this work. An apt comment on the contribution of the British federalist writings to this explosion of intellectual and political activity was the Latin tag cited by Spinelli: 'habent sua fata libelli' (little books have their own destiny).[72]

It is remarkable how swiftly and powerfully the spark crossed, as the interwar period ended and war began, from a northern to a southern pole of federalism. The aim of this essay has been to seek the reasons why.

The rich body of federalist literature written in Britain between 1935 and 1940 by authors such as Beveridge, Jennings, Curtis, Lothian, Mackay, Robbins, Wheare and Wootton, and the associated political action by Federal Union, could only have flourished with its roots in a political culture that was fertile for such a growth. This, we have seen, included the liberal constitutional tradition, inherited from such great nineteenth-century figures as Acton and Mill, with their normative writings on multinational federation, and Bryce and Dicey, with their scholarly evaluations of the federal system in the United States. These in turn stemmed from the achievements of the American federalists, particularly Hamilton, Jay and Madison, whose political philosophy was rooted in Locke, Hume and Montesquieu: on the liberal principle of limiting the power of the sovereign, by means of the rule of law, civil rights and representative government; and on the principle of dividing sovereignty among different levels of government, which they derived from the liberal principle of limiting sovereignty. This liberal philosophy also embraced the empirical method, measuring ideas and ideologies against their performance in the real world and adjusting them when they proved inadequate. The federalists found that national sovereignty was associated with war and economic autarky, so they adjusted their idea of sovereignty to provide for its sharing under a federal constitution. The federalists were also rooted in a radical tradition of action against social ills, of which they saw international anarchy as the greatest.

Most of the Italians who so eagerly adopted the federal idea were rooted in the same philosophy. Einaudi was steeped in the liberal tradition, constitutional as well as economic. C. Rosselli and Rossi had been his disciples. Rosselli brought together in GL many of the radical social liberals who were to help found the federalist movement. Rossi conveyed the liberal philosophy and the British federalist ideas to Spinelli, who established them in the federalist movement, together with his own ideas on how federation should be achieved. The approaches to liberal and federalist principles varied widely across the Italian political spectrum. But the coherence of the hard core of federalists, themselves profoundly influenced by British liberal and federalist ideas, enabled them to exert a pervasive influence on Italian attitudes towards federalism.

Both British and Italian federalists had *virtu*: liberal consitutional principles and zeal to reform the international system in the light of them. But their *fortuna* was diverse. In the interwar period, Italian fascism suppressed liberal principles and exalted the nation-state. Federalism could develop only clandestinely or in exile, whereas in Britain federalists were free to write and work. They felt a strong sense of their responsibility to urge Britain, as a liberal and democratic great power, to act in order to establish a durable peace; and under the pressure of impending war they made a great effort to develop federalist thought (Federal Union Research Institute), action (Federal Union) and policy (European federation based initially on Britain and France).

After the war, however, Britain, its confidence in the British nation-state restored and that in its Continental neighbours for the time-being low, turned its back on the idea of European federation which was spreading like wildfire on the Continent. The Italians, on the contrary, had lost their confidence in the nation-state. Liberal democracy prevailed. Continental neighbours were moving to establish the European Community to replace the prewar European anarchy. The time was ripe for Spinelli, having 'the stuff of a founder of movements', to make Italian federalism a political force to be reckoned with: a powerful influence for developing the Community into a European Union then a European federation.

Britain remains the loser from this change of roles. Now that *fortuna* has changed again, is it too much to expect that reflection on this history will prompt efforts to restore *virtu*?

Notes

1. Luigi Einaudi (Junius), 'La Società delle Nazioni è un ideale possibile?', *Corriere delle Sera*, 5 January 1918, and 'Il dogma della sovranità e l'idea della Società delle nazioni', *Corriere della Sera*, 28 December 1918; reprinted in Luigi Einaudi, *Lettere politiche* (Bari, Laterza, 1920); most recently reprinted in Luigi Einaudi, *La guerra e l'unità europea* (Bologna, il Mulino, 1986).
2. Riccardo Faucci, *Einaudi* (Torino, UTET, 1986), pp. 12–15 and *passim*.
3. Giovanni Agnelli and Attilio Cabiati, *Federazione Europea o Lega delle Nazioni?* (Torino, Bocca, 1918). The book was reproduced in the late 1970s (undated) under the same title and in the same form, but with a preface by Senator Giovanni Agnelli and an introduction by Sergio Pistone (publisher Edizione E.T.L., Torino). A French edition was published in Paris in 1919, entitled *Fédération européenne ou ligue des nations?*
4. Agnelli and Cabiati have been identified as pioneers in the critique of *raison d'état* theorists by Dino Cofranceso, 'Il contributo della resistenza italiano al dibattito teorico sull'unificazione europea', in Sergio Pistone (ed.), *L'idea dell'unificazione europea dalla prima alla seconda guerra mondiale* (Torino, Fondazione Luigi Einaudi, 1975), pp. 151–2. This critique has been developed as an element in

federalist analysis by Pistone, in for example his introduction to Sergio Pistone (ed.), *Politica di potenza e imperialismo* (Milano, Franco Angeli Editore, 1973).

5. Agnelli and Cabiati, *Federazione Europea*, op.cit., pp. 20–5, 27–9.

6. ibid., pp. 8, 11ff., 74, 77, 99–106. The book by Henry Sidgwick that they cite is his *The Elements of Politics* (London, Macmillan, 1891); the article by Wells was from the *Rassegna Italo-Britannica*; the citation from Robertson was from a paper published by the Cobden Club.

7. Agnelli and Cabiati, *Federazione Europea*, op.cit., pp. 20–5.

8. See Lucio Levi, *Federalismo e integrazione europea* (Palermo, Palumbo, 1978), pp. 21–2. Levi's references to Cattaneo's works are from C. Cattaneo, *Stati Uniti d'Italia* (anthology edited by N. Bobbio) (Torino, Chiantore, 1945), pp. 31, 138, 160–1, 185. See also Levi, *Il federalismo* (Milano, Franco Angeli Editore, 1987), pp. 55–7; Edmondo Paolini, *L'idea di Europa* (Firenze, La Nuova Italia Editrice, 1979), pp. 31–3; Sergio Pistone, *L'italia e l'unità europea* (Torino, Loescher Editore, 1982), pp. 48–52.

9. Over a score of references are given in Claudio Pavone, 'Il federalismo europeo', *Libri e riviste*, Nos. xii, xiii, xiv (Rome, February, March, April 1951). See also Paolini, *L'idea di europa*, op.cit., pp. 33–5.

10. Pistone, Introduction to *Federazione Europea*, op. cit., p. xix, where he cites P. Gobetti, 'La Società delle Nazioni', *Energie nuove*, 1–15 January 1919, pp. 65–7.

11. A. Gramsci, 'Un soviet locale', *Avanti!* (edizione torinese), 5 February 1919, cited in Pistone, ibid., pp. xx, xxiv.

12. Faucci, introduction to, *Einaudi*, op.cit., pp. 172–3. Einaudi's review is also discussed in Pistone, *Federazione Europea*, op.cit., pp. xii, xxi–ii.

13. Charles F. Delzell, *Mussolini's Enemies: The Italian Anti-Fascist Resistance* (Princeton, University Press, 1961), p. 88. The citation from Mussolini is from his *La dottrina del fascismo*, Ch. 2., quoted in Paolini, *L'idea di europa*, op.cit., p. 51.

14. Examples from articles by Alberto De Stefani and Camillo Pellizi are to be found in Walter Lipgens (ed.), *Documents on the History of European Integration, Vol. 1, Continental Plans for European Union 1939–1945* (Berlin and New York, de Gruyter, 1985), pp. 187–93; see particularly pp. 189, 193.

15. Philip Kerr (later Lord Lothian) and Lionel Curtis, *The Prevention of War* (New Haven, Yale University Press for the Institute of Politics, Williamstown, 1923); Philip Kerr, 'World problems of today', in the Earl of Birkenhead, General Tasker H. Bliss and Philip Henry Kerr, *Approaches to World Problems* (New Haven, Yale University Press for the Institute of Politics, Williamstown, 1924).

16. The Marquess of Lothian, *Pacificism is not Enough (nor Patriotism Either)* (London, Oxford University Press, 1935: second and third edns, July, October 1941). Translations from Lothian's principal works have been published in Mario Albertini (ed.), *Il federalismo e lo stato federale: Antologia e definizione* (Milano, Giuffrè, 1963); Albertini (ed.), *Il federalismo: Antologia e definizione* (Bologna, il Mulino, 1979); Pistone (ed.), *Politica di potenza e imperialismo* (Milano, Franco Angeli Editori, 1973); Lothian, *Il pacifismo non basta* (Bologna, il Mulino, 1986). See also Giulio Guderzo (ed.), *Lord Lothian. Una vita per la pace* (Firenze, La Nuova Italia Editrice, 1986), particularly the contributions by

Andrea Bosco, Guilio Guderzo and Luigi Vittorio Majocchi.

17. See J.R.M. Butler, *Lord Lothian (Philip Kerr) 1882–1940* (London, Macmillan, 1968), for example, p. 28.

18. Alexander Hamilton, John Jay and James Madison, *The Federalist or, The New Constitution*, first published 1787–8. Curtis and Lothian were also influenced by F.S. Oliver, who wrote *Alexander Hamilton: An Essay on American Union* (London, Macmillan, 1906).

19. Agnelli and Cabiati, *Federazione Europea*, op.cit., pp. 64, 111–6. The book by Lionel Curtis was *The Commonwealth of Nations: An Enquiry into the Nature of Citizenship in the British Commonwealth and into the Mutual Relations of the Several Communities Thereof* (London, Macmillan, 1917), see particularly pp. 702–3.

20. Lionel Curtis, *Civitas Dei* (London, George Allen and Unwin, revised edn, 1950), pp. 655, 714–15, 744 (first edn, 1934–7).

21. Gilbert Murray, *The Ordeal of this Generation: The War, The League and the Future* (London, George Allen and Unwin, 1929), pp. 190–2, 197.

22. Rappard was later to help Einaudi after his escape from Italy to Switzerland in 1943. See Faucci, *Einaudi*, op.cit., pp. 316–18.

23. Lionel Robbins, *Economic Planning and International Order* (London, Macmillan, 1937), pp. 240–1. This passage was cited with strong approval by von Hayek in 'The economic conditions of inter-state federalism', *New Commonwealth Quarterly* (September 1939), reprinted in F.A. Hayek, *Individualism and Economic Order* (London, Routledge and Kegan Paul, 1949), pp. 255–72, here pp. 269–70.

24. Lionel Robbins, *The Economic Causes of War* (London, Jonathan Cape, 1939), pp. 104–9; the citations are from pp. 105–6.

25. Their pamphlets were Lord Lothian, *The Ending of Armageddon* (Federal Union, London, 1939), and Lionel Robbins, *Economic Aspects of Federation* (Federal Tracts No.2, London, Macmillan, 1941), reprinted in Patrick Ransome (ed.), *Studies in Federal Planning* (London, Macmillan, 1943). Italian translations of Lothian's writings are cited in Note 16 above. For Robbins they include Lionel Robbins, *Le cause economiche della guerra* (Torino, Einaudi, 1944); Robbins, 'Aspetti economici della federazione', in *La Federazione Europea* (Firenze, La Nuova Italia, 1948); Robbins, *La base economica dei conflitti di classe* (Firenze, La Nuova Italia, 1952); extracts in Albertini (ed.), *Il federalismo* and in Pistone *Politica di potenza e imperialismo*; and Robbins, *Il federalismo e l'ordine economico internazionale* (Bologna, il Mulino, 1985).

26. See Michael Burgess, 'Empire, Ireland and Europe: a century of British federal ideas', in Burgess (ed.), *Federalism and Federation in Western Europe* (London, Croom Helm, 1986), pp. 137–8.

27. Winston Churchill, 'The United States of Europe', *Saturday Evening Post*, New York, 15 February 1930, reprinted (in English) in Roberto Ducci and Bino Olivi (eds), *L'Europa incompiuta* (Padova, CEDAM, 1970), see particularly pp. 36–7.

28. See Sir Charles Kimber, 'Federal Union', *The Federalist*, Vol. 26 (1984), p. 204; R.H. Tawney, *Equality* (London, George Allen and Unwin, second edn, 1938), cited in R.W.G. Mackay, *Federal Europe* (London, Michael Joseph, 1940), p. 139; G.D.H. Cole, *War Aims* (New Statesman pamphlet, 1939); Ernest Bevin,

speech to Trades Union Congress, 1927; C.R. Attlee, *Labour's Peace Aims* (London, Peace Book Co., 1940), reprinted in C.R. Attlee, Arthur Greenwood and others, *Labour's Aims in War and Peace* (London, Lincolns-Prager, 1940).

29. Harold J. Laski, *Studies in the Problems of Sovereignty* (New Haven, Yale University Press, and London, Oxford University Press, 1917), p. 273; and his *A Grammar of Politics* (London, George Allen and Unwin, 1948, first edn, 1925), pp. 64, 271.

30. Laski, *A Grammar of Politics*, op.cit., Preface to third edn, and pp. v, xiii, xx, xxiii.

31. See, for example, extracts from Barbara Wootton, *Socialism and Federation, Federal Tracts No. 6* (London, Macmillan, 1941), and from Mackay, *Federal Europe*, in Walter Lipgens (ed.), *Documents on the History of European Integration, Vol. 2, Plans for European Union in Great Britain and in Exile 1939–1945* (Berlin and New York, de Gruyter, 1986), pp. 138–42.

32. Lord Acton, *History of Freedom and other Essays*, 1862; J.S. Mill, 'Of federal representative governments', *Considerations on Representative Government*, 1861; Henry Sidgwick, *The Elements of Politics*, 1891; Hamilton, Jay and Madison, *The Federalist*, 1787–8; James Bryce, *The American Commonwealth*, 1888; A.V. Dicey, *Introduction to the Study of the Law of the Constitution*, 1885; E.A. Freeman, *A History of Federal Government in Greece and Italy, 1893* (revised second edn); J.R. Seeley, 'United States of Europe', *Macmillan's Magazine*, Vol. 23 (1871), pp. 441–4; W.T. Stead, *The United States of Europe* (London, 1899).

33. *Federal Union News*, No. 14, 23 December 1939. The foundation and early period of Federal Union are described in Kimber, 'Federal Union', op.cit., and in John Pinder, 'Federal Union 1939–41', in Lipgens, *Documents*, op.cit., pp. 26–34. The full title of Clarence Streit's book was *Union Now: A Proposal for a Federal Union of the Democracies of the North Atlantic* (London, Jonathan Cape, and New York, Harper, 1939).

34. See Luigi Salvatorelli and Giovanni Mira, *Storia del fascismo: l'Italia dal 1919 al 1945* (Rome, 1952), pp. 341, 371, cited in Delzell, *Mussolini's Enemies*, op.cit., pp. 97, 100.

35. See Delzell, ibid., p. 6.

36. See Delzell, ibid., p. 48; Eugenio Guccione, 'Il federalismo europeo in Luigi Sturzo', *Archivio Storico Siciliano*, Serie IV, Vol. IV (1978), pp. 445–93, here p. 448; L. Sturzo, *The International Community and the Right of War* (London, George Allen and Unwin, 1929), pp. 228ff. and 277. The failure to distinguish between a federal and a Commonwealth structure was not unusual in Britain at that time; see, for example, Arnold Toynbee, *World Order or Downfall?* (London, BBC, 1930), pp. 34, 36.

37. L. Sturzo, 'Problemi dell'Europa futura', *Il Mondo*, New York, April 1940, extracts reproduced (in English) in Lipgens, *Documents*, op.cit., Vol. 2, pp. 497–9. It is interesting that Toynbee's thought had undergone the same evolution: see his 'First thoughts on a peace settlement', unpublished memorandum, 26 July 1939, London, Royal Institute of International Affairs Archives 9/18f, p. 7.

38. Delzell, *Mussolini's Enemies*, op.cit., p. 162.

39. Altiero Spinelli, 'The growth of the European Movement since World War II', in G. Grove Haines (ed.), *European Integration* (Baltimore, The Johns Hopkins Press, and London, Oxford University Press, 1957), pp. 44–5.

40. See Guccioni, 'Il federalismo europeo', op.cit., and Don Sturzo in *Il popolo*, 29 April 1948, reprinted in Sturzo, *Politica di questi anni*, Vol. 1 (Bologna, Nicolo Zarichelli, 1954), pp. 421–4.

41. Delzell, *Mussolini's Enemies*, op.cit., p. 217; Sergio Pistone (ed.), *L'idea dell' unificazione europea dalla prima alla seconda guerra mondiale* (Torino, Fondazione Luigi Einaudi, 1975), p. 93; Lipgens, *Documents*, op.cit., Vol. 1, pp. 503–5.

42. Lipgens, ibid., pp. 505–6; Pistone, *L'idea dell'unificazione europea*, op.cit., pp. 94, 134–5.

43. See Mario Albertini, 'La fondazione dello stato europeo', in Luigi Vittorio Majocchi and Francesco Rossolillo, *Il Parlamento europeo* (Napoli, Guida Editori, 1979), pp. 163–216. See also Giulio Andreotti, *De Gasperi e il suo tempo* (Milano, Mondadori, 1956), pp. 313–14; Andreotti, who was one of De Gasperi's closest collaborators, has continued to promote the European federal idea as Foreign Minister in the 1980s, in particular supporting the European Parliament and its European Union Draft Treaty.

44. Pier Carlo Masini, 'Introduzione', in Filippo Turati, *Per gli Stati Uniti d'Europa* (Lettere, discorsi e scritti raccolti da P. Carlo Masini) (Roma, Editore Armando, 1980), p. 14; Turati, 'La decadenza di un uomo illustre', *Critica sociale*, 30 November 1891, reproduced in ibid., pp. 35–7.

45. Masini, ibid., pp. 14, 16; Turati, speech in Parliament on 29 April 1919, reproduced in Turati, ibid., pp. 53–60, here p. 56; and Turati's speech to the Rome Congress of the PSU, 3 October 1922, cited in Masini, ibid., p. 19.

46. Delzell, *Mussolini's Enemies*, op.cit., pp. 52–4; Faucci, *Einaudi*, op.cit., p. 223.

47. Interview in *Le Quotidien*, Paris, 15 December 1929; see Filippo Turati, *Per gli Stati Uniti d'Europa*, op.cit., pp. 74–9, 80–8; and Pistone, *L'idea dell'unificazione europea*, op.cit., pp. 61–3.

48. Delzell, *Mussolini's Enemies*, op.cit., pp. 9, 22 and *passim*; Lipgens *Documents*, op.cit., Vol. 2, pp. 517–19; F.L. Josephy, document on the history of Federal Union 1938–48, typescript in Josephy/Federal Union archive at London School of Economics, pp. 13, 27, 41.

49. Delzell, *Mussolini's Enemies*, op.cit., pp. 78–9, 136; Lipgens, *Documents*, op.cit., Vol. 2, pp. 499–51; Alexandre Marc's ideas are considered in John Laughlin, 'French personalist and federalist movements in the interwar period', Chapter 11 of this book.

50. Lipgens, *Documents*, op.cit., Vol. 2, pp. 521–3; Pistone, *L'idea dell'unificazione europea*, op.cit., pp. 122–3: Altiero Spinelli, *Come ho tentato di diventare saggio: la goccia e la roccia*, posthumously edited by Edmondo Paolini (Bologna, il Mulino, 1987), p. 63 (hereafter cited as *la goccia e la roccia*).

51. Leo Solari, *Eugenio Colorni: Ieri e oggi* (Venezia, Marsilio Editori, 1980), pp. 46, 63–8, 189–90; Eugenio Colorni, 'Prefazione' (unsigned), in A.S. and E.R. (Alberto Spinelli and Ernesto Rossi), *Problemi della Federazione Europea* (Roma, Edizioni del Movimento Italiano per la Federazione Europea, 1944; reprinted at Bologna, Centro Stampa del Movimento Federalista Europeo, 1972). The

Preface is on pp. 3–8 of the reprint. It has also been reprinted, among others, in Solari, *Eugenio Colorni*, op.cit., pp. 129–34, and in Altiero Spinelli, *Il progetto europeo* (Bologna, il Mulino, 1985), pp. 195–9.

52. Faucci, *Einaudi*, op.cit., p. 223, pp. 284–5.
53. ibid., p. 222; Max Salvadori, *Breve storia della Resistenza italiana* (Firenze, Vallecchi, 1974), p. 44.
54. Delzell, *Mussolini's Enemies*, op.cit., p. 18.
55. Salvadori, *Breve storia della Resistenza italiana*, op.cit., p. 55.
56. Pistone, *L'idea dell'unificazione europea*, op.cit., p. 77. See also Delzell, *Mussolini's Enemies*, op.cit., pp. 30–2, 60ff, 73. *Socialismo liberale* was published in Paris in 1930.
57. Delzell, ibid., p. 79; Pistone, op.cit., *L'idea dell'unificazione europea*, pp. 64–8.
58. Charles F. Delzell, 'The European federalist movement in Italy: first phase, 1918–1947', *Journal of Modern History*, (1960), pp. 241–50, here p. 243; Lipgens, *Documents*, op.cit., Vol. 1, p. 290, and Vol. 2, p. 494; Solari, *Eugenio Colorni*, op.cit., pp. 82, 190.
59. Delzell, *Mussolini's Enemies*, op.cit., p. 80; Lipgens, *Documents*, op.cit., Vol. 1, pp. 469–71; Pistone, *L'idea dell'unificazione europea*, op.cit., pp. 89–93. For a list of sources on the relationship between the political culture of the *Partito d'Azione* and the development of federalist thought and action in Italy, see L. Levi and S. Pistone (eds), *Trent'anni di vita del Movimento Federalista Europeo* (Milano, Franco Angeli Editore, 1973), p. 42.
60. Altiero Spinelli, *Come ho tentato di diventare saggio: Io, Ulisse* (Bologna, il Mulino), pp. 296, 301 (hereafter cited as *Io, Ulisse*).
61. ibid., pp. 144, 146, 165, 281, 315.
62. Delzell, *Mussolini's Enemies*, op.cit., p. 60.
63. Spinelli, *Io, Ulisse*, op.cit., p. 301.
64. ibid., p. 302, 306; Spinelli, *la goccia e la roccia*, op.cit., p. 40.
65. Einaudi, *Lettere politiche*, op.cit. See Spinelli, *Io, Ulisse*, op.cit., p. 307; Faucci, *Einaudi*, op.cit., p. 318.
66. Spinelli, *Io, Ulisse*, op.cit., p. 307, and *le progretto europeo*, op.cit., pp. 201–3. The two books by Robbins were *Economic Planning and International Order* and *The Economic Causes of War*; Spinelli's translation was *Le cause economiche della guerra*. The book by von Hayek was *Collectivist Economic Planning* (London, Routledge, 1935); for his participation in the Federal Union Research Institute, see Lipgens, *Documents*, op.cit., Vol. 2, pp. 27, 31–3, 113, 129–34. The two essays by Spinelli were 'Gli Stati Uniti d'Europa e le varie tendenze politiche' and 'Politica marxista e politica federalista', first printed, together with the 'Progetto d'un manifesto' (Ventotene Manifesto) and the Preface by Colorni, in A.S. and E.R., *Problemi della Federazione Europea*, op.cit., in Rome in January 1944; the essays have been reprinted in the edition published in Bologna in 1972 and in Spinelli, *Il progretto europeo*, op. cit.; and extracts translated into English can be found in Lipgens, *Documents*, op.cit., Vol. 1, pp. 484–92. For a note on the original sources, see *Le progretto europeo*, pp. 13–4.
67. See 'Intervista con Altiero Spinelli', in Spinelli, *Il progetto europeo*, op.cit., pp. 201–13, here p. 202. The Federal Union pamphlets available by mid-1940

included Sir William Beveridge, *Peace by Federation?*; H.N. Brailsford, *The Federal Idea*; Lord Lothian, *The Ending of Armageddon.*

68. Spinelli, *Io, Ulisse*, op.cit., pp. 307–8; the English translation of this passage comes from *The Federalist*, Vol. 26 (1984), p. 158.
69. The Ventotene Manifesto was distributed in duplicated form on the Italian mainland from 1941 onwards. For its subsequent publication, see note 66 above.
70. *Problemi della Federazione Europea*, op.cit., 1972 edn, Federalistu Europeo, 1972) pp. 9, 10, 21, 22–3, 27, 28–30; Spinelli, *Il progetto europeo*, op.cit., pp. 17, 18, 28–9, 30, 34, 35–6, 203–4; Lipgens, *Documents*, op.cit., Vol. I, pp. 473–4, 478–9, 481–3; Spinelli, *Io, Ulisse.* op.cit., p. 301.
71. Spinelli, ibid., p. 312.
72. Spinelli, ibid., p. 307.

Index